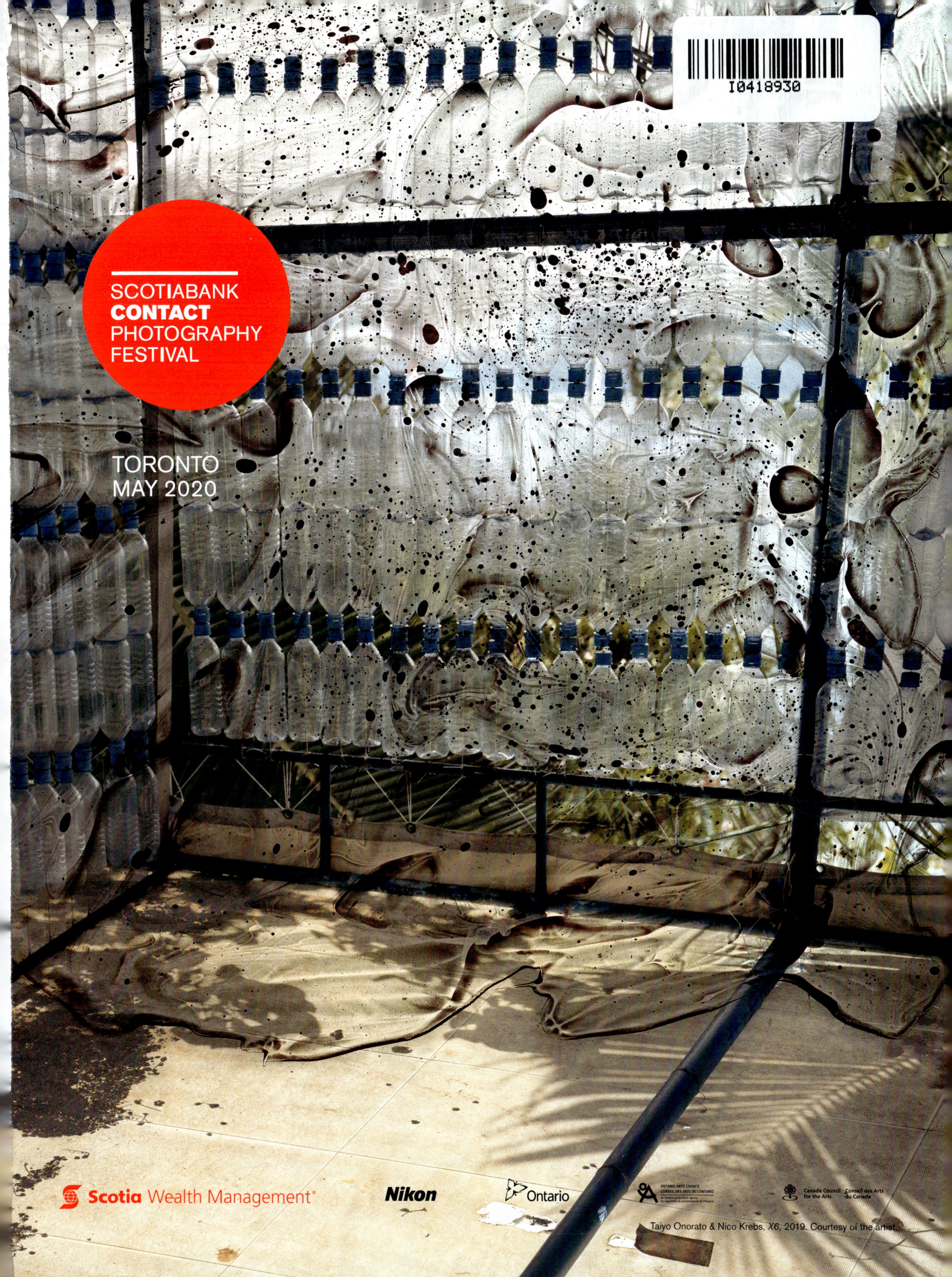

SCOTIABANK
CONTACT
PHOTOGRAPHY
FESTIVAL

TORONTO
MAY 2020

Scotia Wealth Management®

Nikon

Ontario

ONTARIO ARTS COUNCIL
CONSEIL DES ARTS DE L'ONTARIO

Canada Council   Conseil des Arts
for the Arts   du Canada

Taiyo Onorato & Nico Krebs, *X6*, 2019. Courtesy of the artist.

Spring 2020

Words

Pictures

Front

Back

Front cover:
Mauro Restiffe, from the
series *Santo Sospir*, 2018
Courtesy the artist
(See page 86)

Opposite:
Seher Shah & Randhir
Singh, from the series
*Studies in Form
(The Barbican Estate –
London)*, 2018
Courtesy the artists and
Green Art Gallery, Dubai
(See page 72)

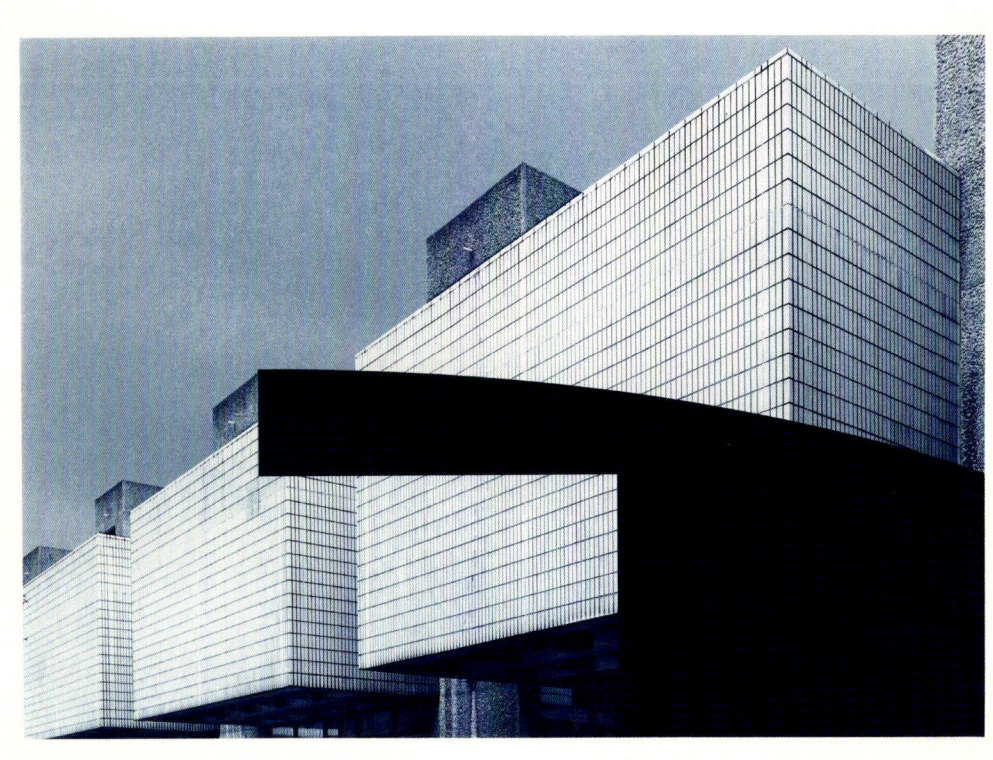

Aperture, a not-for-profit foundation, connects the photo community and its audiences with the most inspiring work, the sharpest ideas, and with each other—in print, in person, and online.

Aperture (ISSN 0003-6420) is published quarterly, in spring, summer, fall, and winter, at 547 West 27th Street, 4th Floor, New York, N.Y. 10001. In the United States, a one-year subscription (four issues) is $75; a two-year subscription (eight issues) is $124. In Canada, a one-year subscription is $95. All other international subscriptions are $105 per year. Visit aperture.org to subscribe. Single copies may be purchased at $24.95 for most issues. Subscribe to the Aperture Digital Archive at aperture.org/archive. Periodicals postage paid at New York and additional offices. Postmaster: Send address changes to Aperture, P.O. Box 3000, Denville, N.J. 07834. Address queries regarding subscriptions, renewals, or gifts to: Aperture Subscription Service, 866-457-4603 (U.S. and Canada), or email custsvc_aperture@fulcoinc.com.

Newsstand distribution in the U.S. is handled by CMG. For international distribution, contact Central Books, centralbooks.com. Other inquiries, email orders@aperture.org or call 212-505-5555.

Become a Member of Aperture to take your interest in and knowledge of photography further. With an annual tax-deductible gift of $250, membership includes invitations to exhibition opening parties and studio visits with world renowned photographers, a complimentary subscription to Aperture magazine, discounts on Aperture's award-winning publications and photography workshops, a special limited-edition gift, and more. To join, visit aperture.org/join, or contact membership@aperture.org.

Library of Congress Catalog Card No: 58-30845.

ISBN 978-1-59711-483-7

Printed in Turkey by Ofset Yapimevi

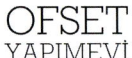

Lead funding for the "House & Home" issue of Aperture magazine is provided by the Henry Luce Foundation. Significant support for Aperture magazine is also provided by The Kanakia Foundation. Further generous support is provided by the New York City Department of Cultural Affairs in partnership with the City Council.

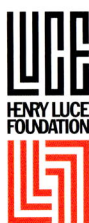

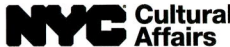

Statement of Ownership, Management, and Circulation (Required by 39 U.S.C. 3685). 1. Publication Title: Aperture; 2. Publication no.: 0003-6420; 3. Filing Date: October 1, 2019 4. Issue Frequency: Quarterly; 5. No. of Issues Published Annually: 4; 6. Annual Subscription Price: $75.00; 7. Complete Mailing Address of Known Office of Publication: Aperture Foundation, 547 West 27th Street, 4th Floor, New York, NY 10001-5511; 8. Complete Mailing Address of Headquarters or General Business Office of Publisher: Aperture Foundation, 547 West 27th Street, 4th Floor, New York, NY 10001-5511; 9. Full Names and Complete Mailing Addresses of Publisher, Editor, and Managing Editor: Publisher: Dana Triwush, Aperture Foundation, 547 West 27th Street, 4th Floor, New York, NY 10001-5511; Editor: Michael Famighetti, Aperture Foundation, 547 West 27th Street, 4th Floor, New York, NY 10001-5511; Managing Editor: Brendan Embser, Aperture Foundation, 547 West 27th Street, 4th Floor, New York, NY 10001-5511; 10. Owner: Aperture Foundation, Inc., 547 West 27th Street, 4th Fl., New York, NY 10001; 11. Known Bondholders, Mortgagees, and Other Security Holders Owning or Holding 1 Percent or More of Total Amount of Bonds, Mortgages, or Other Securities: None; 12. Tax Status: The purpose, function, and nonprofit status of this organization and the exempt status for federal income tax purposes: Has Not Changed During Preceding 12 Months; 13. Publication Title: Aperture; 14. Issue Date for Circulation Data Below: Summer 2019 #235; 15. Extent and Nature of Circulation (Average No. Copies Each Issue During Preceding 12 Months; No. Copies of Single Issue Published Nearest to Filing Date): a. Total Number of Copies (Net press run): 15,012; 15,231; b. Paid Circulation: (1) Mailed Outside-County Paid Subscriptions Stated on PS Form 3541: 5,512; 5,472; (2) Mailed In-County Paid Subscriptions Stated on PS Form 3541: 5; 5; (3) Paid Distribution Outside the Mails Including Sales Through Dealers and Carriers, Street Vendors, Counter Sales, and Other Paid Distribution Outside USPS: 3,855; 3,883; (4) Paid Distribution by Other Classes of Mail Through the USPS: 35; 35; c. Total Paid Distribution: 9,407; 9,395; d. Free or Nominal Rate Distribution: (1) Free or Nominal Rate Outside-County Copies included on PS Form 3541: 355; 353; (2) Free or Nominal Rate In-County Copies Included on PS From 3541: 0; 0; (3) Free or Nominal Rate Copies Mailed at Other Classes Through the USPS: 114; 117; (4) Free or Nominal Rate Distribution Outside the Mail: 525; 600; e. Total Free or Nominal Rate Distribution: 993; 1,070; f. Total Distribution: 10,400; 10,465; g. Copies not Distributed: 4,612; 4,766; h. Total: 15,012; 15,231; i. Percent Paid 90.4%; 89.8%; 16. Electronic Copy Circulation, a. Paid Electronic Copies: 527; 536; b. Total Paid Print Copies + Paid Electronic Copies: 9,933; 9,931; c. Total Print Distribution + Paid Electronic Copies: 10,927; 11,001; d. Percent Paid (Both Print & Electronic Copies); 90.9%; 90.3%; I certify that 50% of all my distributed copies (Electronic & Print) are paid above a nominal price. 17. Publication of Statement of Ownership: Will be printed in the Spring 2020 issue of this publication.; 18. I certify that all information furnished on this form is true and complete. I understand that anyone who furnishes false or misleading information on this form or who omits material or information requested on the form may be subject to criminal sanctions (including fines and imprisonment) and/or civil sanctions (including civil penalties). Signature and Title of Editor, Publisher, Business Manager, or Owner: Dana Triwush, Publisher, October 1, 2019

aperture

The Magazine of Photography and Ideas

Editor
Michael Famighetti

Managing Editor
Brendan Embser

Editorial Assistant
Nicole Acheampong

Copy Editors
Olivia Casa, Donna Ghelerter

Senior Production Manager
True Sims

Production Manager
Bryan Krueger

Work Scholars
Nina Briggs, Eli Cohen, Clay Howard

Art Direction, Design & Typefaces
A2/SW/HK, London

Publisher
Dana Triwush
magazine@aperture.org

Director of Brand Partnerships
Isabelle Friedrich McTwigan
212-946-7118
imctwigan@aperture.org

Advertising
Elizabeth Morina
917-691-2608
emorina@aperture.org

**Executive Director,
Aperture Foundation**
Chris Boot

Minor White, Editor (1952–1974)

Michael E. Hoffman, Publisher and Executive Director (1964–2001)

aperture.org

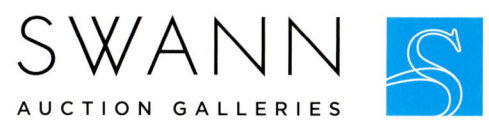

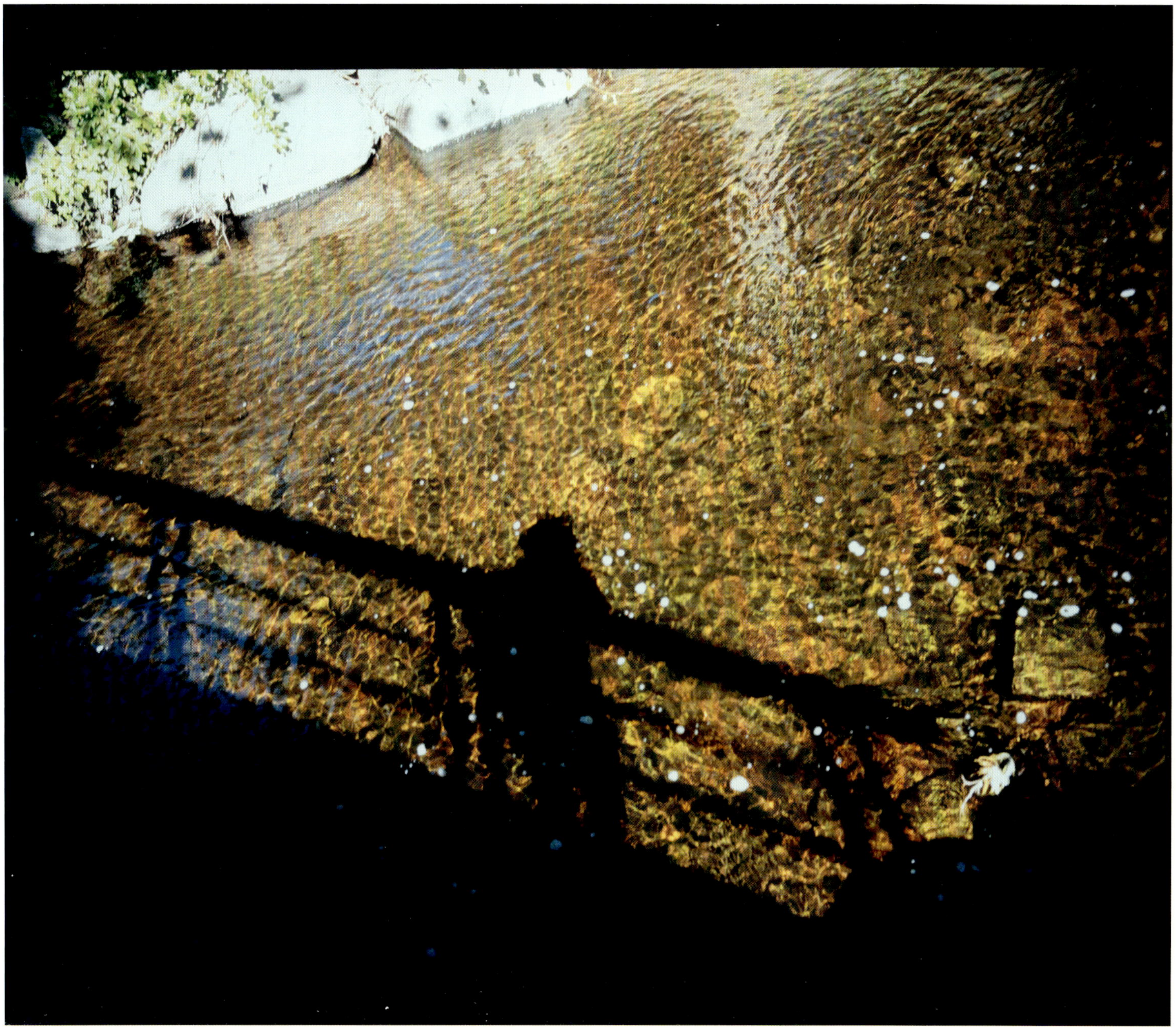

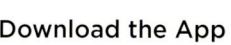

Nan Goldin, *Self Portrait on Golden River, Silver Hill*, 1998, oversized cibachrome print, 1998. Estimate $6,000 to $9,000.

Photographs & Photobooks
April 16

Daile Kaplan • dkaplan@swanngalleries.com

Agenda
Exhibitions to See

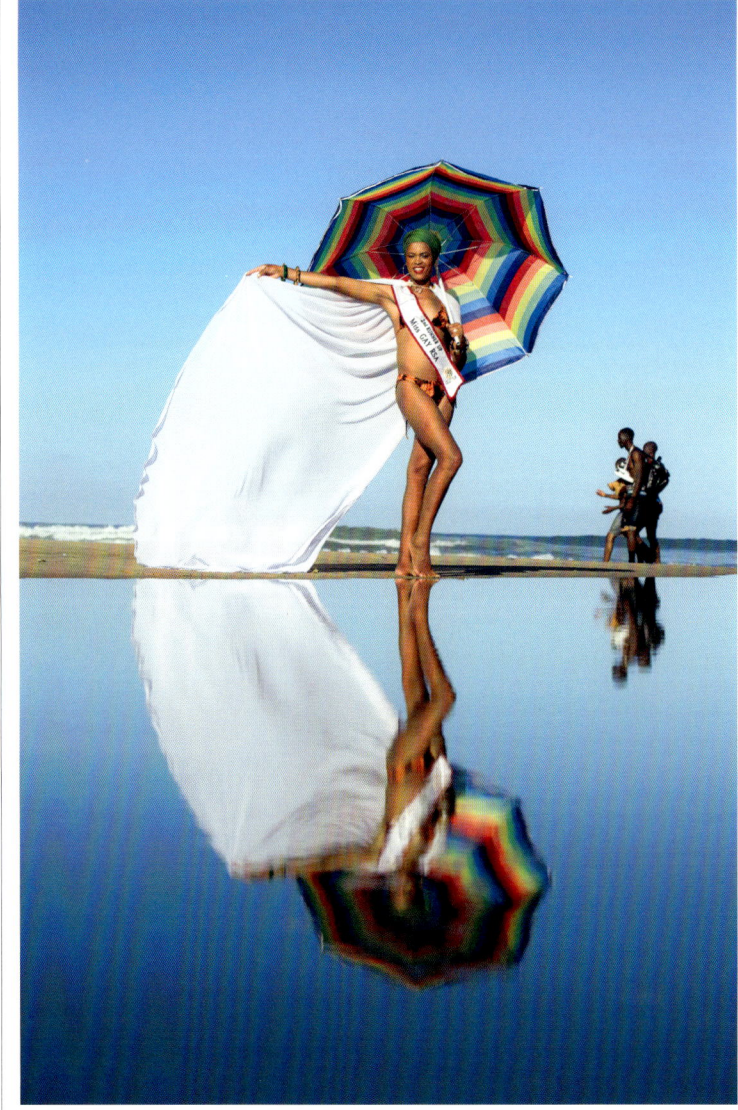

Zanele Muholi

"I'm calling myself a visual activist," Zanele Muholi told *Aperture* in 2015. "That's my stance as a person, before anything else." In Muholi's first major exhibition in the United Kingdom, this visual activism is given due primacy. Featuring approximately 250 works, Tate Modern's survey will lend special focus to Muholi's early work, in particular their expansive, subversively tender portrait series *Faces and Phases*, which they began in 2006. The museum will also delve into South Africa's Gay and Lesbian Memory in Action (GALA) archive. Integral to the project is the programming attached to the images: as is their practice, Muholi will stage conversations with the local community about life for LGBTQIA people in South Africa. "It's not a typical photography exhibition," says the curator Yasufumi Nakamori. "The exhibition is about their activism, seen through their art, seen through their photography. Photography happened to be the medium they chose."

Zanele Muholi at Tate Modern, London,
April 29–October 18, 2020

Zanele Muholi, *Melissa Mbambo, Durban*, 2017
© the artist and courtesy Stevenson, Cape Town/
Johannesburg, and Yancey Richardson, New York

Vera Lutter

A large-scale negative included in Vera Lutter's upcoming exhibition at the Los Angeles County Museum of Art (LACMA), *Vera Lutter: Museum in the Camera*, depicts a ghostly gallery full of old master paintings, reminiscent of the Grande Galerie paintings at the Louvre. Created with a camera obscura the size of a shipping crate, the exposure at LACMA took five weeks; notably, the image shows no traces of the people in the gallery. "There is something poignant in that every visitor to the museum over the five weeks is part of the photograph," says Jennifer King, associate curator of contemporary projects, "even though they are not visible." Lutter's most recent project, completed during the artist's residency at the museum between 2017 and 2019, documents the galleries and campus architecture slated for renovation in LACMA's 2020 makeover, as well as the art within them, constructing uncanny photographs that carry a deep sense of time and memory.

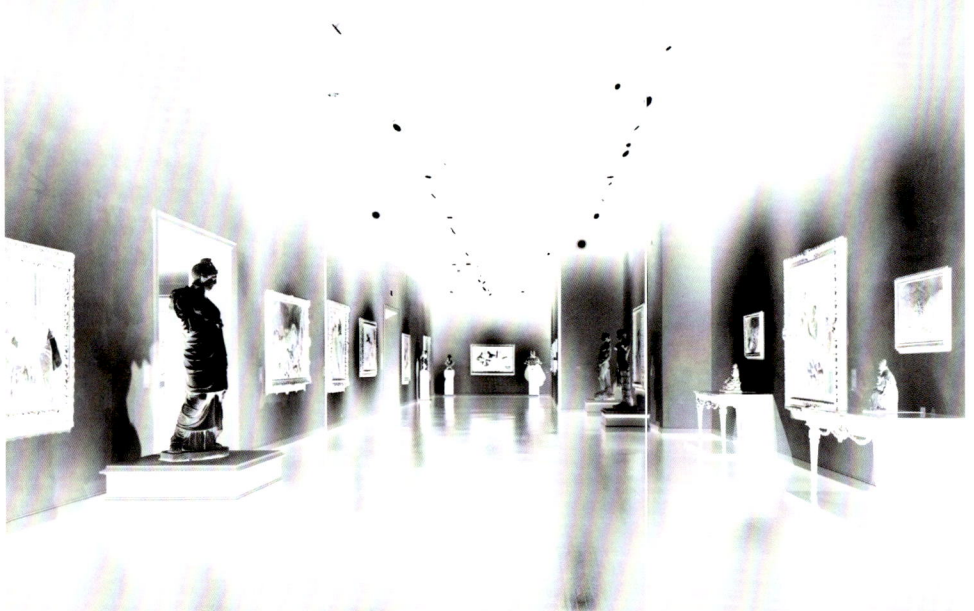

Vera Lutter, *European Old Masters:*
December 7, 2018–January 9, 2019, 2018–19
© the artist and courtesy Gagosian Gallery

Vera Lutter: Museum in the Camera at the Los Angeles
County Museum of Art, **March 29–July 19, 2020**

DAWOUD BEY

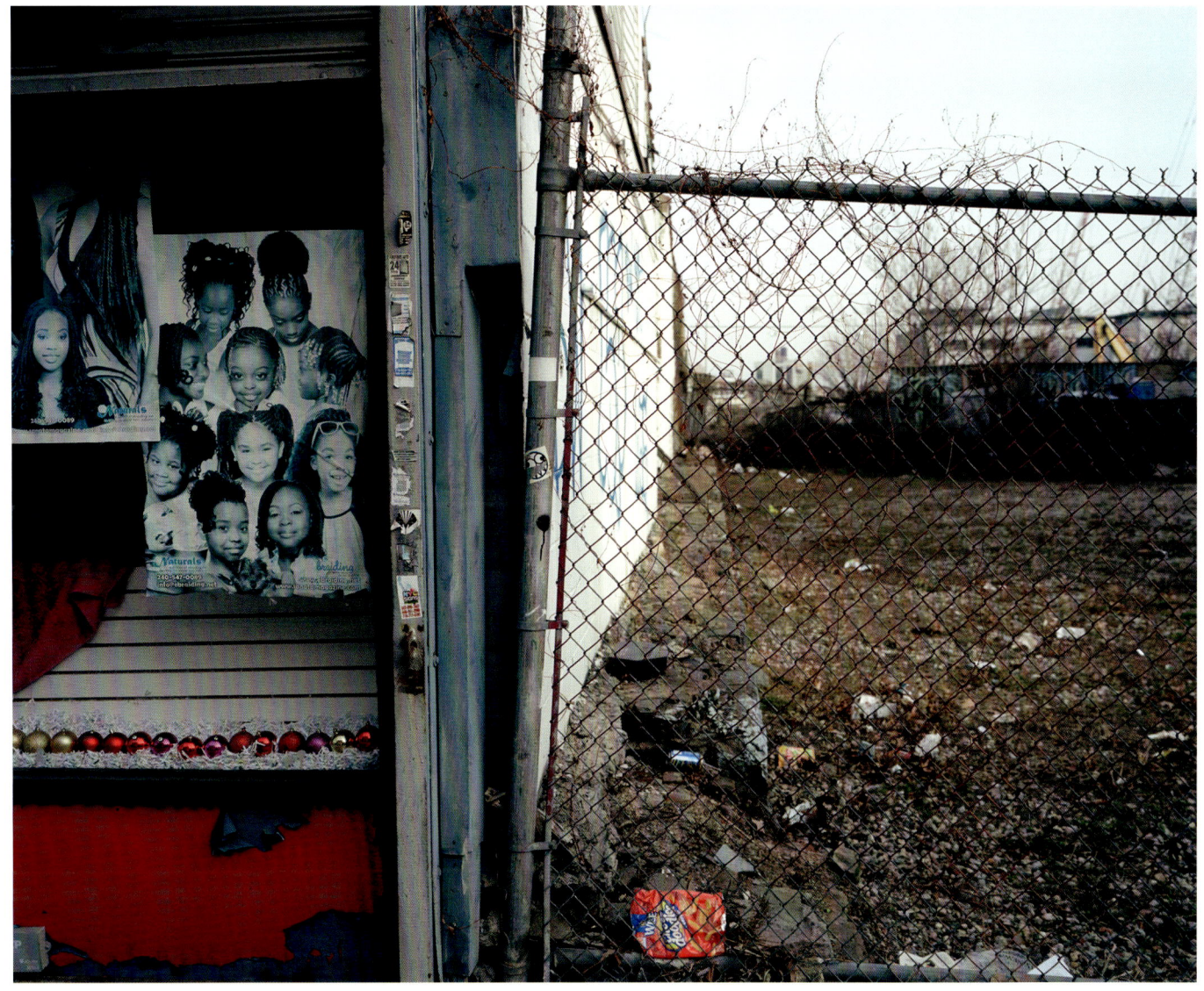

Harlem Redux: Girls, Ornaments, and Vacant Lot, 2016

TRAVELING RETROSPECTIVE, 2020

SFMOMA
San Francisco

High Museum
Atlanta, GA

Whitney Museum
New York

RENA BRANSTEN
GALLERY

1275 MINNESOTA ST. • SAN FRANCISCO CA 94107

Umbo

Like Brassaï and Weegee, Umbo, the German photographer, bohemian, and flaneur, was famous enough in his lifetime to be known by only one name. Following the influential exhibition *Film und Foto*, presented in 1929 in Stuttgart, in which his thirty-nine photographs constituted a solo show within a show, Umbo was hailed as a pioneer of the "New Vision." His inventive compositions and vertiginous angles, and his experiments with photograms and collages, exemplify early twentieth-century German photography, melding objectivity with euphoria. Marking the Berlinische Galerie's recent acquisition of Umbo's estate, *Umbo: Photographer* will feature nearly two hundred works, including Umbo's lesser-known postwar reportage and magazine commissions. "For all his pragmatism," says the curator Ulrich Domröse, "he spent his life trying to find a way to exist that promised maximum personal liberty and freedom from any tethers."

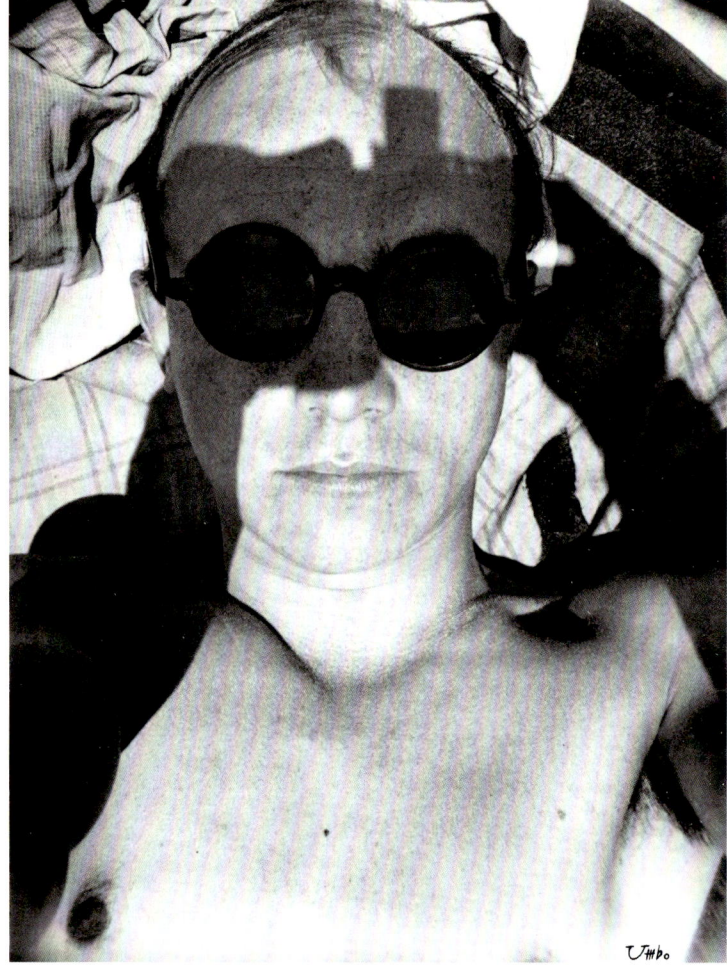

Umbo, *Self-Portrait at the Beach*, ca. 1930
© Phyllis Umbehr/Galerie Kicken Berlin/VG Bild-Kunst, Bonn

Vivian Maier, Location unknown, 1956
© Estate of Vivian Maier and courtesy Maloof Collection and Howard Greenberg Gallery, New York

***Umbo: Photographer* at the Berlinische Galerie, Berlin, February 21–May 25, 2020**

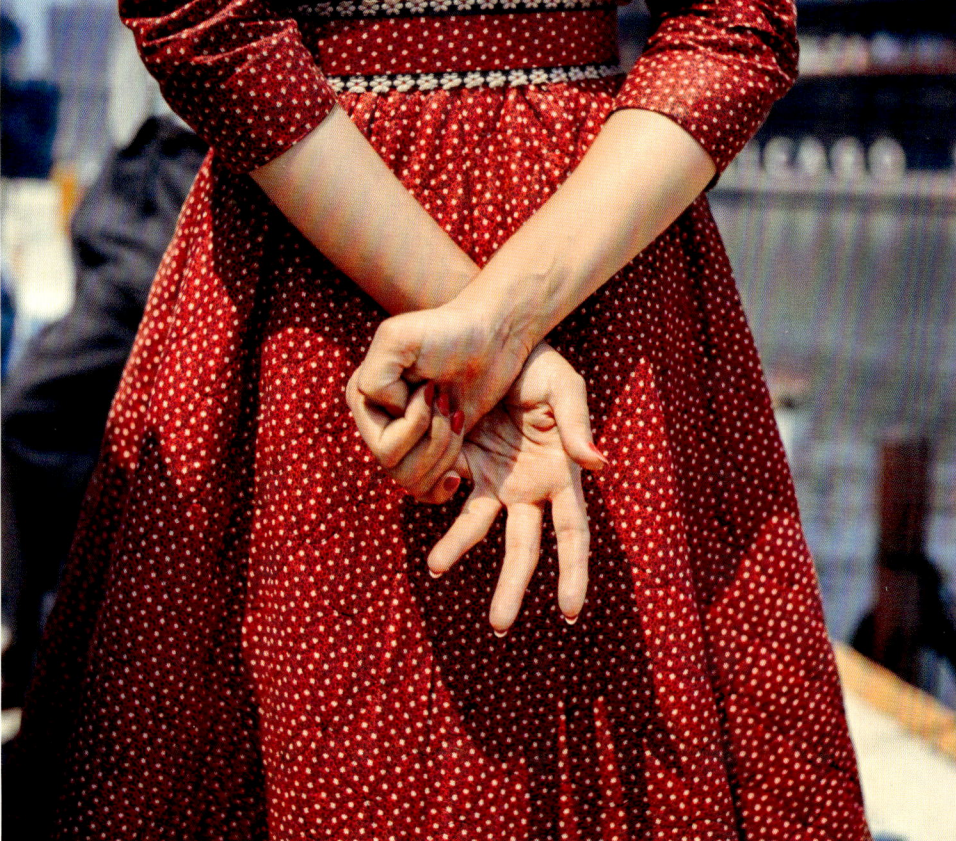

Vivian Maier

When Vivian Dorothy Maier passed away at the age of eighty-three in 2009, her most readily legible legacy was an approximately forty-year career as a nanny. A markedly secluded woman, Maier has earned her artistic acclaim only posthumously when a major body of her photographs was discovered, in 2007, by the Chicago collector John Maloof at a local auction house. A multitude of international exhibitions and documentaries that probe the photographer's mysterious life followed, including the upcoming show *Works in Color* at Foam in Amsterdam. This latest inquiry into the archive and myth of Maier presents approximately sixty color works depicting the eclectic residents of Chicago, as well as the city's equally eye-catching window displays, billboards, and found objects. Trading her go-to Rolleiflex in favor of a Leica, Maier made images that are "a bit more playful and tongue-in-cheek," says the curator Kim Knoppers. The exhibition also celebrates Maier's disruption of street photography's male-dominated canon as well as "her great eye on America."

Vivian Maier—Works in Color at Foam, Amsterdam, April 10–June 28, 2020

Orlando

February 7 – May 2, 2020

Guest curated by Tilda Swinton, organized by Aperture

The West Coast debut of the pioneering exhibition, inspired by the writings of Virginia Woolf

Open for exploration, contemplation, and engagement in the art and ideas of the McEvoy Family Collection

mcevoyarts.org
@mcevoyarts

1150 25th Street, Building B
San Francisco, CA 94107

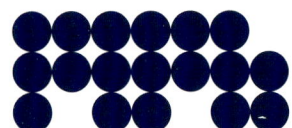

 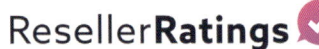

MORE INTO AERODYNAMICS THAN DYNAMIC RANGE NOW?

When your interests move on, move your kit on too. Cash in on your camera gear. Get a free instant quote.

Trusted by 250,000 creatives. Sell or trade in.

mpb.com/sell

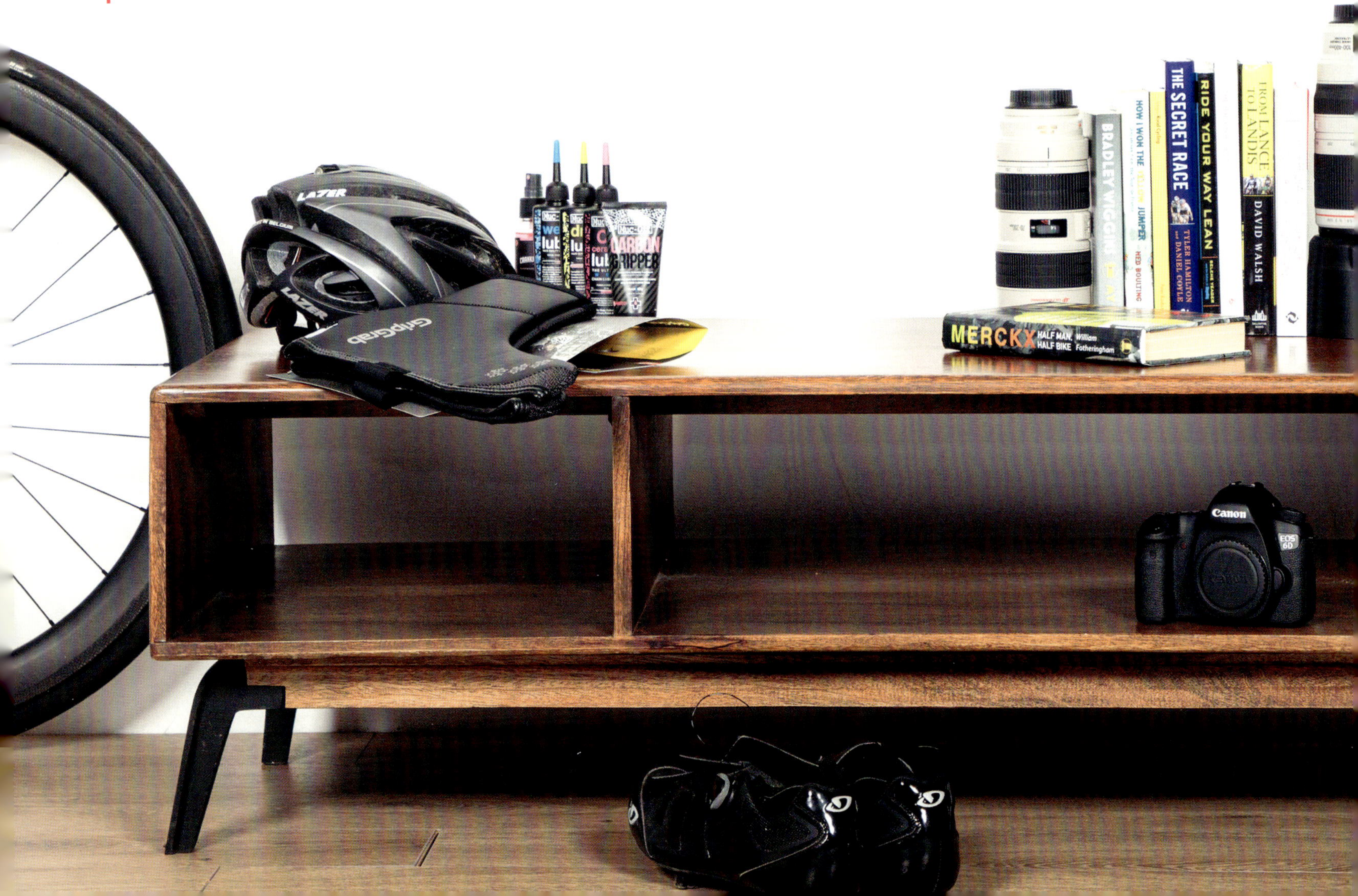

Redux

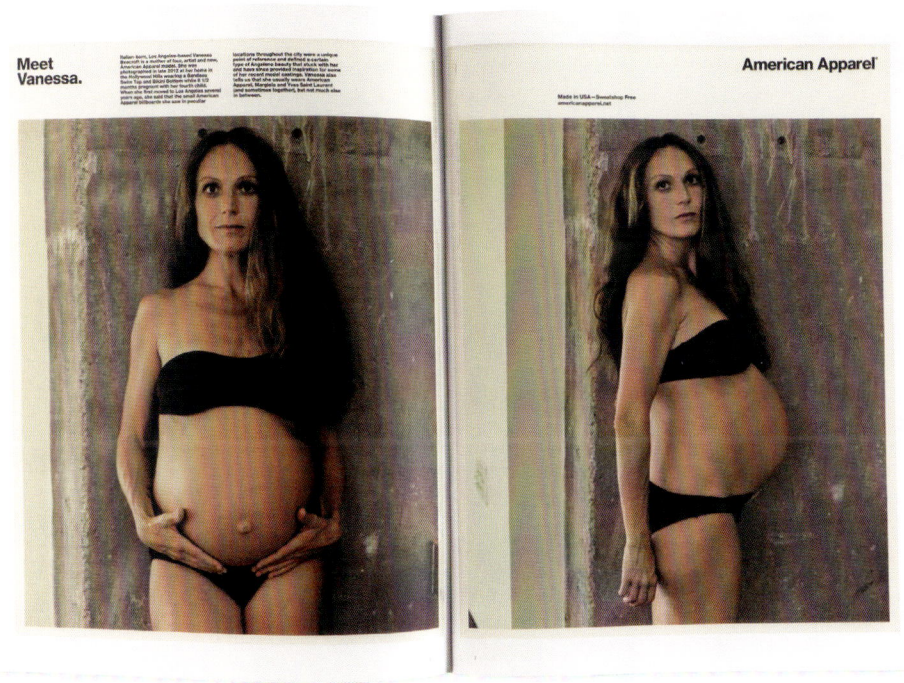

**Norman Rockwell, Jeff Koons, and Vanessa Beecroft
have something to sell you.**
Randy Kennedy

At least since Pop—but, really, going back as far as Pablo Picasso's 1912 newspaper-clipping collages and Gerald Murphy's 1920s paintings of product packaging—high art and advertising have been circling each other slowly, sometimes falling into a rash embrace. By the 1980s, the writer and editor Glenn O'Brien could riff about whether anyone still cared about keeping them apart: "An art-director friend called and said she was making a TV commercial for Barneys New York and she needed some words," he wrote later. "Would I do it? I didn't hesitate for a second. Why not? What is the difference between art and advertising? Quality? Clearly not. The only difference I could come up with for sure was the logo."

It was around the '80s that artists themselves started appearing with greater frequency *in* advertisements, and, as O'Brien would have said, why not? As a group, they might not look as good as celebrities or athletes, but they almost always look better than writers, and

Andy Warhol, who never met a product he wouldn't pimp, had shown the way. The French conceptual artist Pierre Leguillon's new photobook *Ads* (2019) presents full-page images of fifty-five artists in their sometimes cool, sometimes cringy roles as pitch people, arranged with neither commentary nor critique, from Abramović (Marina) to Young (Aaron).

Besides Warhol, the lineup includes a handful of usual suspects, artists you would be surprised have not appeared in far more ads, like Salvador Dalí, Norman Rockwell, and Jeff Koons. But the bulk of the book is like an accidental group show, made up of more than a few artists you probably wouldn't expect to find among the perfumed pages. Jean Cocteau for TV sets? Thomas Hart Benton for commercial aircraft? Robert Mapplethorpe for Rose's lime juice!? My favorite ads are the ones in which the creative director seems to have ceded control to the artist, resulting in some seriously loopy *détournement*: Donald Baechler for Gap, appearing in a

portrait hugging what appears to be a large white ceramic pepper; Robert Rauschenberg for Barneys, grinning in a floor-length shearling coat with a chair floating above him, an apparent reference to Merce Cunningham's *Antic Meet*; Peter Shire for American Apparel cavorting in dad shorts, striped socks, and sandals.

Of course, the selection makes you dream of the campaigns that never were and how they might have looked: Marcel Duchamp for Schwinn? Ad Reinhardt for Rheingold beer? Georgia O'Keeffe for Stetson? Donald Judd for John Deere? Diane Arbus for Disneyland? Tracey Emin for Frette? Why not? As Warhol said: "When you think about it, department stores are kind of like museums." And, more to the point: "Art? That's a man's name."

Randy Kennedy is Editor in Chief of *Ursula* magazine, published by Hauser & Wirth. His first novel, *Presidio*, was published in 2018.

Spread from Pierre Leguillon, *Ads* (Brussels: Triangle Books, 2019)

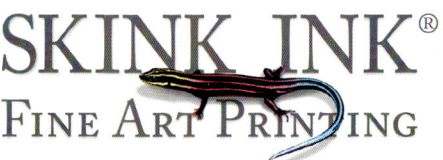

Backstory

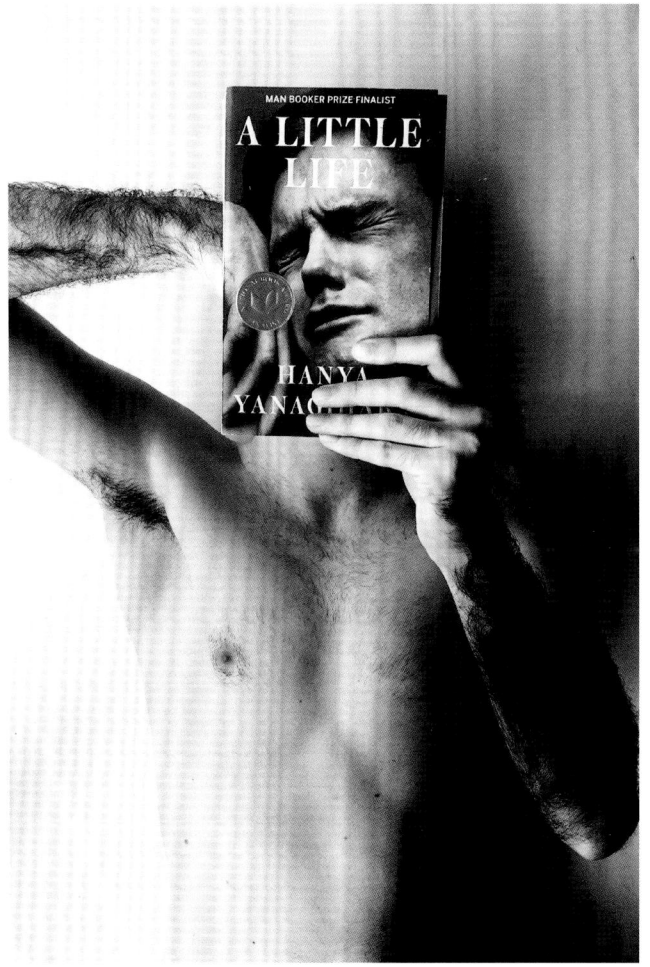

With their clever use of photographs, are book jackets the new record sleeves?

Alistair O'Neill

The British writer Rachel Cusk's celebrated *Outline* trilogy, published between 2014 and 2018, concerns a series of journeys a writer named Faye takes in Europe. In one, Faye encounters a woman who is obsessed with the works of a painter. "What she was trying to say was that she wasn't interested in them objectively, as art," Cusk writes. "They were more like thoughts, thoughts in someone else's head that she could see."

A recent spate of well-regarded novels has taken the use of photographs in book jacket design into new territory, structuring a relationship between word and image. The U.K. Faber and the U.S. Picador editions of Cusk's trilogy, designed by Rodrigo Corral, make use of still lifes by the fashion photographer Charlie Engman. The thick white border and the bold black all-caps text frame an image that offers a way into thinking about what the individual titles of the trilogy might refer to—*Outline*, *Transit*, *Kudos*. But after reading the book, you realize how provisional the cover's illustrative nature is. Corral's design was in reaction to reading Cusk's prose: "It isn't super linear," he says. "It's more about being part of the journey."

The U.S. edition of the American writer and *T Magazine* editor Hanya Yanagihara's novel *A Little Life* (2015) and the U.K. edition of the British writer Olivia Laing's first novel, *Crudo* (2018), turn this observation concrete. Both novelists were inspired to use photographs for their book jackets after seeing them in galleries. Yanagihara saw Peter Hujar's *Orgasmic Man* (1969); Laing saw Wolfgang Tillmans's *astro crusto* (2012). Laing has noted that Tillmans's image of a post-prandial crustacean shell connects to a scene in the book where her lead character, Kathy, smashes a crab open with a hammer.

But the principle of using someone else's work to frame your own rises above the evident linkage. Laing's use of the American writer Kathy Acker as her protagonist—partly quoting Acker's work, largely fictionalizing her life—is a feature of her style of autofiction, but it is also bound up with how writing is described in the novel: "She wrote fiction, sure, but she populated it with the already extant, the pre-packaged and ready-made." Laing's Kathy is described as "Warhol's daughter," someone who is "happy to snatch what she needed but also morally invested in the cause."

It's a description that is as much about image use in publishing as it is about writing. The cover of *A Little Life* reproduces

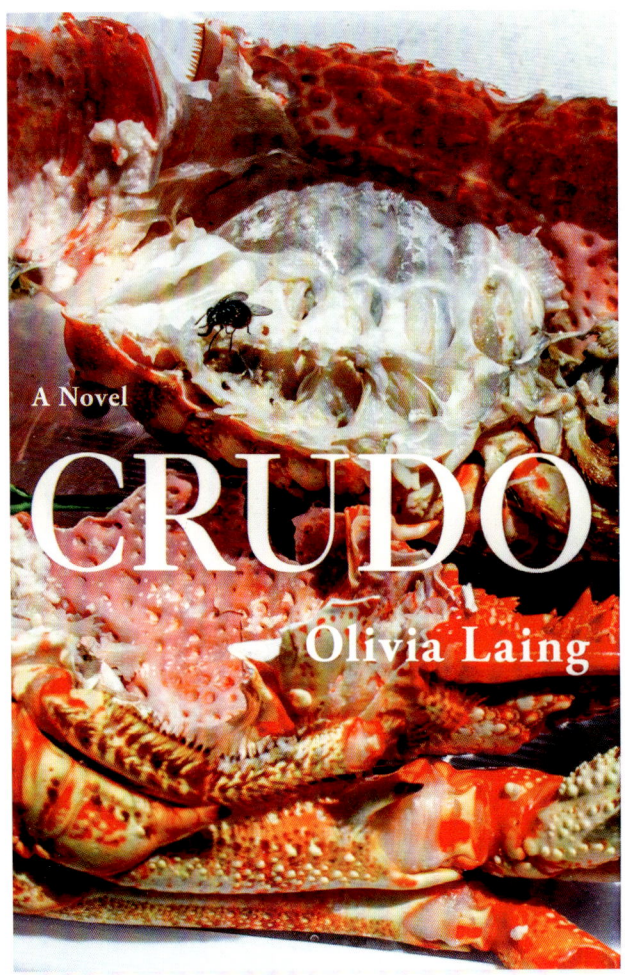

Hujar's photograph of a close-up of a man's face at the point of orgasm; although shorn of its title, the ambivalence about whether it's a face in agony or ecstasy is ramped up. Yanagihara has described the cover as a "sensation—of witness and also of trespass—that I wanted the reader to feel as well." *A Little Life* opens in New York in the early 1980s, a time when Hujar was still working, and chronicles the lives of four young men with a tight focus on private and inner worlds as represented by the cover. One of the four, JB, is an artist, and the photographs he takes of his friends—depicting them in his artworks without their consent—is what begins his distance from them. "*Tonight, I am a camera*, he told himself, *and tomorrow I will be JB again.*"

The novel's Instagram account, set up by Yanagihara and her social-media manager, has spawned similar reactions in readers—not through posting portraits of their friends as the book's character does, but by posting portraits of themselves with the book itself. As one London-based reader's body extends out from the jacket, it's as if a novel can be slipped on and off like an alternate, temporary identity or a thing worn. It's a performance that resonates with something the feminist art historian Linda Nochlin wrote: "That the self is a condition of disguise and that we can move back and forth in terms of sexualities, in terms of social being, in terms of all kinds of sense of who we are."

What these book jackets illuminate is the way the contemporary novel, both in content and cover, performs the idea of the self continually collapsing back onto other ideas, other images—as if somehow the prose operates as a written means of interconnectedness between visual ideas, a kind of long-form resort to the pictorial. It's a queer way of defining things, a privileging of final looks over how things might first be written down. It seems somehow reminiscent of record covers and not book jackets, of the photographs Steven Patrick Morrissey once chose for the singles and albums The Smiths released, or of the covers Peter Saville once designed for Joy Division and New Order that made use of sourced photographs. Perhaps it is the realization that novels are now the sleeve notes of our time.

Alistair O'Neill is Professor of Fashion History and Theory at Central Saint Martins, London.

Previous page: Marc Garcia Vilella's Instagram post of himself with a copy of Hanya Yanagihara's *A Little Life*, 2015, with photograph by Peter Hujar
Courtesy the photographer

This page, left: Cover of Olivia Laing, *Crudo*, 2018, with photograph by Wolfgang Tillmans; right: cover of Rachel Cusk, *Transit*, 2018, with photograph by Charlie Engman

PHOTOGRAPHS
April 4 | New York | Live & Online

Including a Collection of Weegee Photographs Unseen for 82 Years.

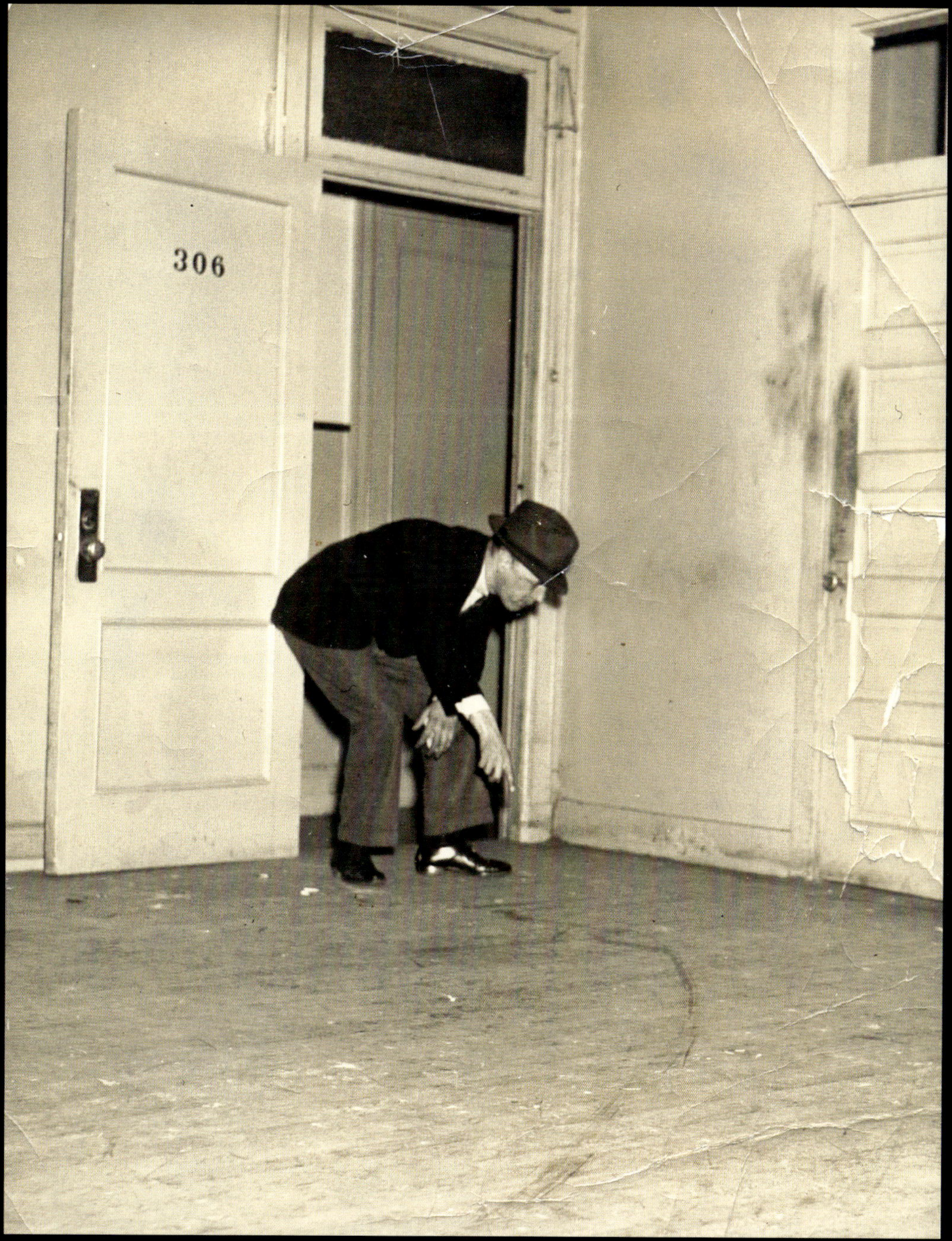

Weegee (American, 1899-1968)
Spurned Suitor Clubs Violinist to Death, April 18, 1937

VIEW | TRACK | BID HA.com/8002

Consignments and Inquiries:
Nigel Russell | NigelR@HA.com | 212.486.3659

DALLAS | NEW YORK | BEVERLY HILLS | SAN FRANCISCO | CHICAGO | PALM BEACH
LONDON | PARIS | GENEVA | AMSTERDAM | HONG KONG

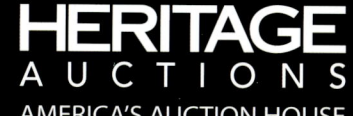

HERITAGE
AUCTIONS
AMERICA'S AUCTION HOUSE

Curriculum
By Rosalind Fox Solomon

"I'm not looking for the outer coating," says the New York photographer Rosalind Fox Solomon. "I want a few moments when we stare into one another, exchanging our histories and feelings in a glance." Across Solomon's work, from Poland to South Africa, from AIDS patients in the 1980s to racial tensions in Chattanooga, Tennessee, those glances are marked by a pure constancy of vision. Her photographs—often square-format and distinguished by the silver sheen of an on-camera flash—extend the sharpened humor and interrogative style of Lisette Model, her mentor. For Solomon, who started taking pictures in her late thirties and has since built a decades-long career, photography is all about the public performance of private emotions.

Hassan Fazili, *Midnight Traveler*, 2019

For photographers and filmmakers, the fact that this well-edited and moving film was made with cellphones is reason enough to see it. *Midnight Traveler* is the saga of an Afghan family on the run, seeking political asylum. Threatened with assassination, Hassan Fazili, his wife, who is also a filmmaker, and their two children left Afghanistan in 2015, crossing borders and staying within fenced camps, with no promise of finding permanent refuge. We watch them acclimate to the unexpected, not having any idea of where they might be allowed to begin a new life. It humanizes the fate of others escaping dangers who are stuck in camps. It reminds us of the deplorable situation on our southern border, where those who seek safer lives in the United States are blocked and detained.

Satyajit Ray, *Pather Panchali*, 1955

Pather Panchali, considered one of the best films of all time, is about a poor, rural, Bengali family struggling to manage their life. It is excellent in every aspect: the quality of the black-and-white film, the sensitivity of the actors, and Ravi Shankar's nuanced music. Satyajit Ray was a filmmaker, screenwriter, composer, graphic artist—a renaissance man. I first saw the film in 1981. When I went to Calcutta later that year, I was told to look up his number in the phone book and call him. I did, and I photographed him the next day.

Lisette Model

As a young woman in early twentieth-century Vienna, Lisette Model studied piano with the composer Arnold Schoenberg, but switched to photography. In 1938, she and her husband left Europe and settled in New York, where she drew the attention of Alexey Brodovitch, art director of *Harper's Bazaar*. Lisette said she never spoke to her subjects. She saw a picture and took it. She created her art in the darkroom, with crops and tilts of the easel. Lisette taught many photographers, including Diane Arbus. I studied with her when I was forty-two, four years after I first took up the camera. Encouraging me to make photography my life's priority, she advised, "Do what you have to do without a fight. Follow your intuition."

Memoirs

From the *New York Times*' 2019 list of the fifty best memoirs of the past fifty years, here is a small selection from the many that I read and liked: *Negroland* (2015), by Margo Jefferson, on the struggles of the upper strata of nonwhite society; *Close to the Knives* (1991), by David Wojnarowicz, the heartbreaking memoir of an artist with AIDS; *Fierce Attachments* (1987), by Vivian Gornick, on the strife and humor of her relationship with her mother; *Dancing with Cuba* (2004), by Alma Guillermoprieto (translated from the Spanish by Esther Allen), on her life in Havana during the early aftermath of the Cuban Revolution.

Jason Eckardt

Contemporary ensemble music began to enrich my life after I met Jason Eckardt at the MacDowell Colony in 2001. My own image, *Statue of Liberty Scaffolded* (1976), is imprinted on the cover of *Subject*, his 2015 album. A section of Eckardt's *Tongues* (2001) is part of the soundtrack of my audiovisual piece *Scintillation* (2016).

Alexander Technique

In the 1890s, F. M. Alexander, an Australian actor born in 1869, originated a technique for feeling better as you move and breathe when he lost his voice and then regained it by learning about his body and his habits. While the technique was often used by musicians and actors, the practice quickly expanded beyond those groups. For me, it's helpful for aging gracefully, by learning to let go of unnecessary habits.

Joseph Losey, *Mr. Klein*, 1976

This film, set in 1942 during the German occupation of France, is a favorite because of its excellent direction, cinematography, and substance. Its narrative, based on mistaken identity, reinforces concern about anti-Semitism today and past historic horrors. It begins with a Jewish man selling valuable family art to a wealthy collector for much less than it is worth because he desperately needs the money in order to feed his family. The film was unpopular in France when it came out because of its portrayal of French collaboration with the Nazi roundups of Jews. In its final scene, we see children being pulled away from their parents before being pushed into trains headed for the gas chambers.

Faith Ringgold

Faith Ringgold is an artist, author, and civil-rights activist. Her painting *American People Series #20: Die* (1967), in the Museum of Modern Art's permanent collection, presents a disturbing scene from her series on 1960s race relations. Ringgold antedates Kara Walker and other younger artists whose works address the ethos of violence, slavery, and racism in the United States.

Lynne Tillman, *Men and Apparitions*, 2018

Lynne Tillman's brilliant musings in this novel range from the profound to the hilarious. Headings include "Seeing Proves Nothing," "Family Drama: Growing Up More Crazy," "The Guilt of Images," "Undocumenting the Document." Here are some of Tillman's many commentaries on photography:

> With digitization, possibilities multiply for what humanity can imagine itself as, which it might one day be or fulfill.
> A photograph infers, doesn't confer.
> Humans split the atom, but can't split themselves from their images.
> "I love the activity of sound … sound that doesn't mean anything."—Cage
> Pictures don't have to mean anything. Life doesn't have to.

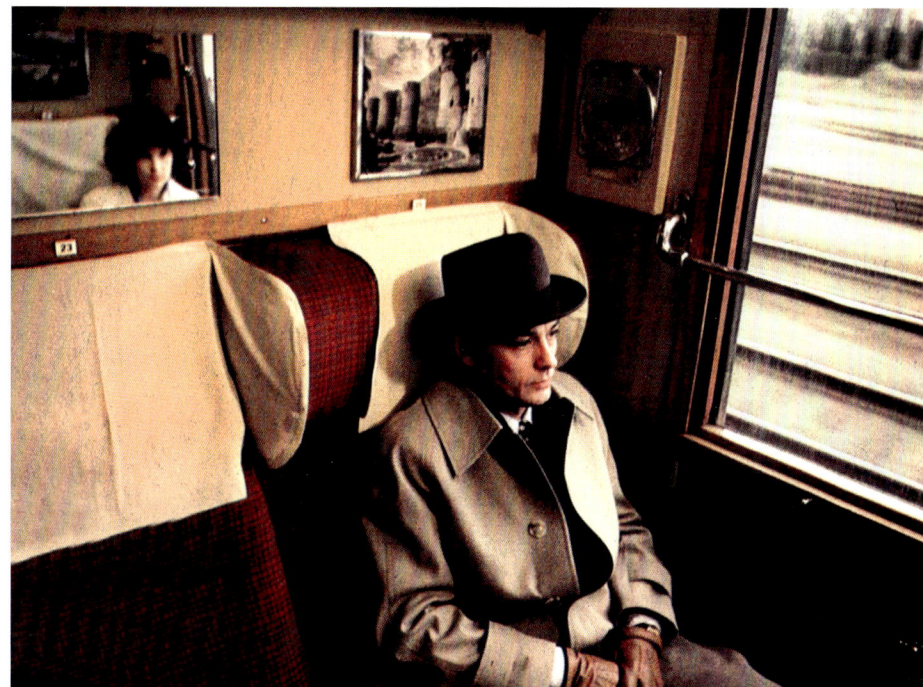

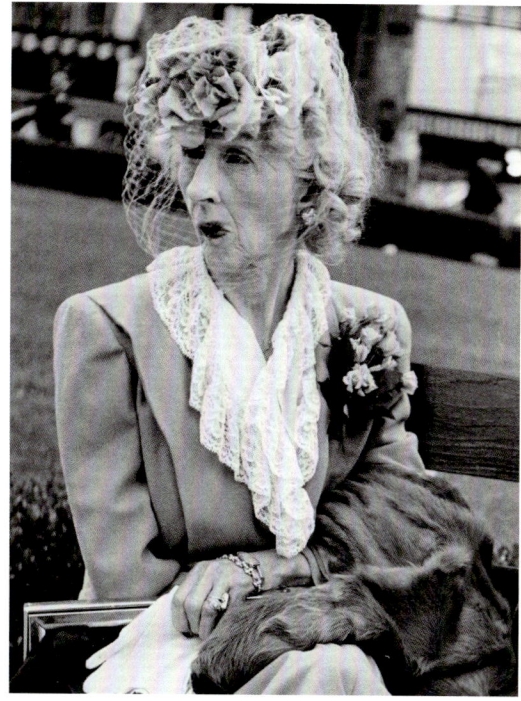

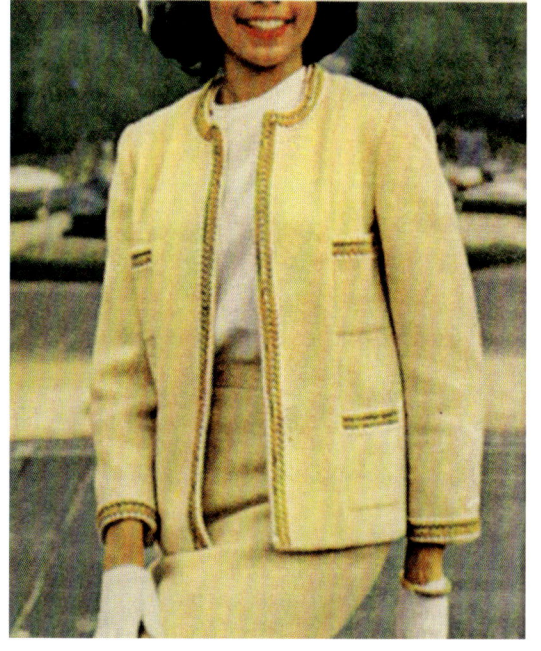

Negroland a memoir
Margo Jefferson

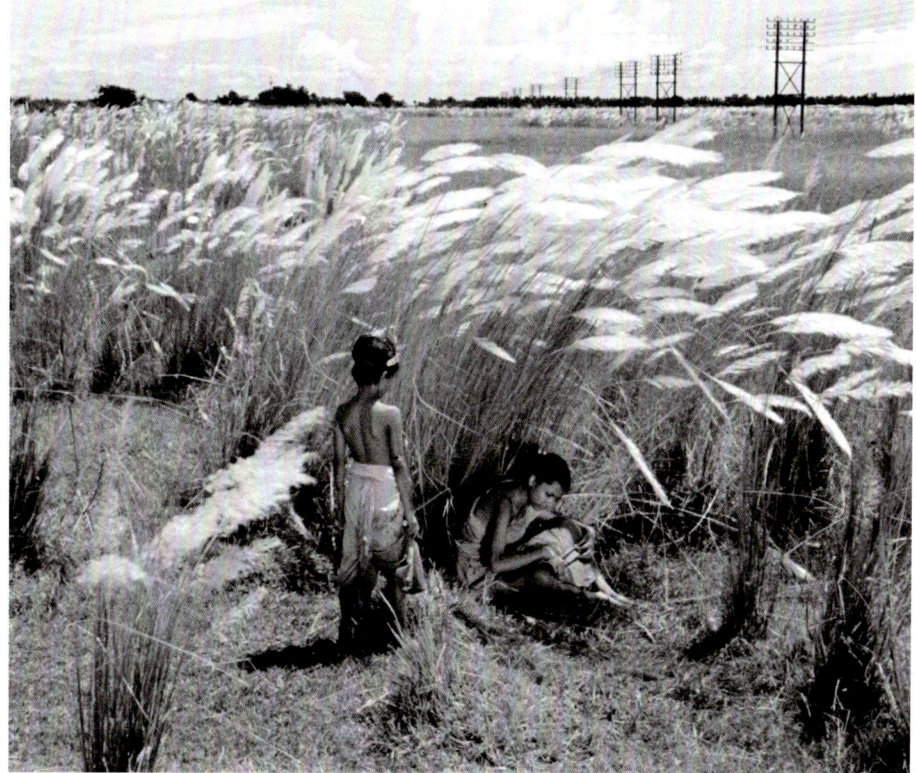

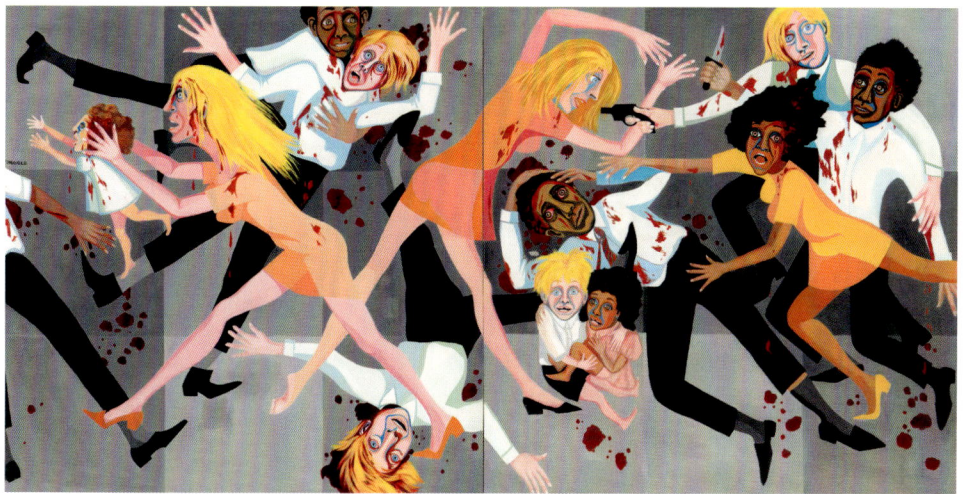

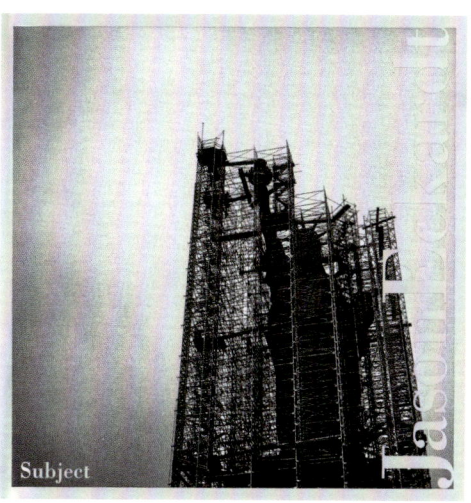

Subject

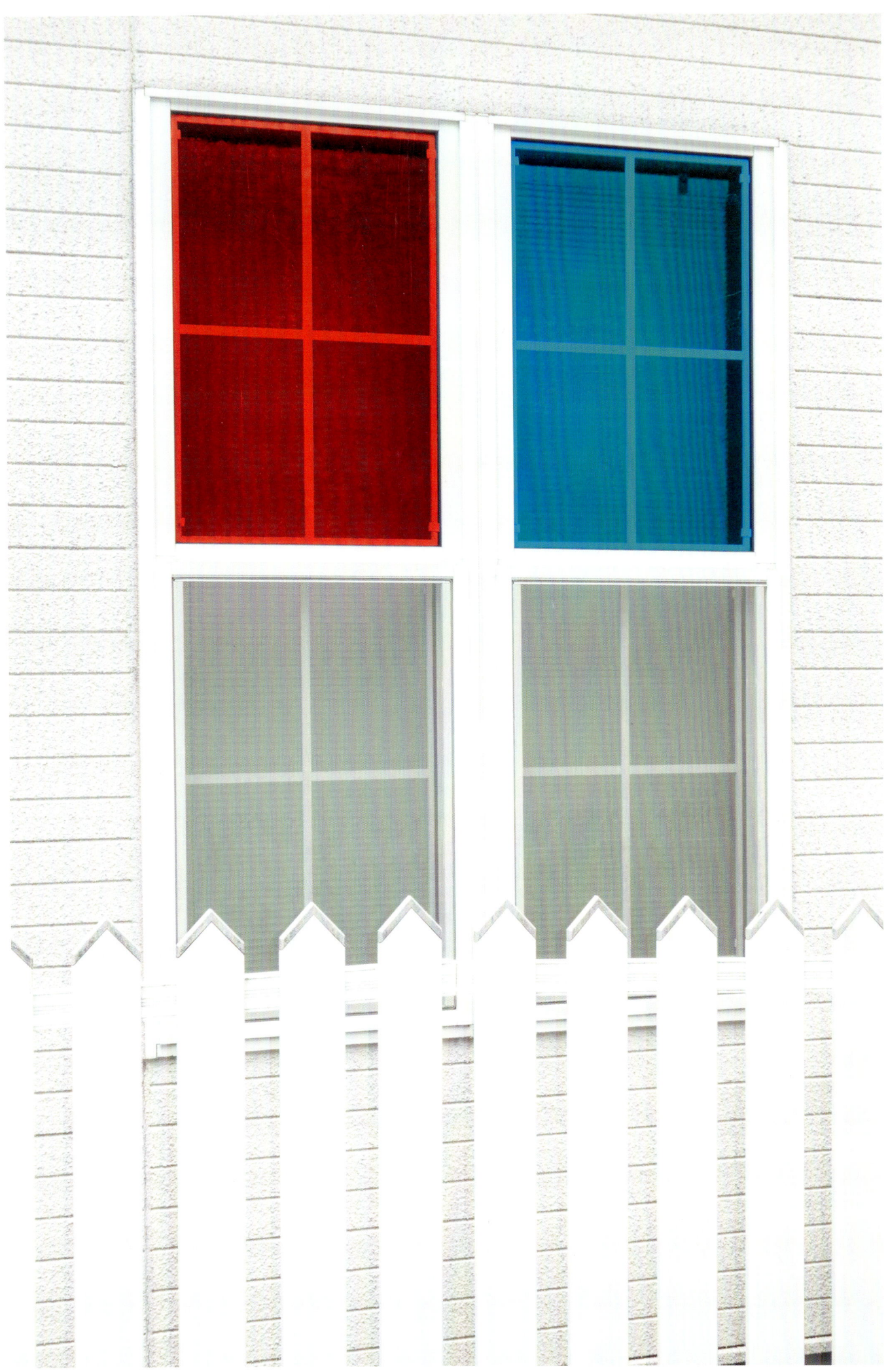

Fumi Ishino, from the series *Loom*, Japan, 2018
Courtesy the artist
(See page 64)

House & Home

In 1835, William Henry Fox Talbot used his new invention to make a photographic image of his own residence, Lacock Abbey, in England, proclaiming it to be "the first instance on record, of a house having painted its own portrait." Since then, through myriad revolutions in technologies, the forms and goings-on of the domestic realm have remained a preoccupation for photographers, who, like writers, often depict what they know. "I wanted just to show what lay within the houses that were a part of my primary subject, the new western landscape," says Robert Adams of his austere interiors of suburban housing schemes in the United States. "I also hoped, however, to find evidence of human caring."

Just as photographers have trained their lenses on the built environment, architects have equally been drawn to photography. In this issue, four visionary architects discuss how they conceive of homes, civic spaces, and the fabric of our cities. "Photography is not just images of places," says David Adjaye, whose own Instagram "sketchbook" is a lesson in looking at buildings and thinking through urbanism. It is "a whole set of information that really captures the narrative about a time, or a place, or a form … or even just a sensation."

Whether as a form of inspiration, a means of documentation, or a vital component of the design process, architects rely on photographs. Since the 1950s, Denise Scott Brown has made thousands, often while traveling the globe, and most famously as part of her Las Vegas Studio, with Robert Venturi, which studied the signs and symbols of the city's iconic neon-decorated strip. From her Art Nouveau home outside Philadelphia, she sums up her motivations to get behind the camera: "We wanted a record." She now plans to collect this record in a book of her life's work.

More recently, Frida Escobedo designed a house that is partly based on a camera obscura, featuring a large window that frames her hometown of Mexico City—a place of social contradictions examined through her creative practice. While Annabelle Selldorf acknowledges the photographs that have been important to her and discusses her collaborative process of working with a photographer, she also reminds us that architecture is about being *in* spaces, not just consuming images of spaces. "We live in an age where everything is event-driven and, for me, that's overwhelming," she says. "What I care about is a kind of calm, or tranquility, that creates a setting."

From Seher Shah and Randhir Singh's abstracted cyanotypes of the brutalist geometries of London's Barbican Estate to Ezra Stoller's luminous images of mid-century modern designs, we see how artists are more interested in interpreting than rendering buildings: they go beyond converting three-dimensional form into two-dimensional surface. Mauro Restiffe's approach is almost like drawing. In his recent series made in Villa Santo Sospir—known as the "tattooed villa"—in the South of France, he captures the artist Jean Cocteau's mythological sketches that flow over its ceilings and walls. The space feels magical, timeless. "My approach is to get into the textures of places," says Restiffe. "I want to give more warmth to architecture, to offer traces of human life." —**The Editors**

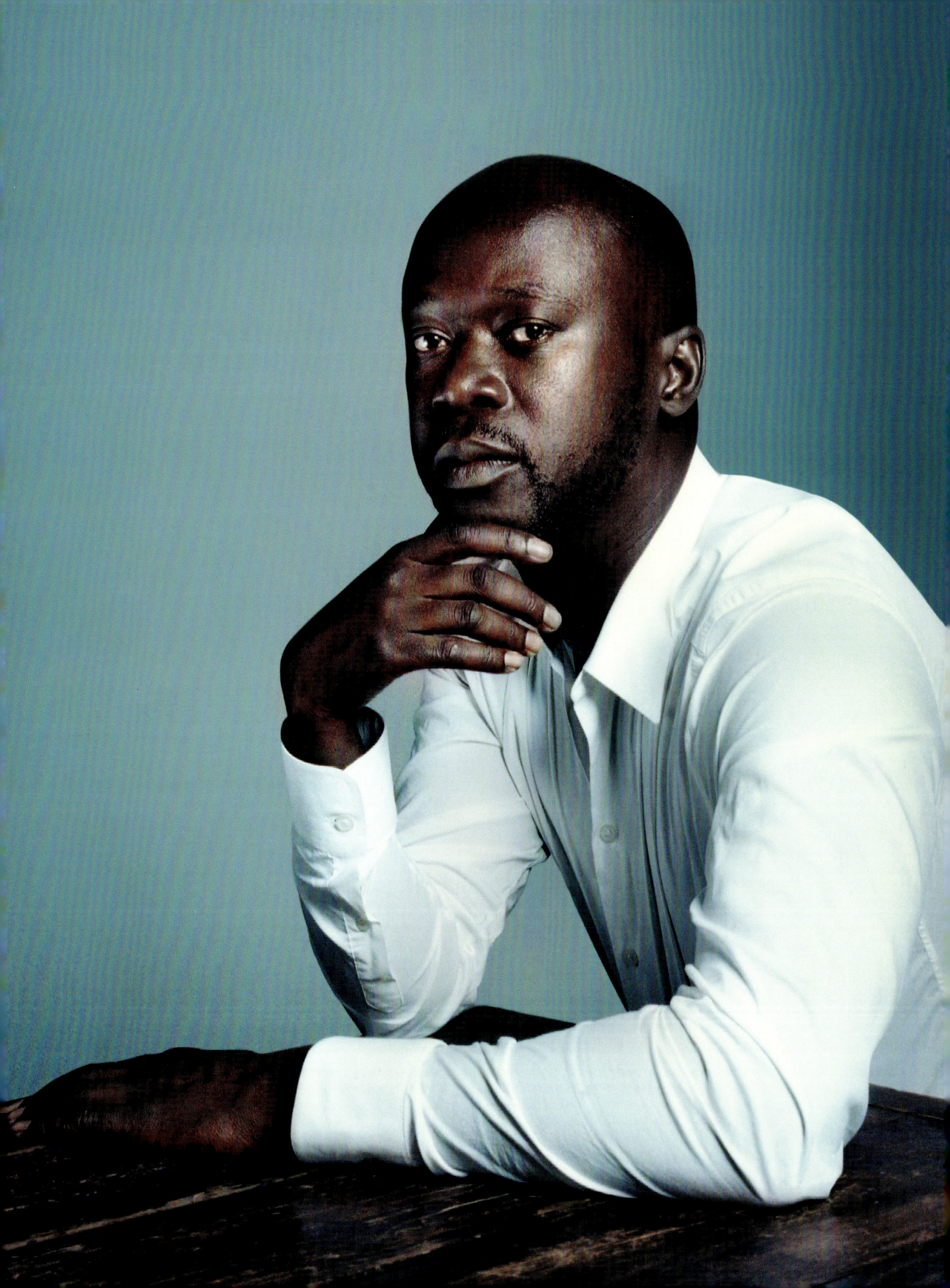

David Adjaye

"Intimacy is profoundly at the heart of my work."

A Conversation with Emmanuel Iduma

In the course of the nearly thirty years of his practice, Sir David Adjaye's projects have been realized on five continents. They include cultural and historical landmarks—such as the National Museum of African American History and Culture, in Washington, D.C., and the planned Holocaust Memorial, in London—and sites that show the possibilities of civic engagement, such as the Moscow School of Management SKOLKOVO and the new building for the Studio Museum in Harlem. His practice, based in New York, London, and Accra, is like a body, he says, "implanting itself globally across many geographies."

During a recent conversation with the writer Emmanuel Iduma, Adjaye was most impassioned when he spoke of drastic changes ahead, in which cities of the future will be increasingly brutal. He has the credentials to make these claims. An artist's architect, Adjaye has worked with Chris Ofili, Lorna Simpson, and Olafur Eliasson, all of whom push the boundaries of the imagination. Yet it seems clear to him that there are distinctions to make with regard to scale: between the domestic and official, the intimate and public. Here, Adjaye, whose own photographs of architecture in Africa and around the world have been collected in books and shared widely on Instagram, reflects on the sensibilities that inform what kinds of homes we build, and how we live in them. Change might be inevitable, but Adjaye believes the home must be designed as a refuge.

Emmanuel Iduma: When you begin designing a home, what kind of visual references do you use, and how do you approach that kind of research?

David Adjaye: It's quite a specific task, especially if you have the luxury of being able to make a home at the beginning of the twenty-first century. For me, it's not so much about visual references or trying to make relationships to other things, but really about starting from the inside out, moving from the person to the enclosure. In a way, the idea of making homes is about what I call a "unique intimacy." We don't do homes like you see in big magazines. We do them for some very particular people who want to create intimate scenarios.

The research comes from the place that they want to make their home, whatever that idea is, and then we move out from there. If you look at the houses that we've done, there's always either a reference to the local area, or to the construction, or to the materiality. But more than that, which is the last part of that layer, it's this kind of reference to the person, or the couple, or the family, whether it's about art, or a certain kind of labor, or a certain kind of cooperation.

EI: **Your 2011 book, *African Metropolitan Architecture*, includes numerous photographs that you made throughout the continent. How do photographs by artists or architectural photographers, or even your own photographs, play into your design process, and help you develop your thinking on architecture and urbanism?**

DA: Photography is critically important to me because photography is not just images of places, but it encodes within the eye of the photographer a whole set of information that really captures the narrative about a time, or a place, or a form, or an object, or an experience, or even just a sensation.

When I was making my journey around the continent, I was shooting and cropping and editing my images very specifically. They had a certain kind of casual manner, because I was making a critique against a kind of highly choreographed photography. I was very specific and deliberate. Those images are taken in an honest way to share exactly how I look at things, and how that information is constantly in a feedback loop with me. They are shot a certain way to give me thoughts about a certain region, or a certain place, or to trigger certain emotions about a place. And they are constantly reused to delve into issues that I'm very interested in.

EI: **The first major project that you designed in the United States, Pitch Black (2006), was the artist Lorna Simpson's studio in Brooklyn. I'm curious whether her work informed the building of the studio, or whether, in general, your relationships with artists inform the homes, the studios, and even the museums that you build?**

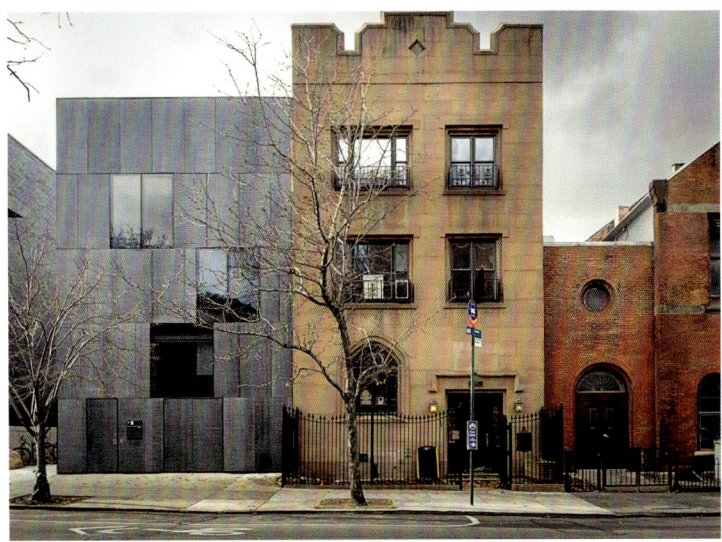

DA: Lorna is probably one of my favorite artists in the world. She asked me to work on her studio with her partner at the time, Jim Casebere. I was fascinated by both of their practices. The project was drawn from her incredible gazes, these gazes of the phenomenon of architecture and the phenomenon of the body in architectural space, and the way in which the body can be dismembered to have narratives about memory and cultural scenarios.

So the building is a kind of game in that way. It's really a fragment of a set piece, which has to do with how close it is to a church and a rectory. When you look at that building, it's really a composition about religion and black culture, and then the reappropriation of topology, the phenomenon of form, the use of different space—those are all working through it. And it's really a direct critique/discourse with her work in a very profound way.

If you look at the houses that we've done, there's always either a reference to the local area, or to the construction, or to the materiality.

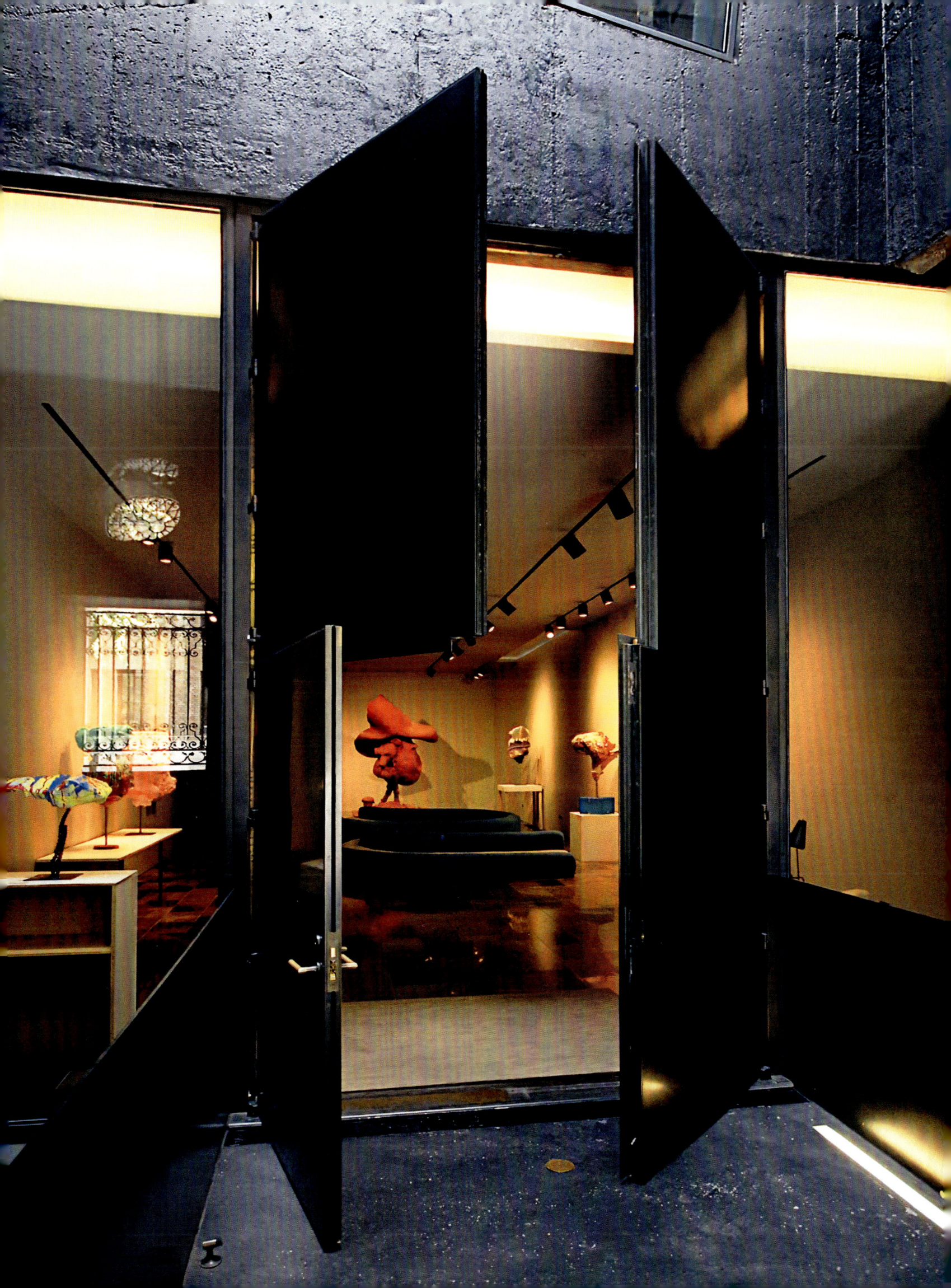

People look at the architecture of West Africa and they think of it as a kind of material primitive but actually don't realize the sophistication.

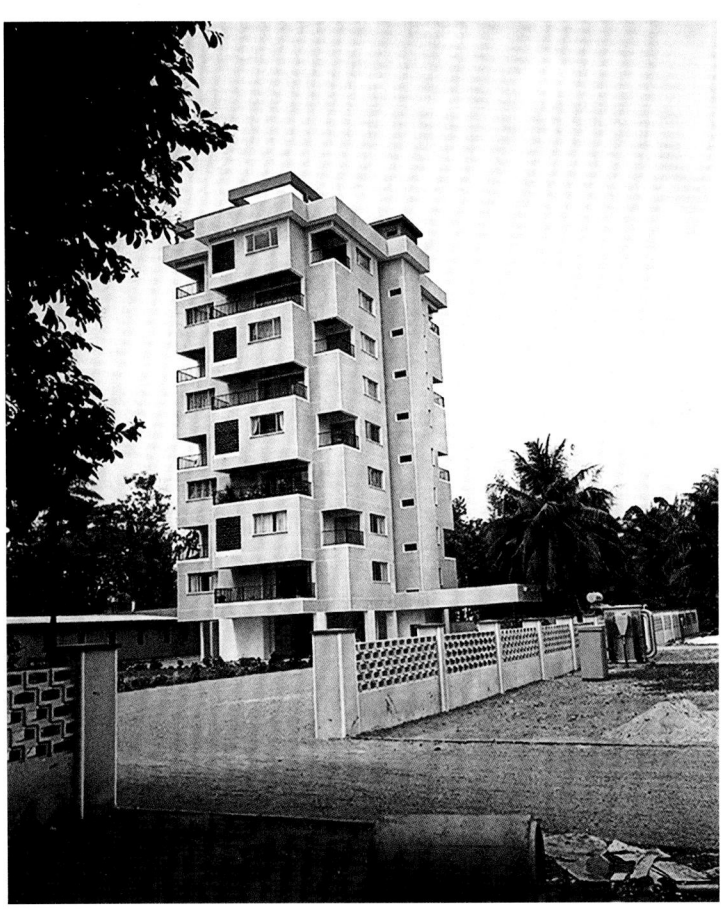

EI: **I am also thinking about an interview you granted to the Design Museum, where you were speaking about the Smithsonian's National Museum of African American History and Culture (2016), in Washington, D.C., and one of the things you say is that you wanted to create a design that transforms the museum from a viewing experience into a narrative experience. Does this particular form of museology also impact the kind of work you do with artists or museums, if you're thinking critically about the kind of storytelling experience that a viewer can have?**

DA: Absolutely. Museums have gone so far as to become almost an archive of history; I think that the complexity of our time has been missing from the way in which museums have organized their spatial narrative. In making the Smithsonian, I really wanted to avoid that problem. I wanted to make content that, even though it's dense, has a kind of trajectory and a direction to it, for people to really engage in increments—in bite-size pieces, knowing where the story is and how to sample it. Almost all my public projects have a curatorial or narrative base to do with trying to impart some kind of experience through other media.

EI: **Yes. Perhaps that's a good place to segue into talking about this turn from designing residential spaces to designing public spaces. Is the process similar, or is it different?**

DA: They share a common kind of research root, but they are, to me, expressed very differently. Public spaces really are about speaking to the time and to the powerful narratives that are in the space. And residential spaces are slightly different, because they have to do with the kind of changing nature of the city, and the different densities. The residential buildings are more about a kind of specific beauty, and the public spaces are about a kind of collective beauty.

EI: **I was reflecting on your ideas in relation to the work you did with Carriage House (2010) with Adam Lindemann and Amalia Dayan, who are art collectors. They were collecting work that normally would fit in museums, institutional spaces, and now they wanted a space in which they could live with this kind of work. You speak about this "schizophrenia," as you called it, between the domestic and the institutional, or the domestic (in my own thinking) and the undomestic. Do you still think about those kinds of distinctions?**

DA: Adam and Amalia's house—that's something almost iconic in my portfolio. Really an assessment of the blur between the two worlds. In a way, their kind of ravenous attempt at collecting at the institutional as well as the domestic scale was fascinating for me, because that's the schizophrenia that I thought was extraordinary— collecting for the home, the palace built with specific pieces, the ravenous idea to collect what is relevant irrespective of the scale. So the house is a dialogue between the institutional-commercial scale and the residential. In the entire house, there's nothing in the sense of conventional proportion; it's either exaggerated or extremely intricate. It avoids the middle ground.

EI: **One other idea that I'm interested in with relation to photography is the idea of the vernacular, which has always been important in photography, and seems to be equally important to the London homes you designed, like Glass House or Dirty House (both 2002), or even the more recent National Museum of African American History and Culture. I am curious if you still think about these notions of the vernacular, and how they might not only inform your material sources, but, say, show up in 130 William, your current high-rise project in New York.**

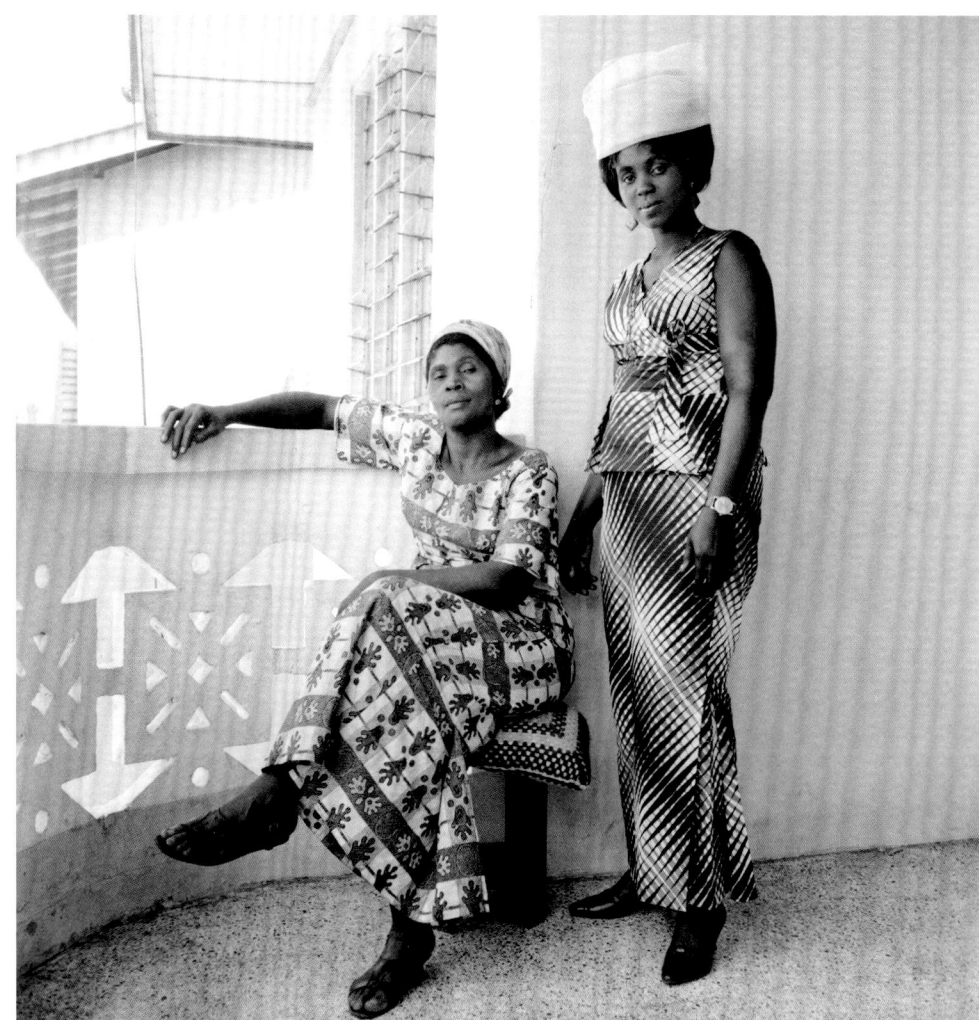

James Barnor, Two Sisters-in-law, Florence and Gifty, 1973–74
Courtesy the artist and October Gallery, London

DA: In a way, my work has a kind of new vernacular. [*Laughs*] It's kind of like a new body that's implanting itself globally across many geographies, but it's actually a new reading of the body. And it's an attempt to rescript the dominance of Western architecture and to hybridize it, to implicate it with other phenomenology. It always assumes some of what I call a "slip" with the existing conditions and also, at the same time, a resonance. That's deliberate.

EI: Is this something in particular that you're thinking about in relation to the design of the new Studio Museum in Harlem?

DA: Yes. It's such an important moment. It's a critical mark in the sand, especially after the National Museum of African American History and Culture, which is a federal project. This is a project that was generated within a city by a group of supporters and patrons and was eventually supported by the city, recognizing that it is fundamentally important. For diverse communities and communities of color who find themselves in the minority, it's a big statement. So, for me, it's like the first big cultural open house in New York—the first real one for black people.

There are all these institutions, but in a way, they were built not really for the audience of black folk or brown folk. They were built exclusively for a certain idea of the population. That's the kind of context of being an immigrant, you hybridize—in that Du Boisian sense—you can inhabit many bodies and be in many spaces. But it feels really wonderful to be able to make a space that is not about trying to assimilate into a dominant culture; it's kind of the other way around. So, in a way, everything about the Studio Museum originates from the profound experience of Harlem, and being in Harlem, and the time that has passed now, and the hybridization that has happened with the architecture, which was built by Europeans.

EI: Yes.

DA: But hybridized by people of color across the entire spectrum, and remade in a different way. Rescripting what's already happened. This is one of those moments where the rescripting now presents the opportunity of an architecture, because the rescripting, the appropriating, has been kind of completed, so that it makes its own reference, and then reimagines the city another way, which allows the city to go, "What the hell is that?" But it doesn't realize that it's actually from itself. It's birthed from the very premise of the city, but the way in which the city creates suppression can also birth a form that is surprising, generous, and opportunistic.

EI: I imagine it's a tenuous connection, but I am thinking about the notion of intimacy in your architecture and this idea of thinking about the body as some kind of metaphorical notion that guides the work you do. If one can make connections between, say, the buildings that you are making as some kind of body and the notion of intimacy in architecture, in general.

DA: Completely. I think understanding the body as architecture is a very central way to understand what I am doing. It's a very West African way of thinking, actually, that people don't realize. Most of West Africa is the city as the body—the architecture is really about the body. It's about the face, the arms; it's about the organs, the systems. People look at the architecture of West Africa—what is left, what wasn't destroyed—and they think of it as a kind of material primitive but actually don't realize the sophistication, which was about the whole way in which you organized the society.

EI: **Absolutely.**

DA: Especially in a metropolitan world, where everything is being mixed, do we make a machine aesthetic of the city, which is simply a tool, a machine to be used? Is architecture simply a machine for living in? Or is architecture an extension of the body? And I am interested in the latter.

So intimacy is profoundly at the heart of my work. And that intimacy has to do with the idea of the person in the construction called space, called the city, called whatever typology. Yes?

EI: **Yes. Thinking about typology, I just want to go back to your thinking around the photographer J. D. 'Okhai Ojeikere's work. It is possible to think that there is a so-called disjuncture between the buildings and the headgear or hairstyles. But some scholars have argued that there is no disjuncture there, that it's essentially the same vision—the attempt to capture with compositional acuity what towers above.**

DA: Correct.

EI: **Are there other photographers' works where you've seen that kind of through line between how the body is depicted, and then how buildings, or how landscape in general, is depicted?**

DA: I am not a photography expert, but I have a particular fascination with that generation that was post-independence, and the way in which they were trying to deal with the past and potentially project a body of work that speaks to the future. James Barnor is really that kind of photographer for me—he photographs West Africans in London, and speaks about the hybridity of West Africans in London,

but also photographs the West Africans in independence architecture. I am interested in them because of this relationship between the ideas of figure and space, and the way in which they try to speak about the connectivity of it. I think that the trajectory of West Africa specifically, if it hadn't been colonized, would have been really powerful in helping the world to understand how to make that architecture.

EI: **Could you speak about your concerns with gentrification, particularly if there is a difference for you between the idea of housing and the idea of home?**

DA: Gentrification is a big topic, and it's a trauma. There's gentrification that is the opportunity of capitalism and its horrible desire to gain as much as possible—especially now at the beginning of the twenty-first century. I always say that we've forgotten that we've moved from a population of one to eight billion in a hundred years, which has never happened in the history of humanity. We've gotten bigger in a hundred years than in the previous ten thousand years. And we have just started to invent tools to deal with this extraordinary explosion. People talk about housing shortages. In a hundred years' time, that magnitude is going to be even more profoundly acute, because we simply cannot build fast enough for the population explosion that's happening through the advances in medical science.

So the planet is going to change, and our ideas of the city are going to radically change. The privilege of saying "I want my space to look like what it always looked like" is a kind of hopeless fantasy, to be honest. It's a kind of wonderful fantasy, and it's romantic but not sustainable. There's the lack of ability to build in what has become of the city, and we don't want to make any more suburbs. We have to aggregate and, in fact, shrink in the center.

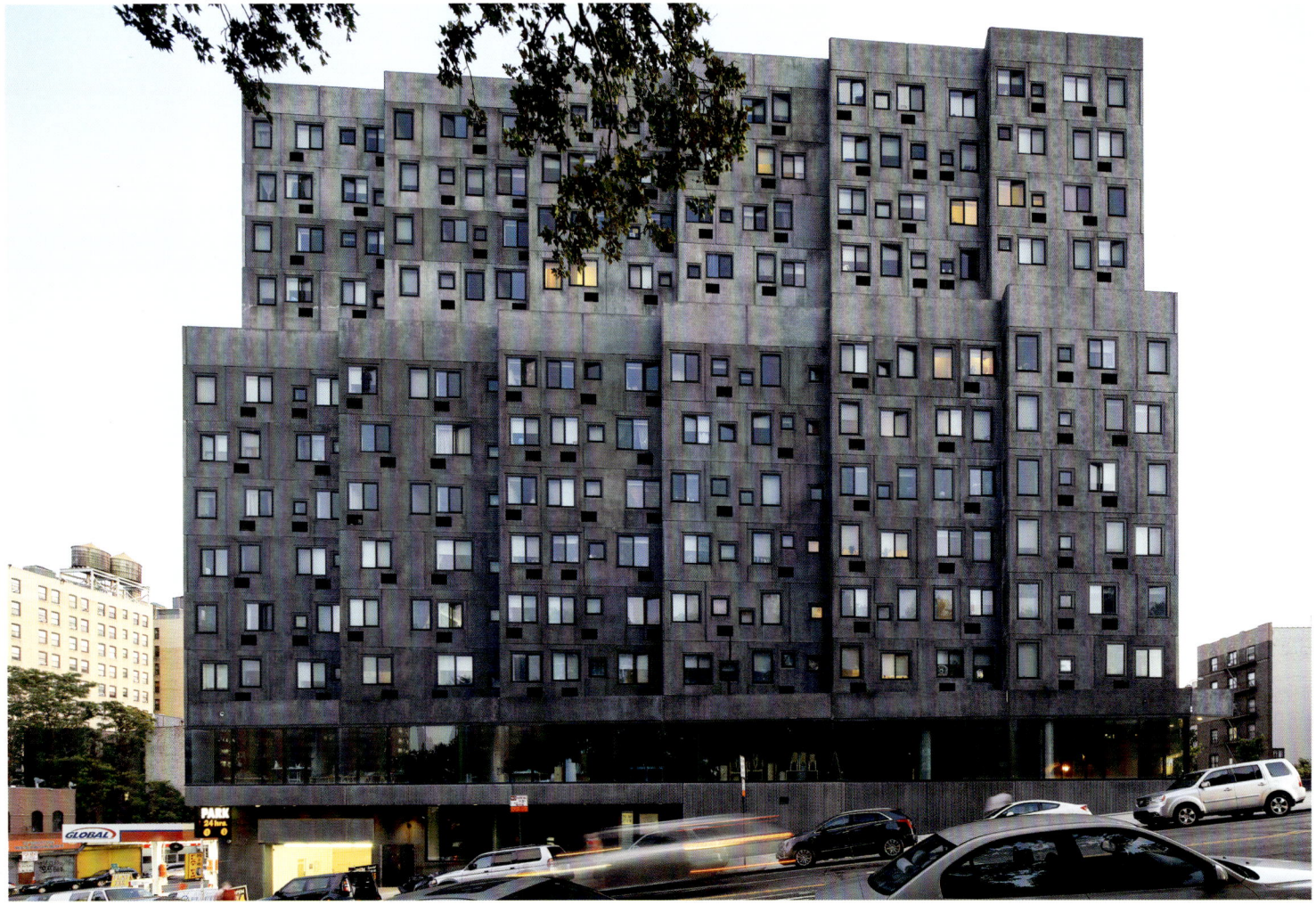

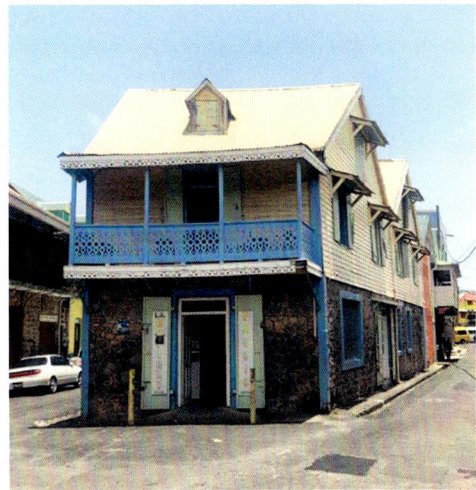

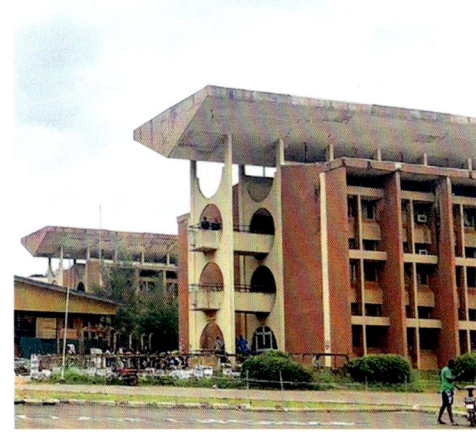

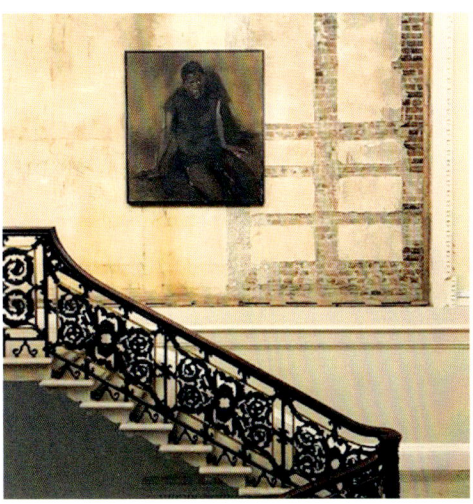

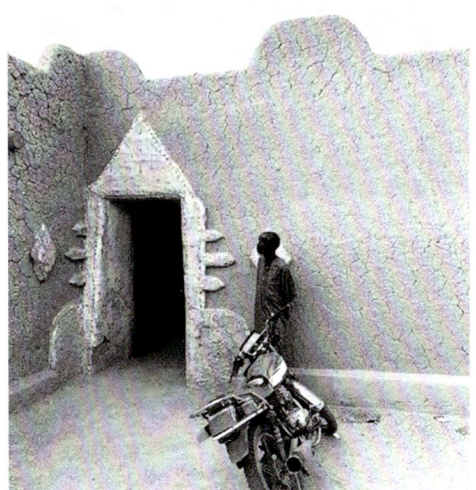

Record the city now, because in a hundred years it will not look like this. It is all going to change because we simply have changed as a civilization on this planet, and either we are going to destroy the planet by taking over all the land, or we're going to change it, we're going to shift it. And, you know, capitalism, and the way in which it creates value, has a little check in it. Markets collapse and restart. I always say to people, "Don't believe capitalism; it's a kind of game." So, yes, I am completely invested in thinking about the trauma of gentrification, especially in communities that are the least able to resist change—I am totally empathetic. But I also realize that just holding on to what it is, exactly as it is, is not the answer.

EI: **I feel like I would call that a pre-apocalyptic vision.**

DA: Totally.

EI: **But what then?**

DA: It's not quite the apocalypse. The apocalypse is much, much worse. [*Laughs*]

EI: **What kind of sensibilities do you think will be important to develop when thinking about home going into the next fifty years, or even twenty-five years?**

DA: For me, the crisis of the home is in this idea of the refuge, or the respite. If New York, or Manhattan, is a model of the relentlessness of how the city can punish the body, it's a warning at the same time of the brutality of the city against the body in the future. If you're lucky, you can create a refuge, which is your shield against the city. If you're making homes, they have to become no longer just components of the city, but refuges. They are a battery recharge for

the body before going back into the world—restorative, committed to nature, connected to a source of individuality that allows the body to breathe.

EI: **Finally, I wanted to ask about your use of Instagram. You call your page a "visual sketchbook," or that's the name of your account. I'm curious what have been the peculiar pleasures of sharing the mélange of built forms you encounter in the course of your travels, and how that has informed your practice since you started using Instagram.**

DA: Instagram allows me to perform one of my public duties as a public person. I don't have any interest in Instagram as a kind of business tool or extension of myself. As I've become more successful in what I'm doing, I don't have time to be in schools and teaching in the way that I used to. Instagram became a tool where I could simply share what is going on in the lens of my eyes and my thoughts with anybody who was interested in my work. So instead of waiting to hear from me at a lecture, a young kid in Malawi, or in Vietnam, or in the Philippines can actually know what I'm doing and what I'm looking at. I think as a public person who is making form in the city, it's a responsibility.

The documentation and the making of images become part of a collective memory, the memory that informs the next generation. I am making a body of images that I hope becomes a kind of reflexive space, one that allows another generation to look at a body of references that's different from the canon that they're supposed to look at. I hope that mine will give them another way of looking.

Emmanuel Iduma is a writer based in
New York and Lagos and is the author,
most recently, of *A Stranger's Pose* (2018).

To find beauty where others see only emptiness, or junk: that might be one of the artist's greatest gifts. To bring clear eyes to what the rest of us overlook, and never forget that the same light that shines on the postcard sites of our vacations shines alike on the gas stations and strip malls where we go to make those vacations possible (and fashion our everyday lives).

When Robert Adams showed us a deserted drive-in theater screen against Cheyenne Mountain—in his indelible 1974 book, *The New West*—as well as a stop sign, a cross, and a cluster of flimsy vacation homes set against the majestic landscapes of Colorado, he was not so much diminishing the glory of our wilderness as reminding us of the poignancy, and touching hopefulness, of our attempts to make a home within it. Yes, the great peaks and open spaces of the West put us in place and make our subdivisions and motel blocks seem fragile indeed; but the interplay of such temporary structures and an enduring landscape is what has given rise to the deeply human and almost religious art of both the filmmaker Terrence Malick and the writer Cormac McCarthy.

In the seldom-seen works we get to view here, Adams trains his quiet and observant eye on interiors instead. The majesty of nature is entirely absent. But the brave fragility of our constructs, what we gather as stays against eternity, is no less affecting. A cruel eye might see the stuff we collect as silly, unbecoming; a sympathetic eye sees that it is all we have.

I don't know what exactly I feel when I see the latest evidence Adams has assembled of our attempts to build a home here on an Earth so much larger than we are. There's no question that loneliness and an Edward Hopper-like sense of abandonment are part of it. But these works also make me think of the classic postwar films of the Japanese director Yasujiro Ozu, such as *Late Spring* (1949) or *Tokyo Story* (1953). Ozu's still, low camera,

in many scenes, registers four regular guys talking around a low table. But it's only when the humans leave, and the camera remains fixed for many seconds, silently taking the measure of the room that's left behind them, that the emotion (even the humanity) becomes almost overwhelming.

Absence can fill us up as much as presence does, Adams knows, and something beyond us remains even as we come and go. The light that's so much a part of all these works is as everywhere as the TV sets and trifles we set against it. We won't last and the crags and deserts all around us will, we know; yet what else can we fill the emptiness with but whatever gives us a sense of perhaps doomed security?

I questioned the master photographer recently about these images in which, as ever, he blends an unquenchable tenderness with an acute sense of all that we're destroying. "Overall," Adams wrote back, in three exquisite pages of handwritten answers, "I wanted just to show what lay within the houses that were a part of my primary subject, the new western landscape. I also hoped, however, to find evidence of human caring."

In high school, he recalled, his family had lived in a small tract house, where there was "a lack of relation to the outside (was this innocent, willful, or coerced?) … between the cramped interior and the vast, plastic, and living green."

His sense of social fragility had increased, he continued, especially given what's happening to our democracy, but "the sublime seems more and more certain. And the sublime is evident even in a ditch, a road, or in a backyard."

Then Adams concluded, "Yes, joy is still possible, either because of the love of friends and family, or owing to the inextinguishable beauty revealed by natural light. Every day can be the first day."

Robert Adams
The Light All Around Us

Pico Iyer

Pico Iyer is the author of fifteen books including, most recently, *Autumn Light: Season of Fire and Farewells* (2019) and *A Beginner's Guide to Japan: Observations and Provocations* (2019).

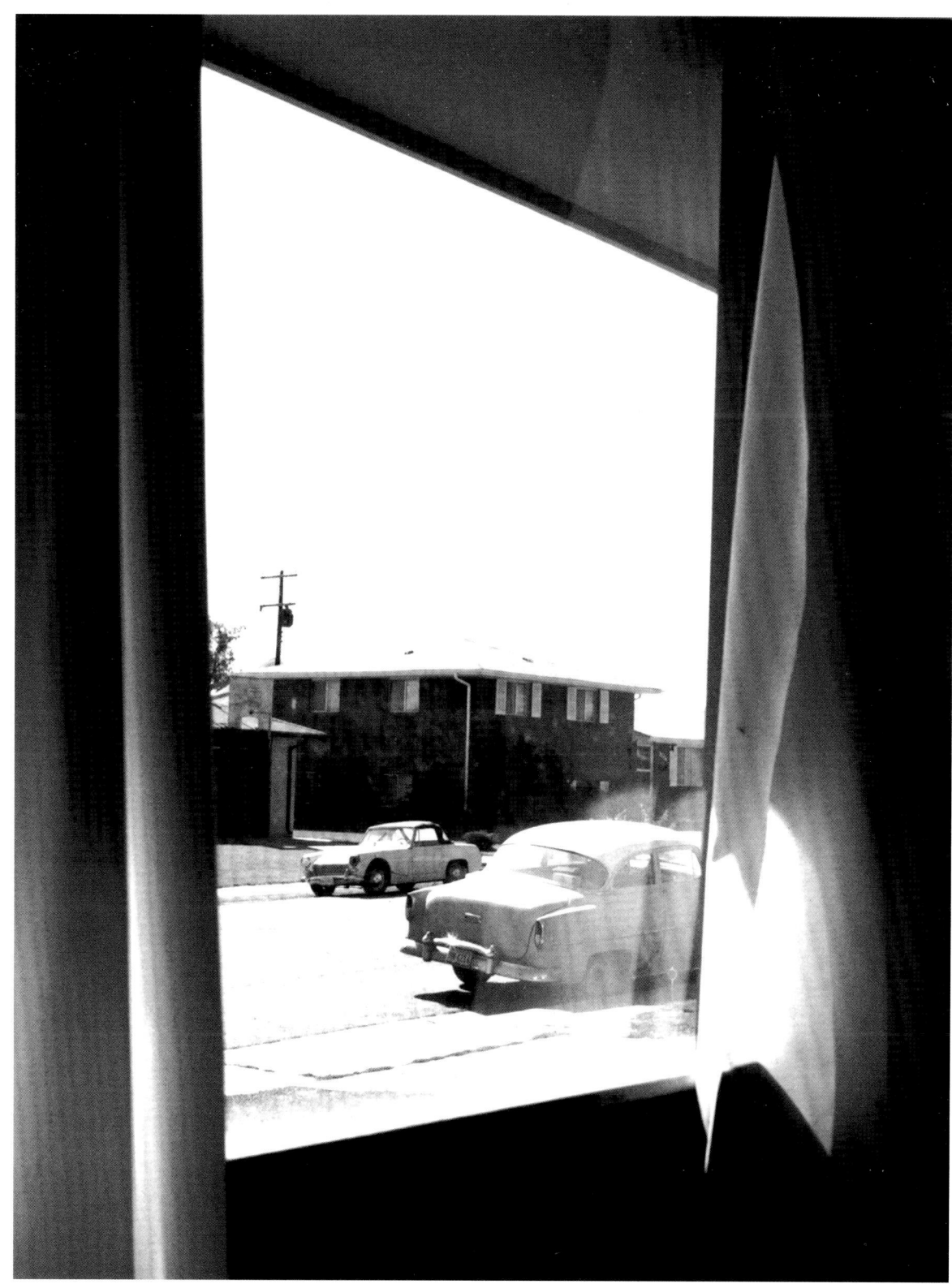

Longmont, Colorado, 1971-72

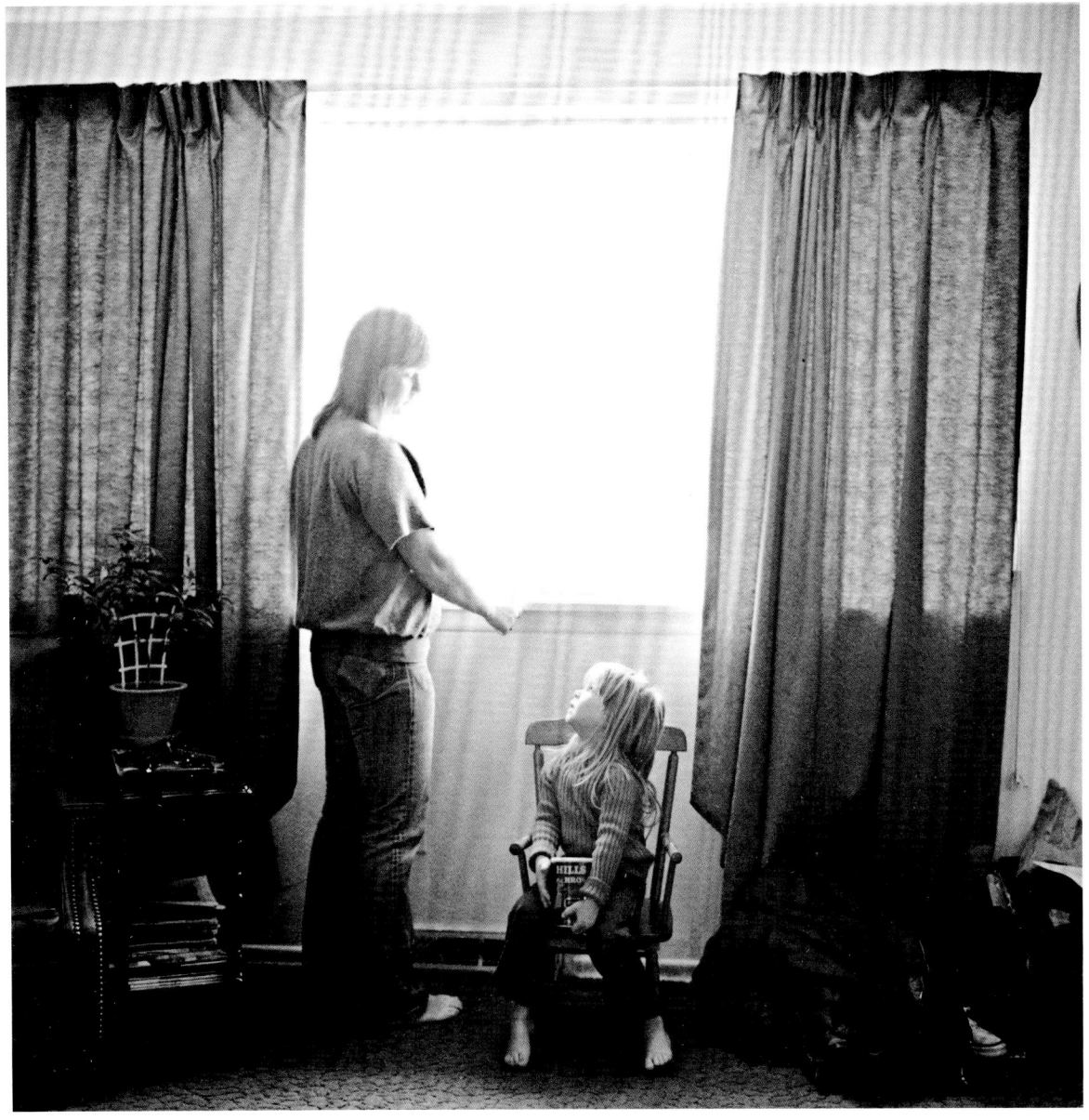

Colorado, ca. 1973

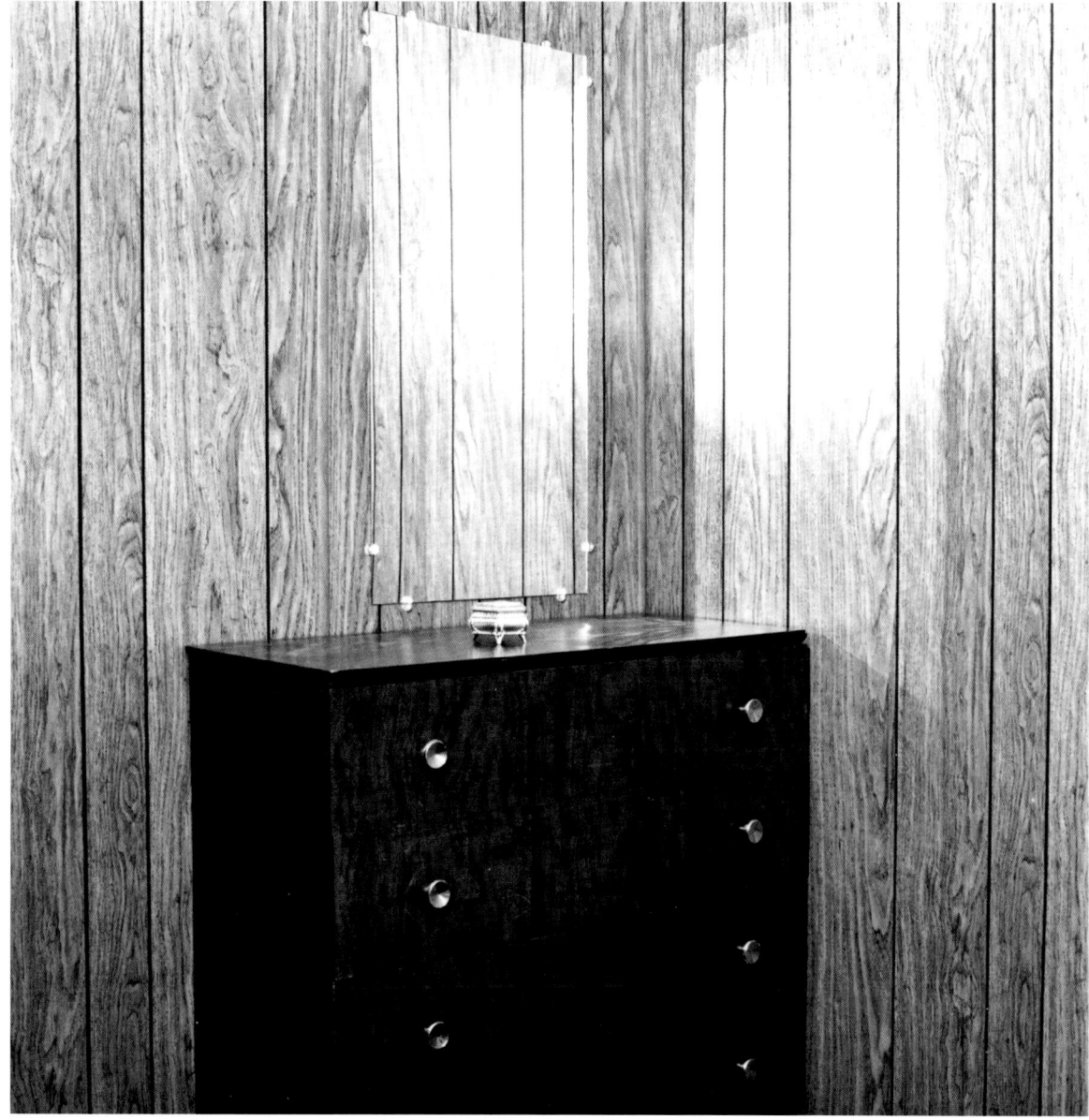

Denver, ca. 1973-74

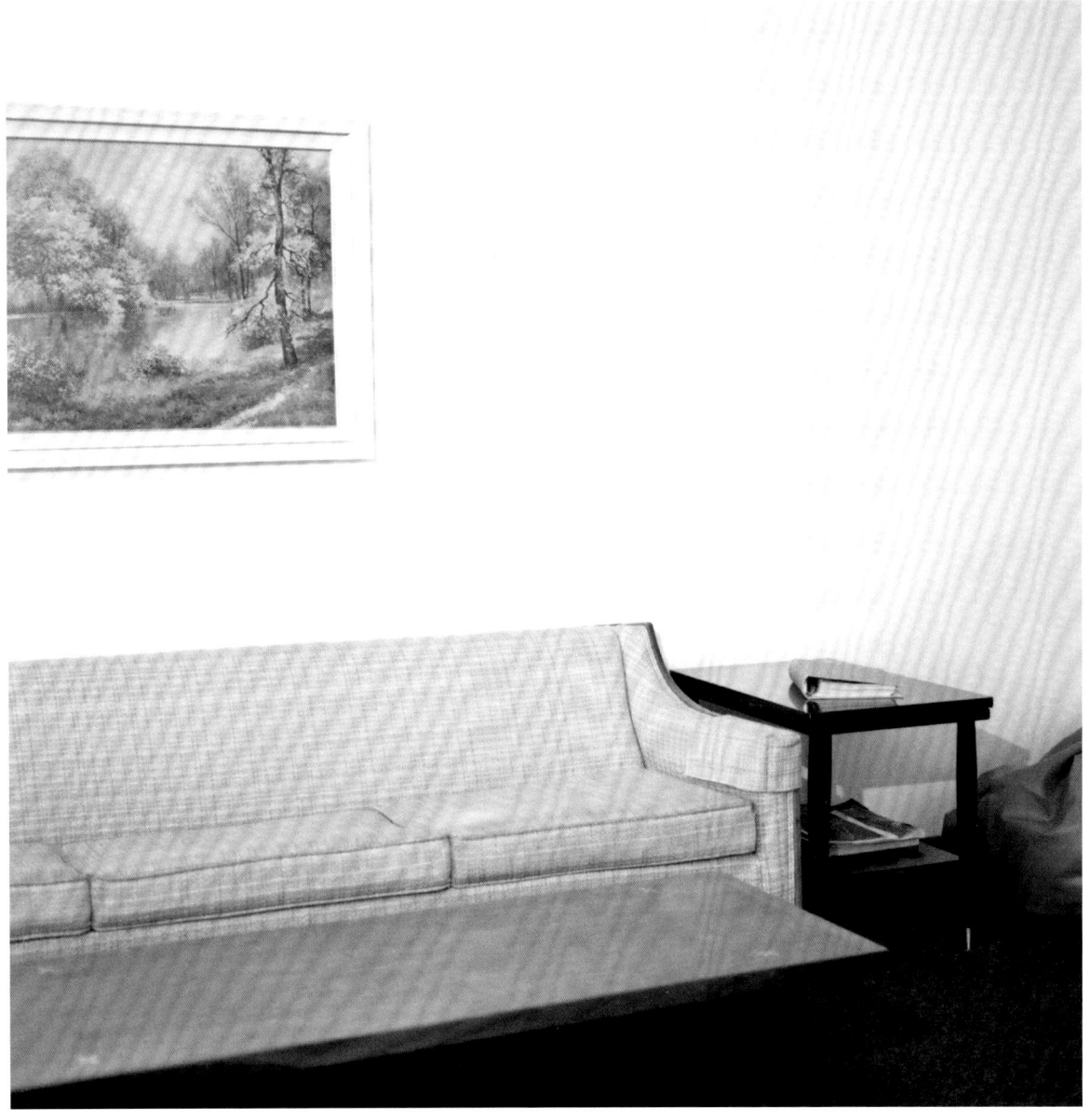

Lakewood, Colorado, 1973-74

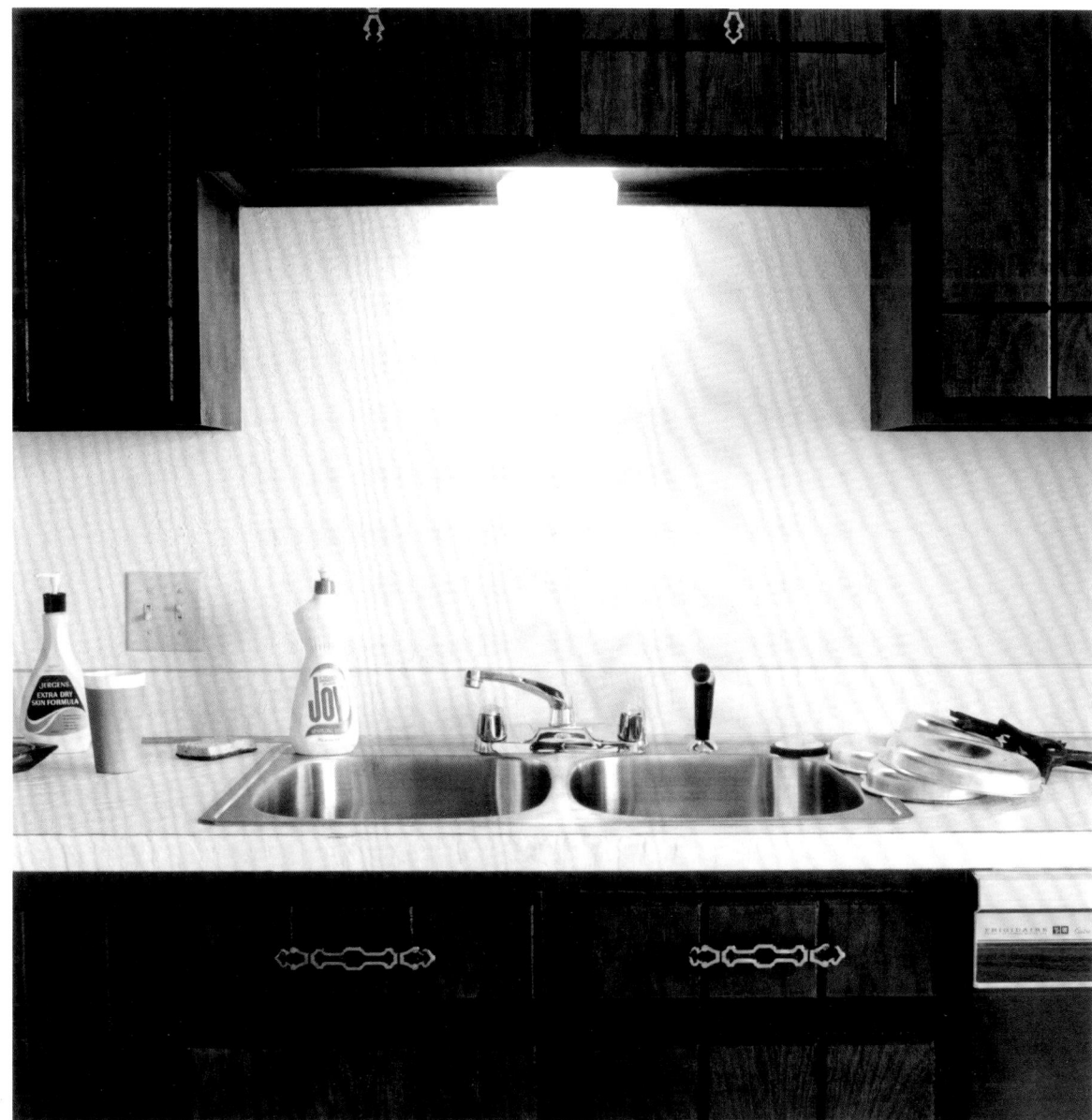

***Untitled*, 1973–74**
All photographs © the
artist and courtesy Fraenkel
Gallery, San Francisco, and
Matthew Marks, New York
and Los Angeles

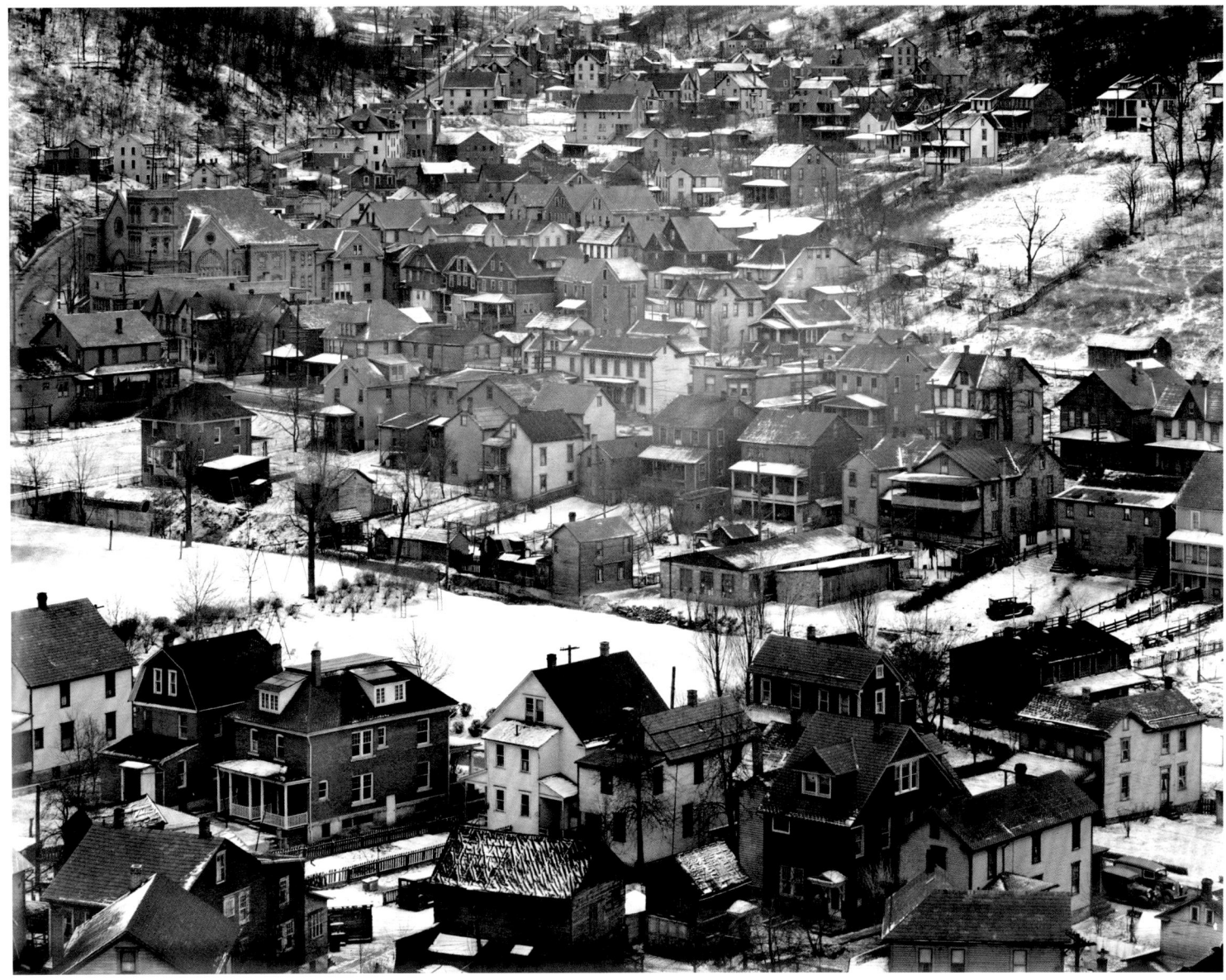

Walker Evans, *Johnstown housing. Pennsylvania,* **1935**
Library of Congress

Ed Panar
Walking Through Walker Evans

David Campany

David Campany is the curator of the 2020 Biennale für aktuelle Fotografie, Germany, and the author, most recently, of the forthcoming book *On Photographs*.

At the recent show of Garry Winogrand's color photography from the 1950s and '60s, presented at the Brooklyn Museum, a woman in her seventies was surprised to see her teenage self on a sidewalk with friends. There she was, frozen in her youth by Winogrand's camera. The anonymity of the street, a subject so dear to photographers, was suddenly deeply personal. Generally, the images and photographers we admire feel a little remote. In a sense, admiration *is* remote, requiring distance. But we can never rule out the possibility of something suddenly closing the gap. An image can jump into our lives with quite unexpected resonance.

For a long time, Ed Panar has been a great admirer of the work of Walker Evans. He was aware that Evans had photographed in and around Pittsburgh, a place Panar has known all his life, but in 2014, he came across an Evans photograph that resonated much more deeply. It was a 1935 image of dwellings in Johnstown, Panar's hometown, a little east of Pittsburgh. Evans made quite a few images like this. He would find some high ground and look across a valley and fill his composition with houses. Although he liked to compress the perspective into an almost flat pattern, Evans wasn't after abstraction. On the contrary, he brought out the subtle repetitions and differences of homes built in the same vernacular. Panar realized he could see the street where he grew up, in the working-class area of Walnut Grove, in the picture. Moreover, for the past fifteen years or so, he had been photographing the neighborhood within Evans's frame.

Panar placed a grid over Evans's image, and then looked to maps to help him identify different areas. He scoured his archive for pictures taken in these same locations. He also kept photographing, adding new work to a project titled *Walking Through Walker Evans* (1999–2019), which combines his own photographs with fragments of Evans's picture, now looking back *and* forward in time. In fact, it was looking back and forth in space too. Panar noticed that many of his images were taken facing toward Evans's vantage point. So he ventured over to that high ground on the edge of town to retake Evans's shot. The vista hadn't changed much, although trees now obscured the view somewhat. Several houses are still standing from 1935, and the newer ones have that traditional look. Only small modern details betray the passing of many decades.

Of all the major photographers of the last century, Evans has perhaps proved the most enduring. Rather than a style, he had an idiom, and a disposition toward the world that was curious and generous. A contemporary photographer can work in Evans's way, inhabit his disposition, without fear of imitation. By contrast, the images of Johnstown by two other well-known photographers, Lee Friedlander and Chauncey Hare, are so visually distinctive, so *theirs*, that they open far fewer doors.

The list of image makers working in Evans's wake is long, and photography in the United States is unimaginable without them, from Stephen Shore and Lewis Baltz to Justine Kurland, Vanessa Winship, Bryan Schutmaat, and LaToya Ruby Frazier. Then there is a second Evans legacy, which has to do with revisiting. Mark Ruwedel, Bernd and Hilla Becher, Camille Fallet, and many others have photographed where Evans did, and with him very much in mind. And, as if that were not enough, there is a third legacy: the direct remaking of Evans's actual images. From Sherrie Levine's postmodern appropriations to projects by Julia Curtin, Jessica Potter, and Darren Harvey Regan, artists have taken Evans's photographs as raw material to be shaped to new ends. Panar's *Walking Through Walker Evans* has the rare distinction of belonging to all three legacies: Panar photographs in Evans's idiom, revisits his location, and remakes his original image.

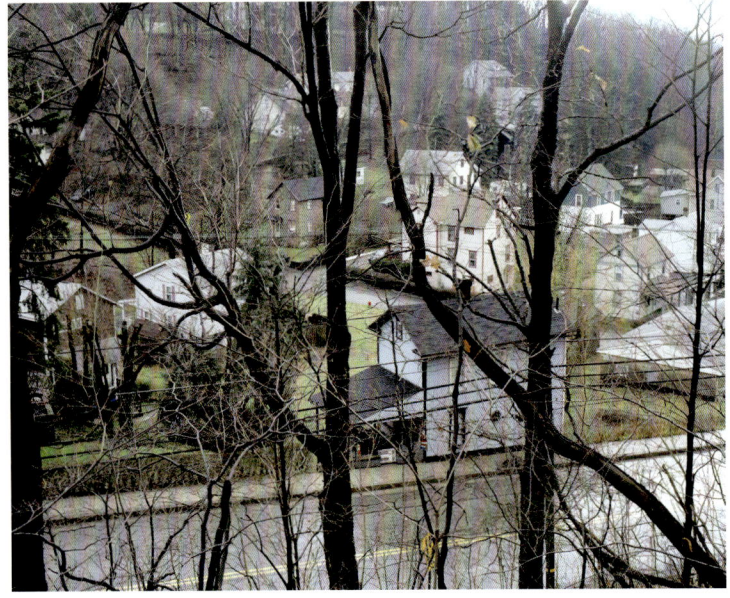
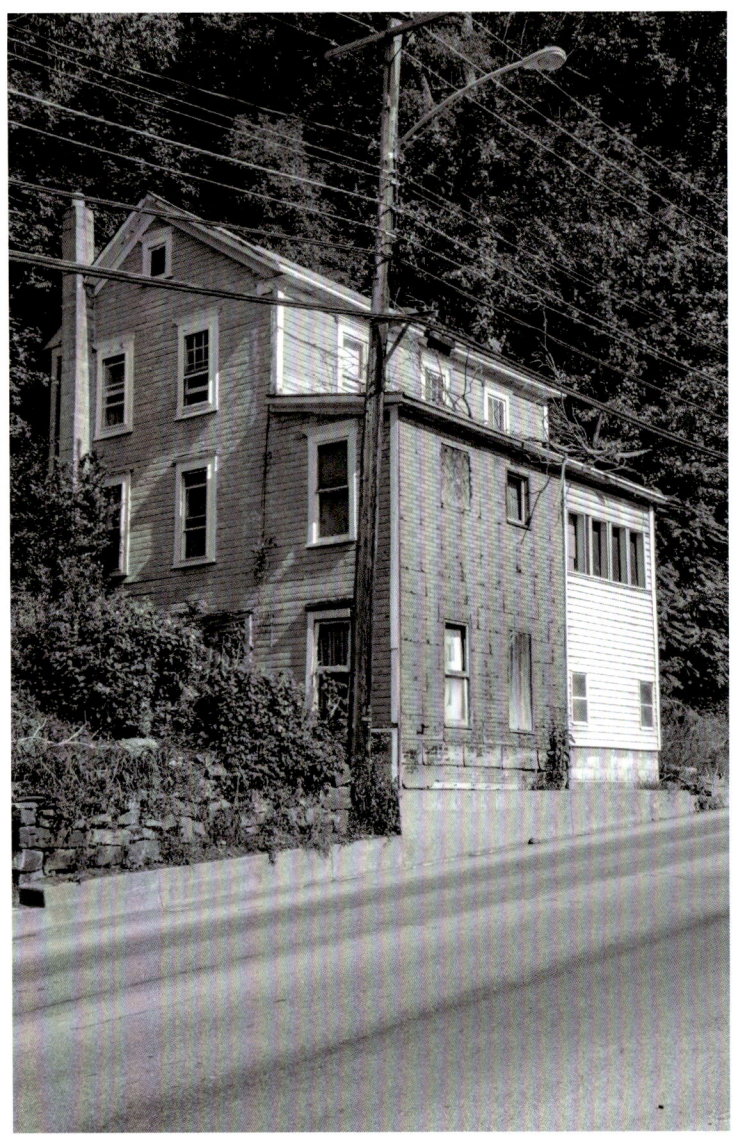
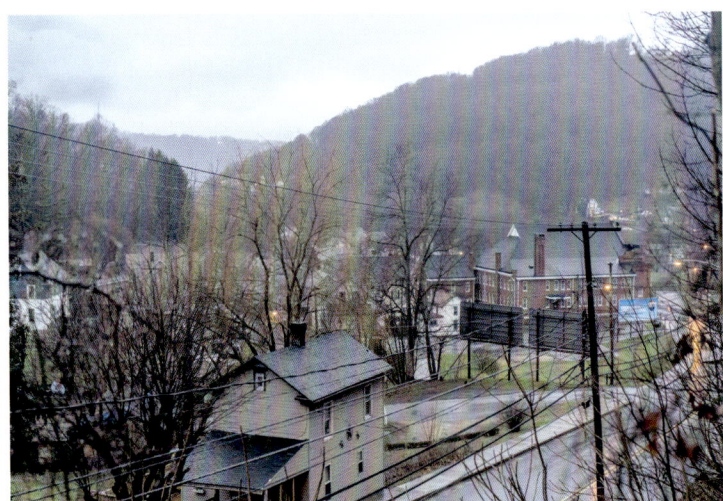
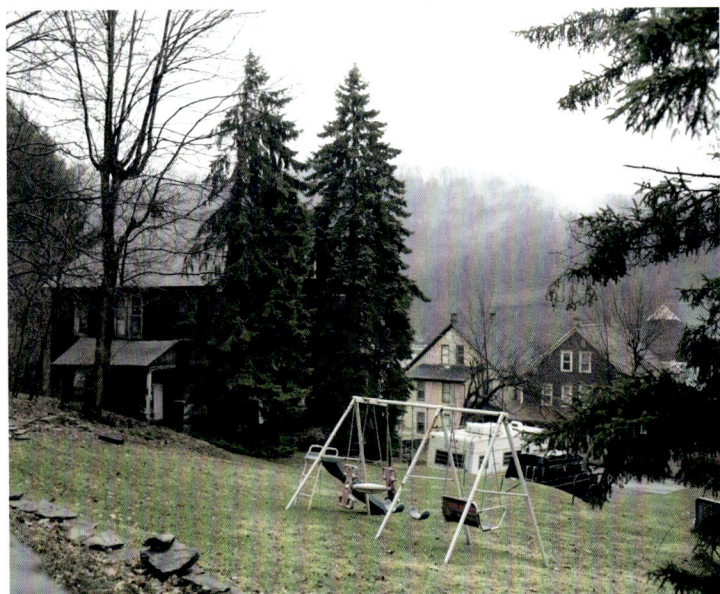
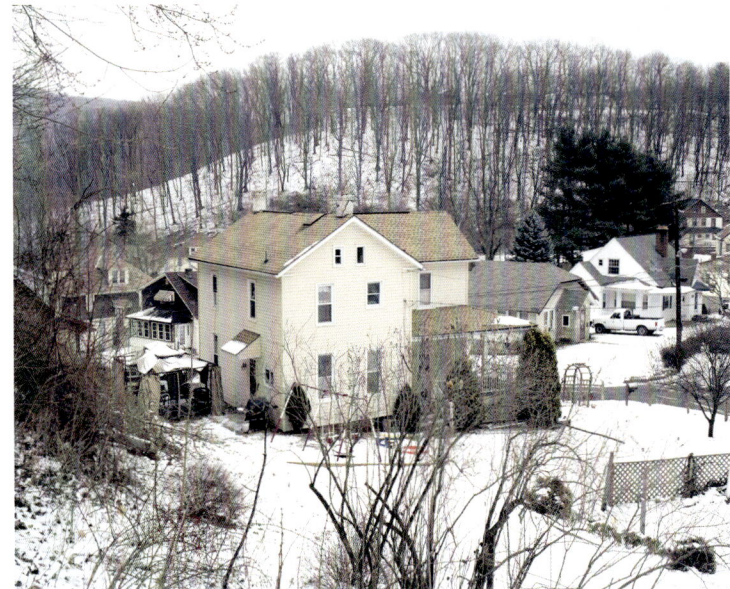

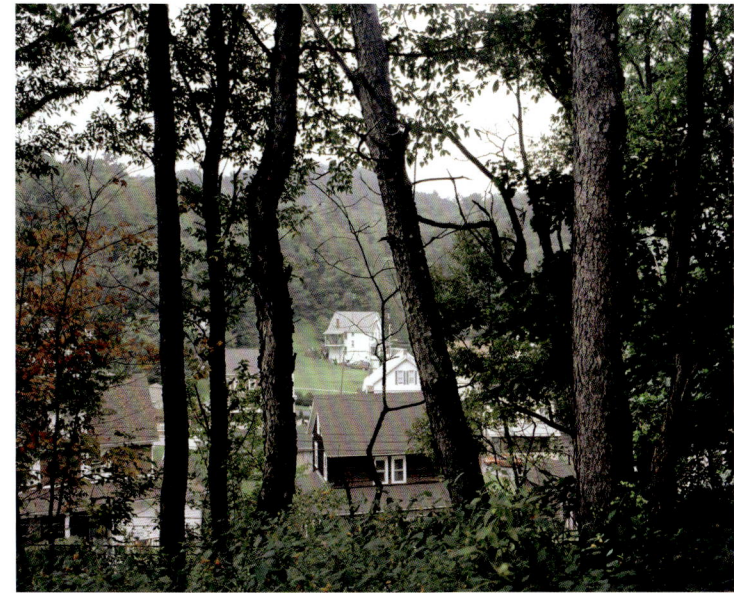
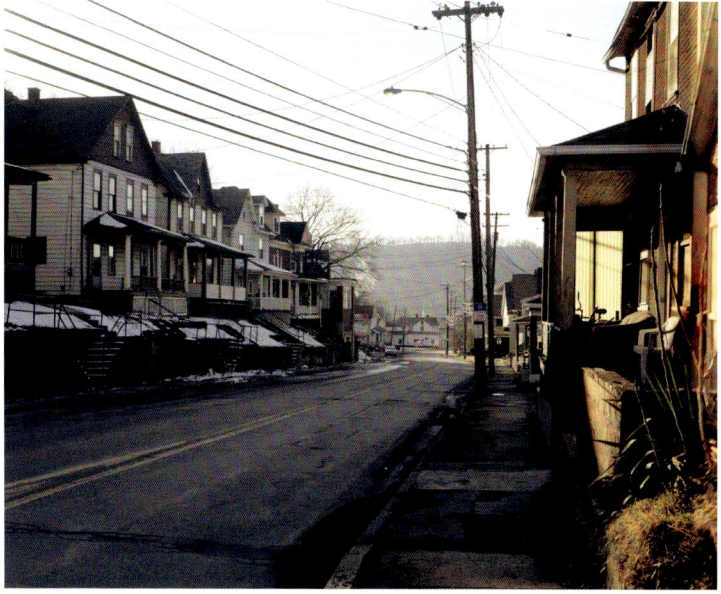
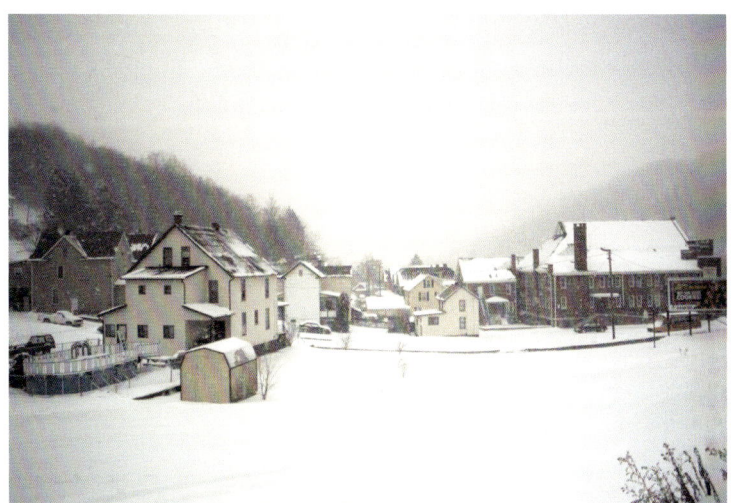
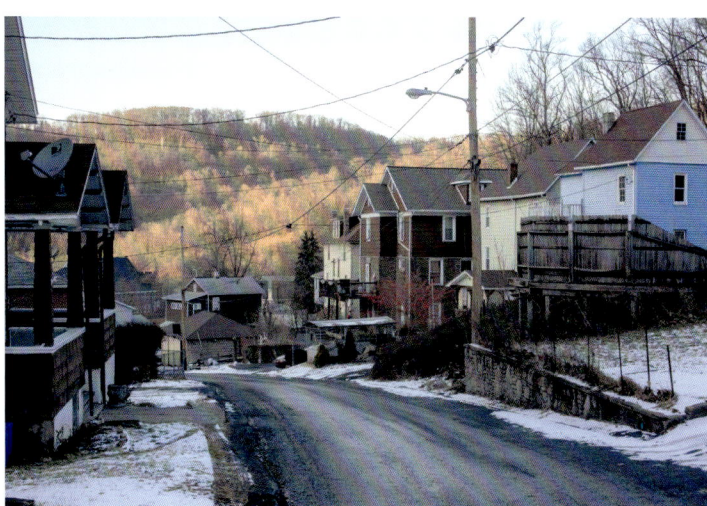
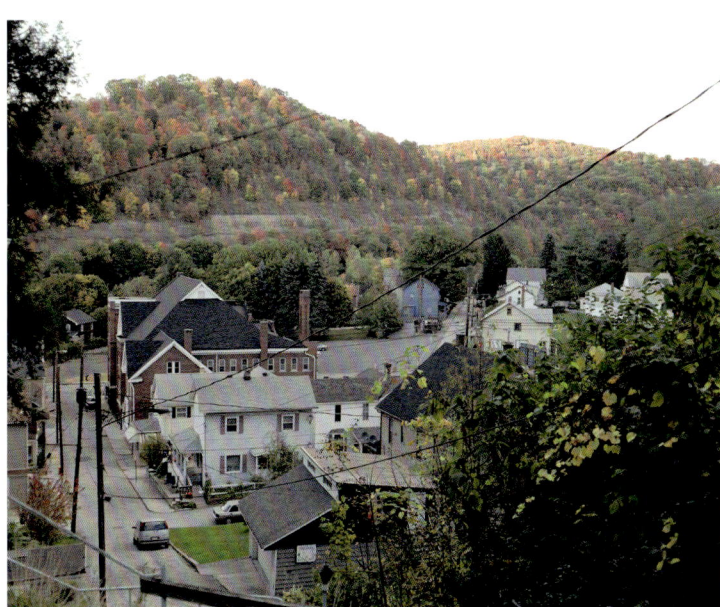
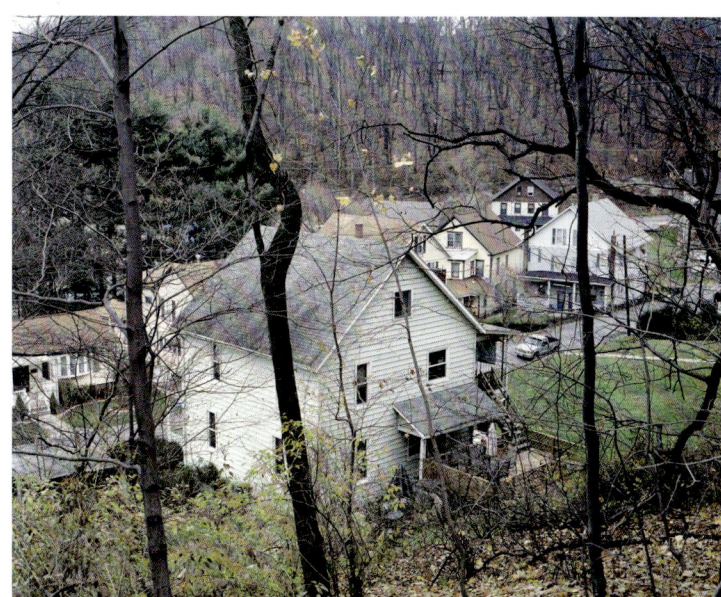

All photographs from the series *Walking Through Walker Evans*, 1999–2019
Courtesy the artist

Alejandro Cartagena

A Small Guide To Homeownership

Yxta Maya Murray

"My images are trying to present the more complex situation that's never told in the commercial and ideological stories of homeownership," Cartagena says. "The idea of buying a home is that it will bring social mobility, safety, love, a family, the whole Hollywood, Disneyland version. But there exist loopholes in this story, particularly in how homeownership had been photographed, always from the outside."

In 2010, Cartagena published *Suburbia Mexicana: Fragmented Cities* with Daylight/Photolucida. This project recorded the suburban sprawl in Monterrey, a city that had 339,282 residents in 1950 but today lodges over 3.8 million. *Suburbia Mexicana* features images of 328-square-foot houses that typically billet four to six people and look like the cookie-cutter "little boxes" lampooned by folk singer-songwriter Malvina Reynolds in her song by that title. In 2014, Cartagena self-published *Carpoolers*: on Monterrey's Highway 85, a route carrying men from their homes in the new suburbs to their work sites, he captured his voyagers lying down, eating, and sleeping in the backs of trucks, often amid the detritus of their jobs.

Cartagena's recent series *A Small Guide To Homeownership: Case Study: Mexico* (2019) takes the form of a photo-collaged proto-*Dummies* manual that blithely, and blindly, gives tips on financing residential real estate and managing thirty-year, fixed-rate mortgages. It tucks images from *Suburbia Mexicana* and *Carpoolers* into found text from home-buying guidebooks. In a particularly lacerating chapter, Cartagena layers the pictures of the little boxes over the real estate–industrial complex's conventional rah-rah fantasies, which counsel that if your family has "two who cook, you need … a big kitchen," and if you have "small children, you need … lots of bedrooms," conveying how unrealistic the own-your-own-home cult can be.

Cartagena observes that his photographs fill in the gaps left by government and development propaganda that pushes the idea of homeownership as an unqualified good. "If you connect a picture of a house in the suburbs with a picture of carpoolers, with a picture of a desiccated river—those images weren't meant to be together," he says. "But if you connect those dots, the story becomes more complex, and the questions open up to 'What are we really doing?'"

The photographer Alejandro Cartagena knows you want to go home. You yearn for a house *that really feels like home*— an affordable space of serenity or happy chaos, with easy access to work, clean air, and clean water. Where you can become fully human and maybe raise a family. Not a site of destruction or pollution. Not a place that will bankrupt you or pen you in or poison you. Home.

The failure of the world's metropolitan areas to fulfill this dream for all of its residents drives Cartagena's work. Cartagena, who was born in the Dominican Republic in 1977 and now lives in Monterrey, Mexico, has photographed Mexican suburban architecture and its housing-challenged inhabitants for the past fourteen years. His images of cheap structures and exhausted commuters critique the international club of politicians and urban planners whose model of quick and unequal development has left many people bereft of a safe place to call home. The housing boom started in Mexico in the early 2000s, when aspiring landholders began acquiring properties financed by mortgages. Though this practice has allowed more people to acquire homes built out of permanent materials, government loans are only available to those with salaried employment, a status that sixty percent of the Mexican working population can claim. Salaried workers thus possess a greater likelihood of living in such sound structures than those surviving in seasonal or gig economies.

Yxta Maya Murray is Professor of Law at Loyola Law School, Los Angeles, and the author of the forthcoming novel *Art Is Everything*.

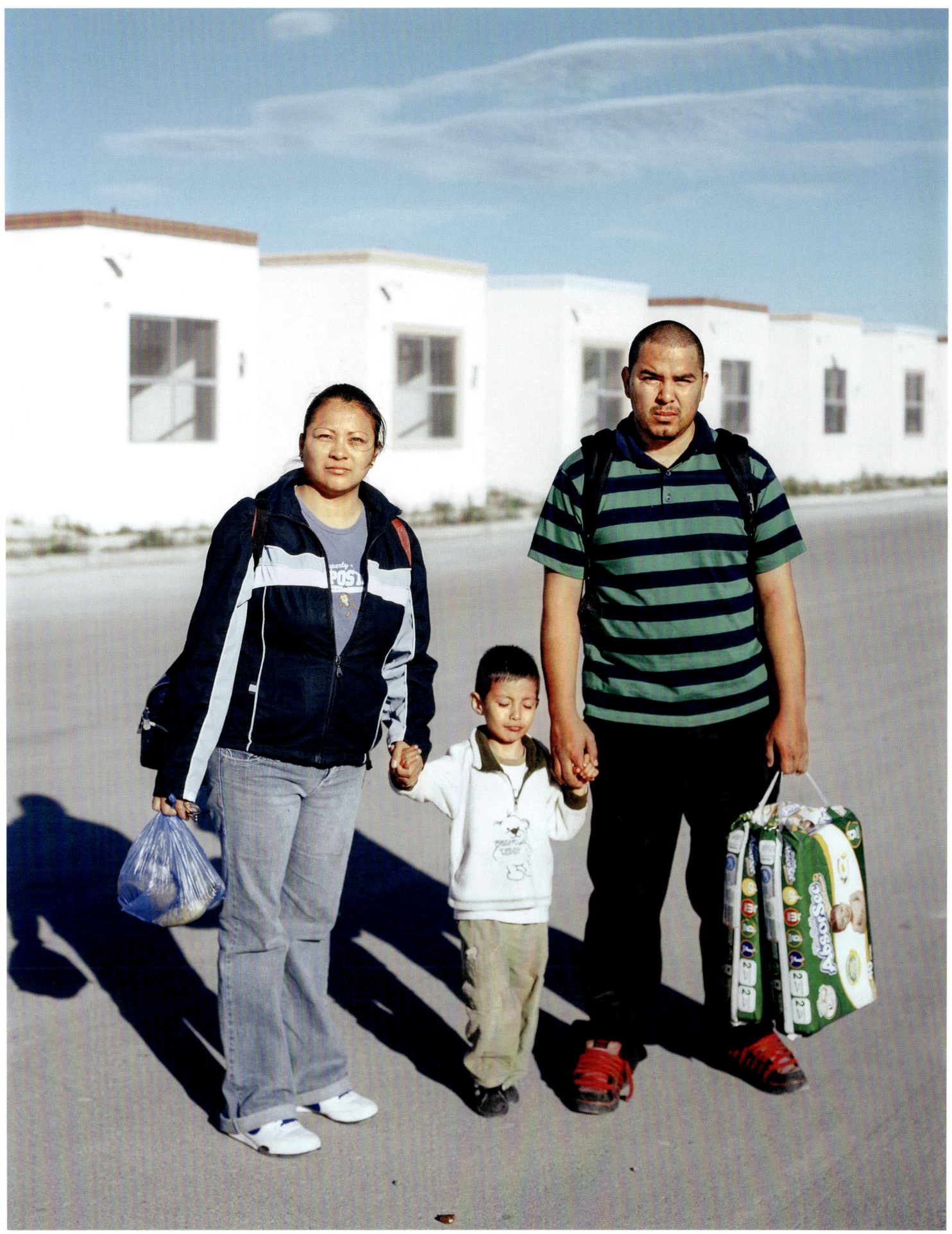

Family walking back from store in Juárez suburb, 2009

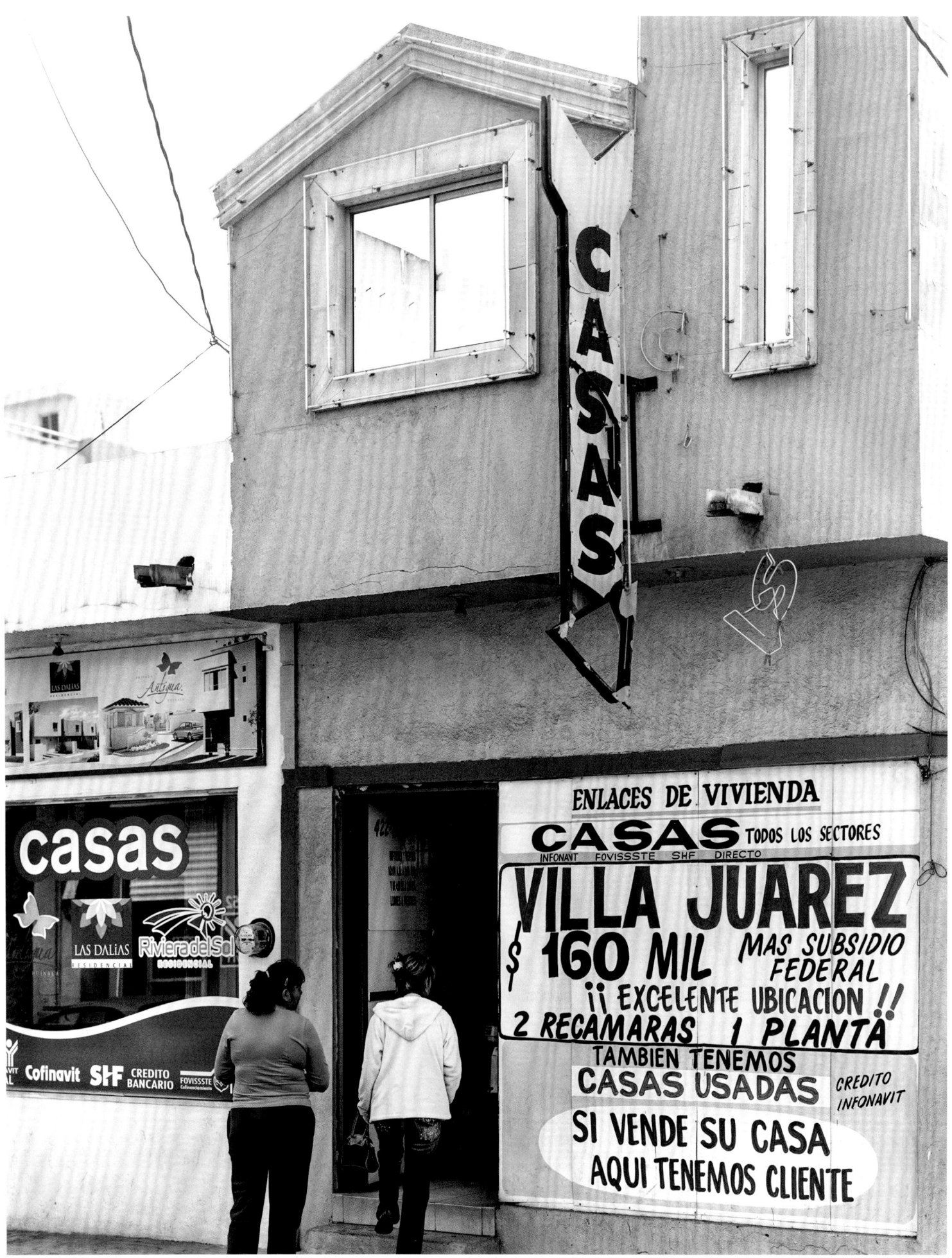

Housing agency, Monterrey,
2011

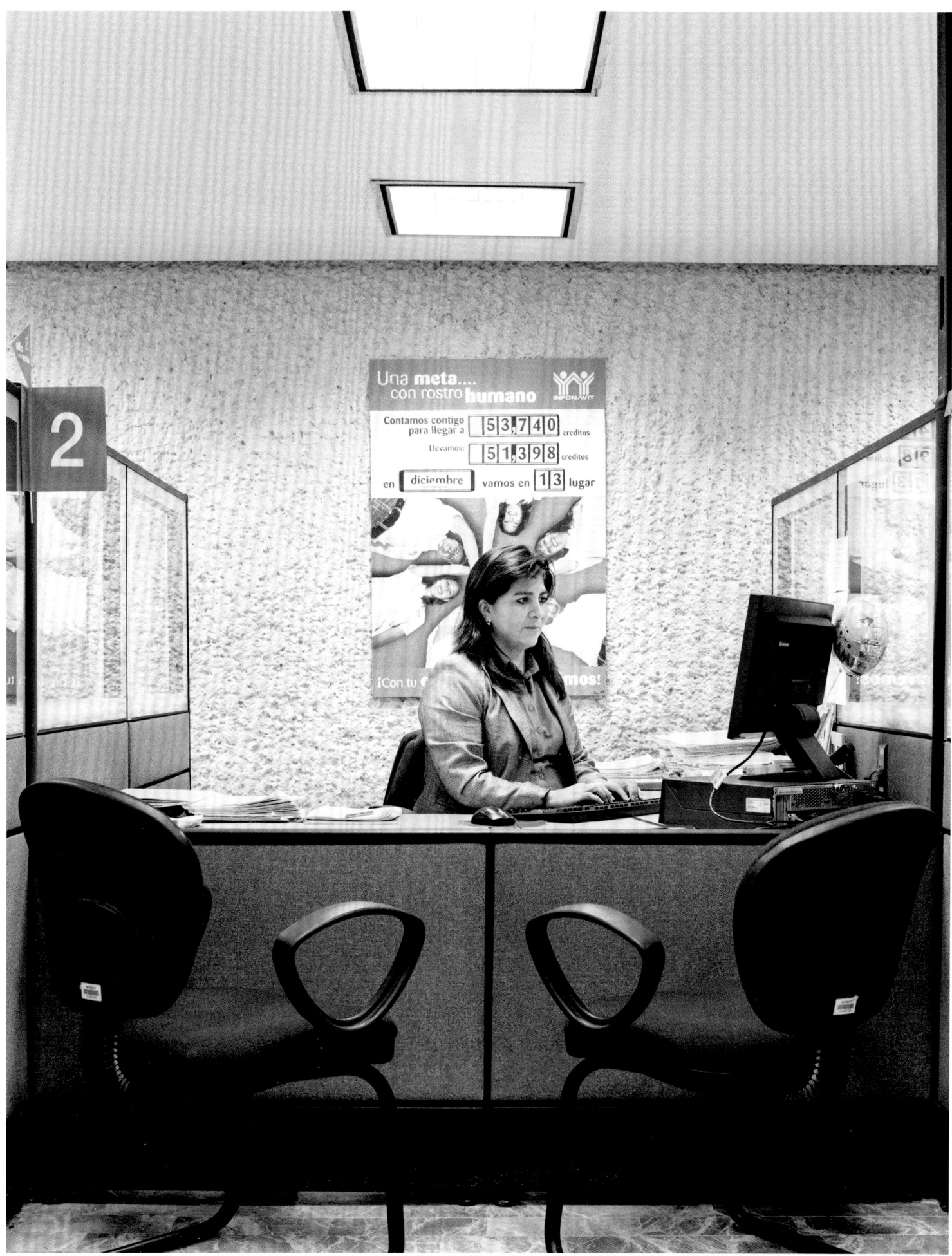

Bureaucrat at her desk at
the INFONAVIT, Monterrey,
2011

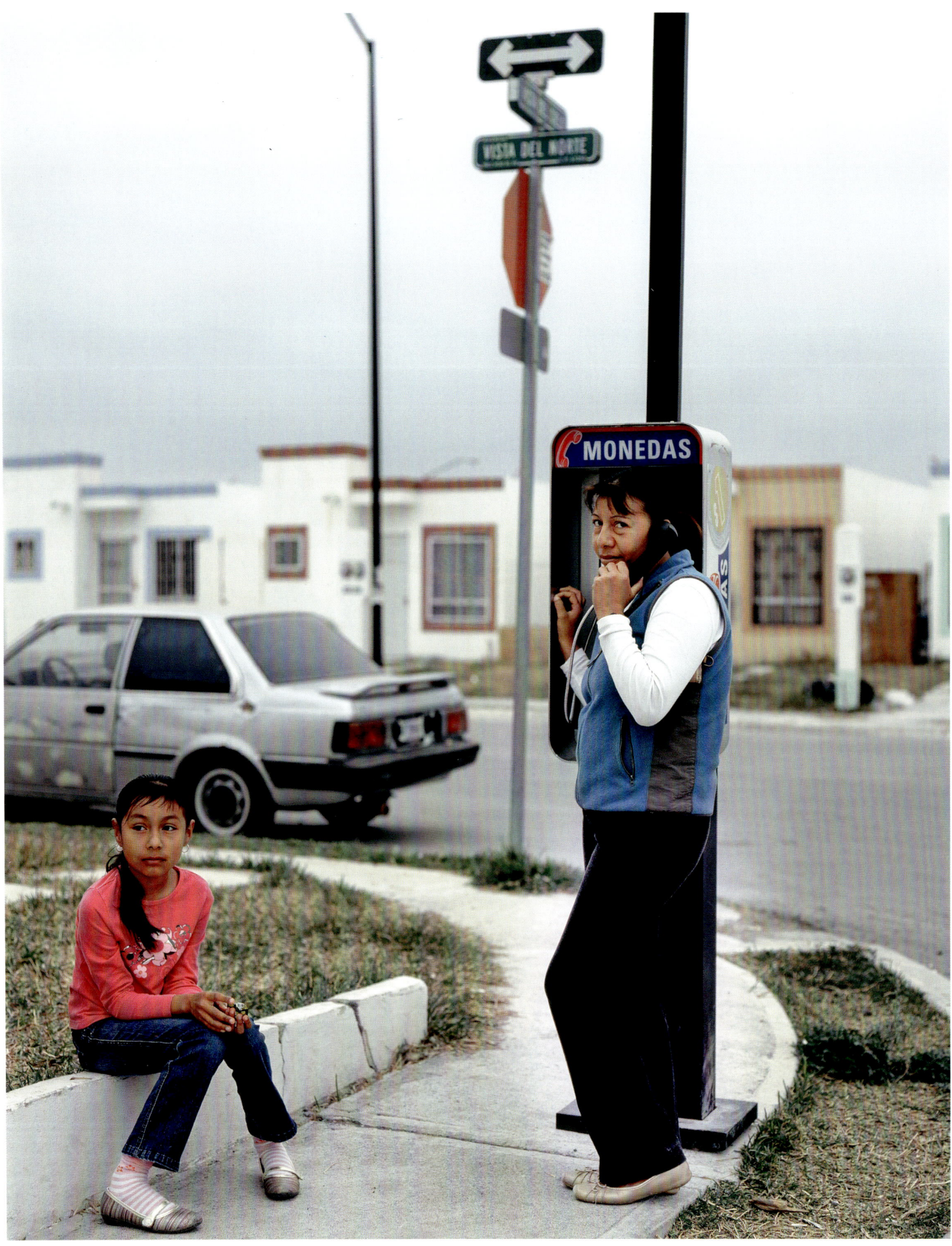

Mother and daughter at
public phone in Juárez
suburb, 2009

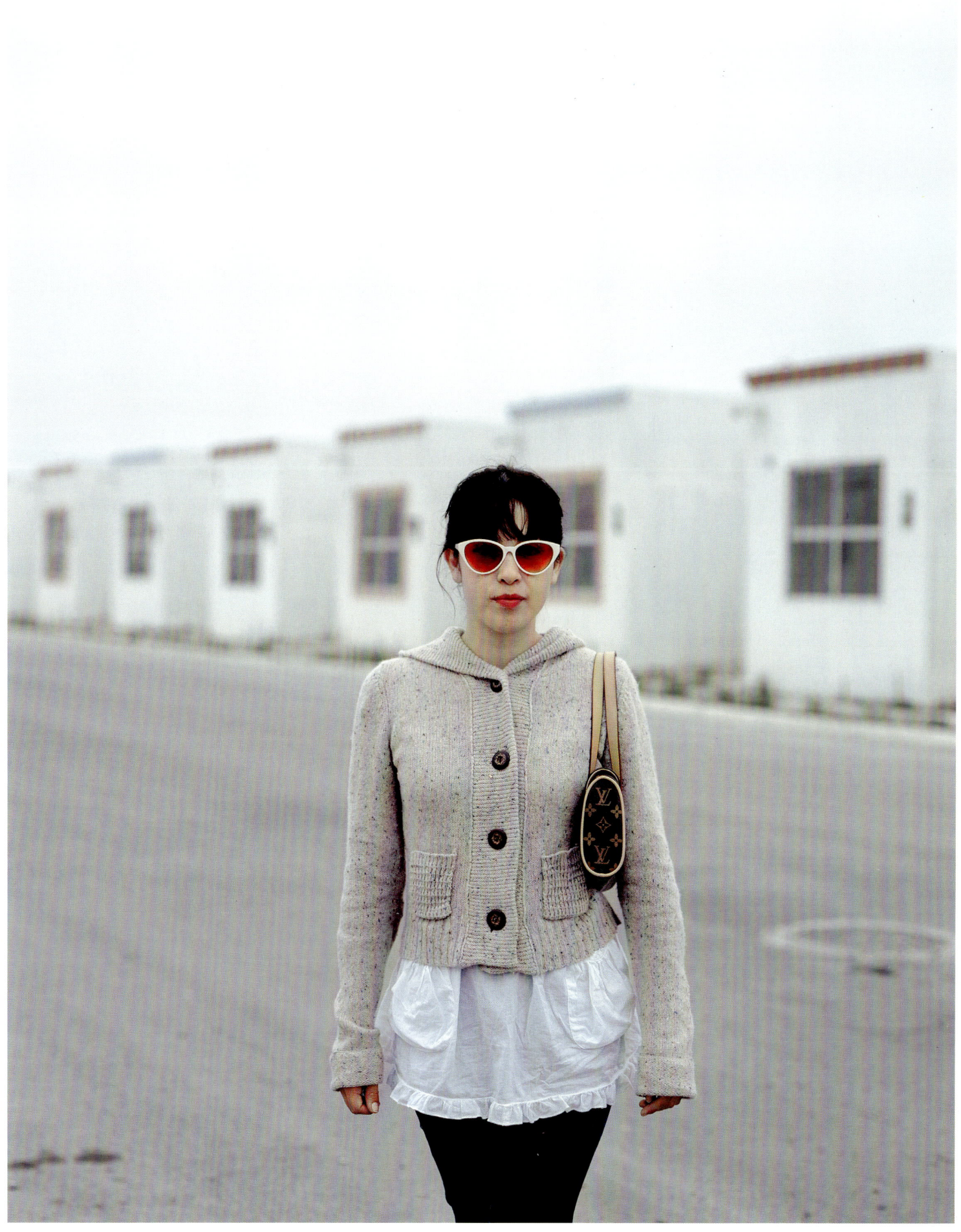

Girl coming home to
suburb in Juárez from a
night out in the city, 2009

Apodaca, 2007
All photographs courtesy the
artist and Kopeikin Gallery,
Los Angeles

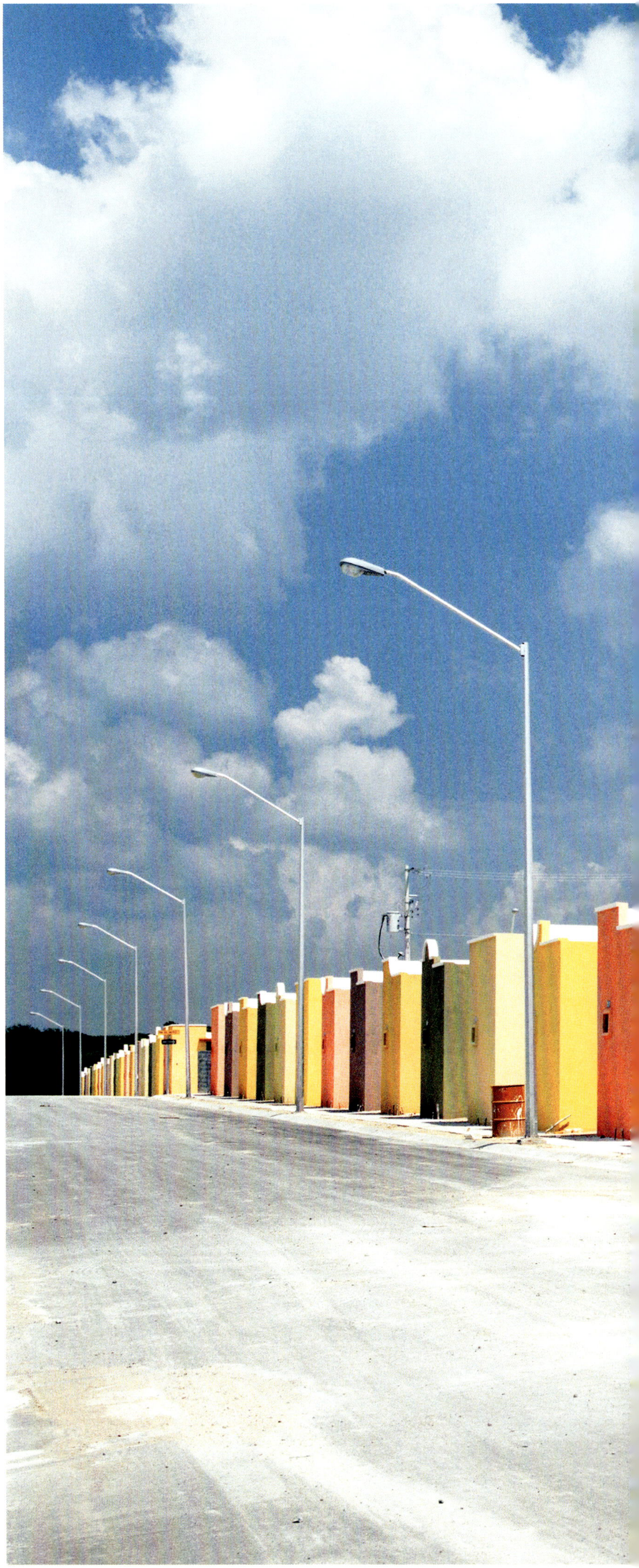

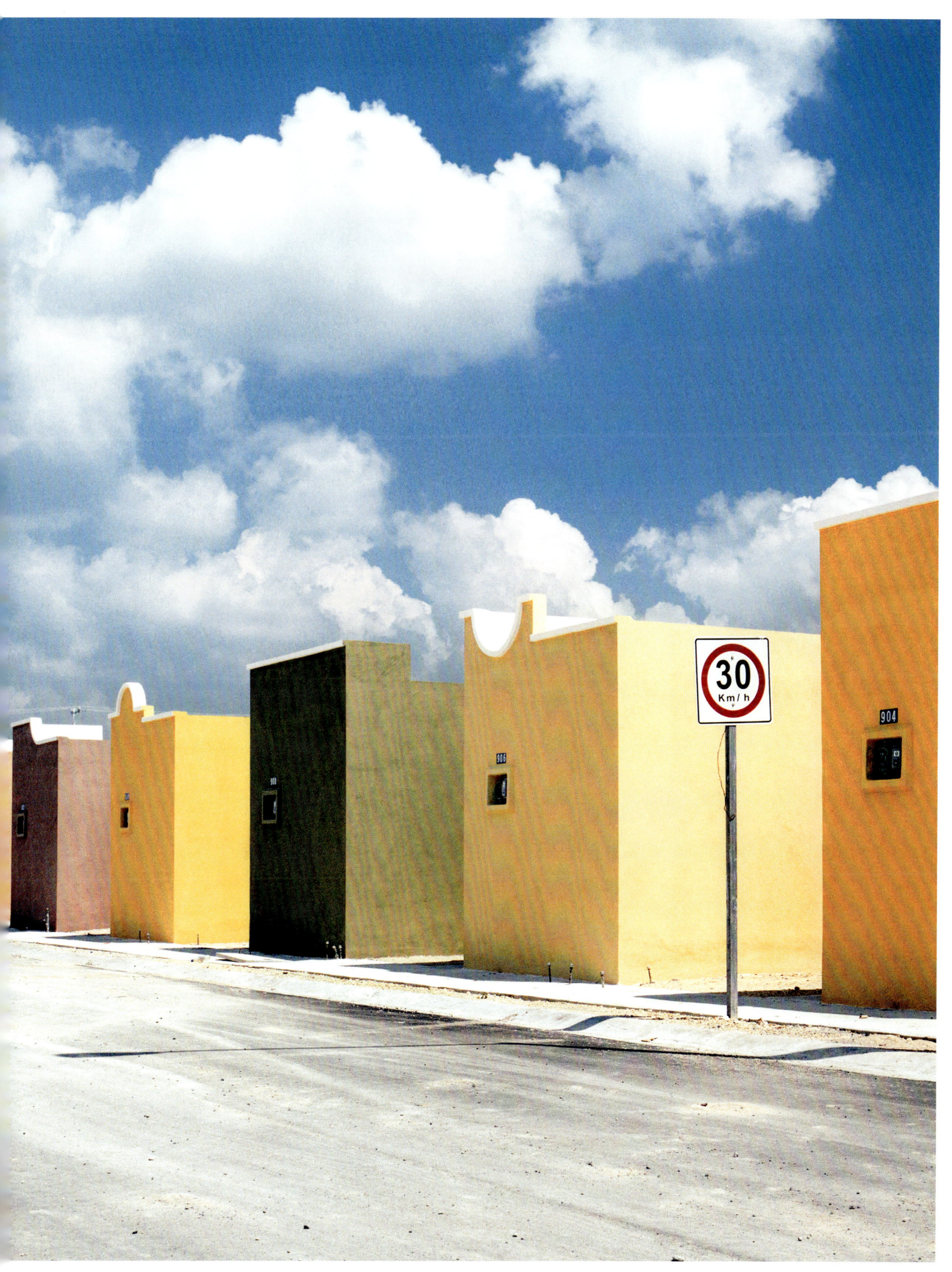

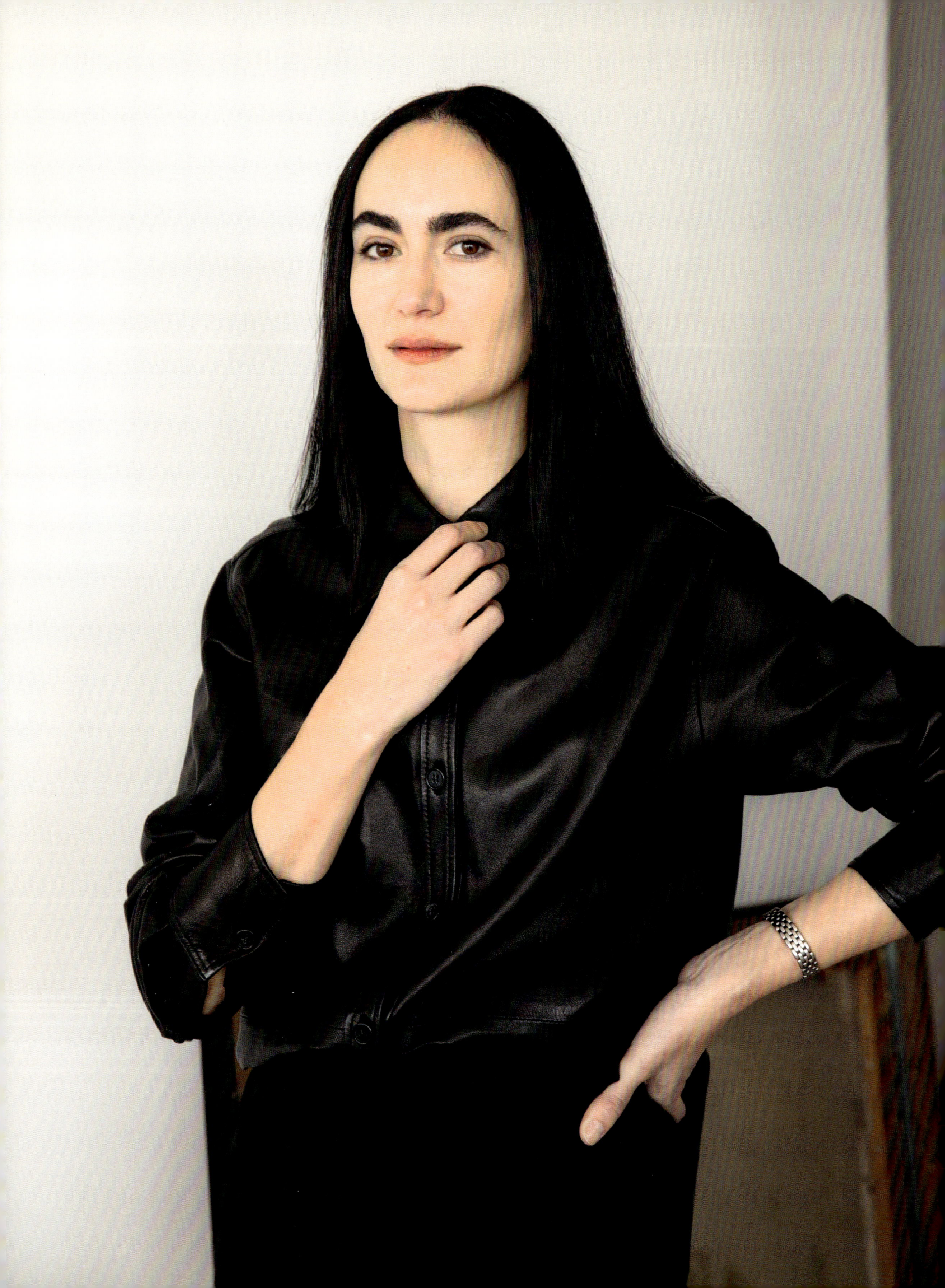

Frida Escobedo

"I don't think there should only be one concept of home."

A Conversation with Alejandra González Romo

When she landed the commission to design London's Serpentine Pavilion in 2018, Frida Escobedo established herself as a young architect with a compelling vision. By that time, she already had a number of accomplished projects under her belt, from the renovation of La Tallera, the former studio of the painter David Alfaro Siqueiros turned public art gallery, to Casa Negra, a house featuring wide-screen views of her native Mexico City, designed for a photographer and inspired by the concept of a camera obscura. Escobedo's works—often made with raw materials like perforated concrete blocks—opt for flexibility and a restrained yet daring form to create simple visual gestures.

Though Escobedo says she was too intimidated to apply to art school, deciding on an architecture path instead, her creative process is close to that of a visual artist who lets her pieces speak for themselves. But she also has an eye on the cultural landscape in which her work exists—Mexico's social divisions and class dynamics have often been a concern in her investigations of buildings and housing—as well as on the storied history of built environments in her home country. "Mexican architecture is informed by its context," she has remarked. "I think it's more like a spirit rather than a style." Here, she speaks about transforming lives through design and space, and her own spirit of invention.

Page 46:
Frida Escobedo, Mexico
City, November 2019
Photograph by Yvonne
Venegas for *Aperture*

This page:
A photograph by Frida
Escobedo's sister,
Ana Gómez de León,
at Escobedo's house,
Mexico City, 2019
Photograph by Yvonne
Venegas for *Aperture*

Casa Negra is a type of camera aiming at the city, but, at the same time, it's spatially functional.

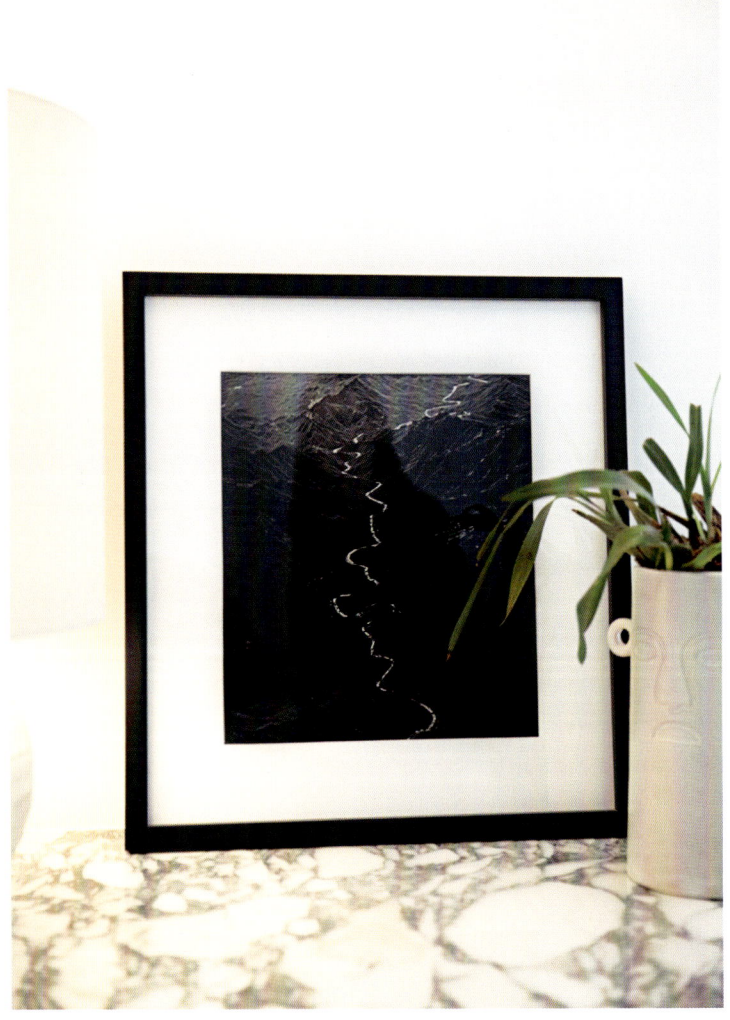

Alejandra González Romo: One of your first projects was the Casa Negra (2006) on the outskirts of Mexico City, which resembles a dark camera. Is there any connection between the concept for that house and that of an old camera?

Frida Escobedo: The first two projects I worked on were house renovations, so this was indeed the first one I developed from scratch. I was twenty-three back then, fresh out of college, and a small, very simple house had to be built with limited resources. The idea was to build a one-room studio with a mezzanine as a quick solution. The owner, who is a photographer, had inherited that plot on the outskirts of Mexico City, on the road to Cuernavaca. A small space, it had to be made permeable to light, and the solution was to build a huge window looking out onto the city, which frames the view. It is a black box standing on columns. One enters by a bridge. When entering the box, one immediately sees the landscape, a mixture of forest and city. At night, especially, the box creates a camera-obscura effect with the city lights visible in the distance.

AGR: **How would you describe the way natural light comes into the space?**

FE: The light comes in from the north. Therefore, the house works perfectly as a studio. The only risk was that the house turns out to be very cold. For this reason, we installed an L-shaped skylight, so it has an additional light inlet from the south, thus warming it a bit. We painted it dark gray—almost black—so that it attracts more light and heat. It also has a ramp that goes from the kitchen up to a terrace. Therefore, the social space is doubled, the peripheral view from the roof offering a whole different experience. It is indeed a type of camera aiming at the city, but, at the same time, it's spatially functional. Also, its position and angle resemble the way any photographer would choose to set a tripod.

AGR: **Looking at the documentation of your projects, I can see the signature of the photographer Rafael Gamo is on practically every single piece. What is the role of photography in your creative process?**

FE: The process behind architecture is overflowing with images. But if we talk of photography's recording value, my interest is in having documentation done on more than one occasion. I like working with Rafael, because he always comes back to the sites to capture the way a project evolves. Neither of us is interested in the perfect picture. All we want is a living record. Even though, in many cases, owners make it difficult to keep that record, I am interested in capturing how each construction ages.

AGR: **What other photographers have influenced your way of seeing?**

FE: Josef Koudelka, Sebastião Salgado, Graciela Iturbide, Manuel Álvarez Bravo, and Gerhard Richter—their interventions with photographs. My sister Ana Gómez de León is also a photographer. A photograph of hers sits by the entrance of my house. I forced her to give it to me as a present. She took the photograph from a plane, where you can see a river crossing the mountains. When I saw it, I thought of Salgado and his endless journeys to shoot such images. This one was taken through a filthy window using an iPhone. I love it. It is my favorite photograph. Here, in my office, I have a postcard taken by the architect Mauricio Rocha, in 1988. It is an image of a wooden wagon with glass doors reflecting a lake. It is a photograph he took at a very young age, and I interpreted it as some sort of acknowledgment of what I was doing in my first years as an architect.

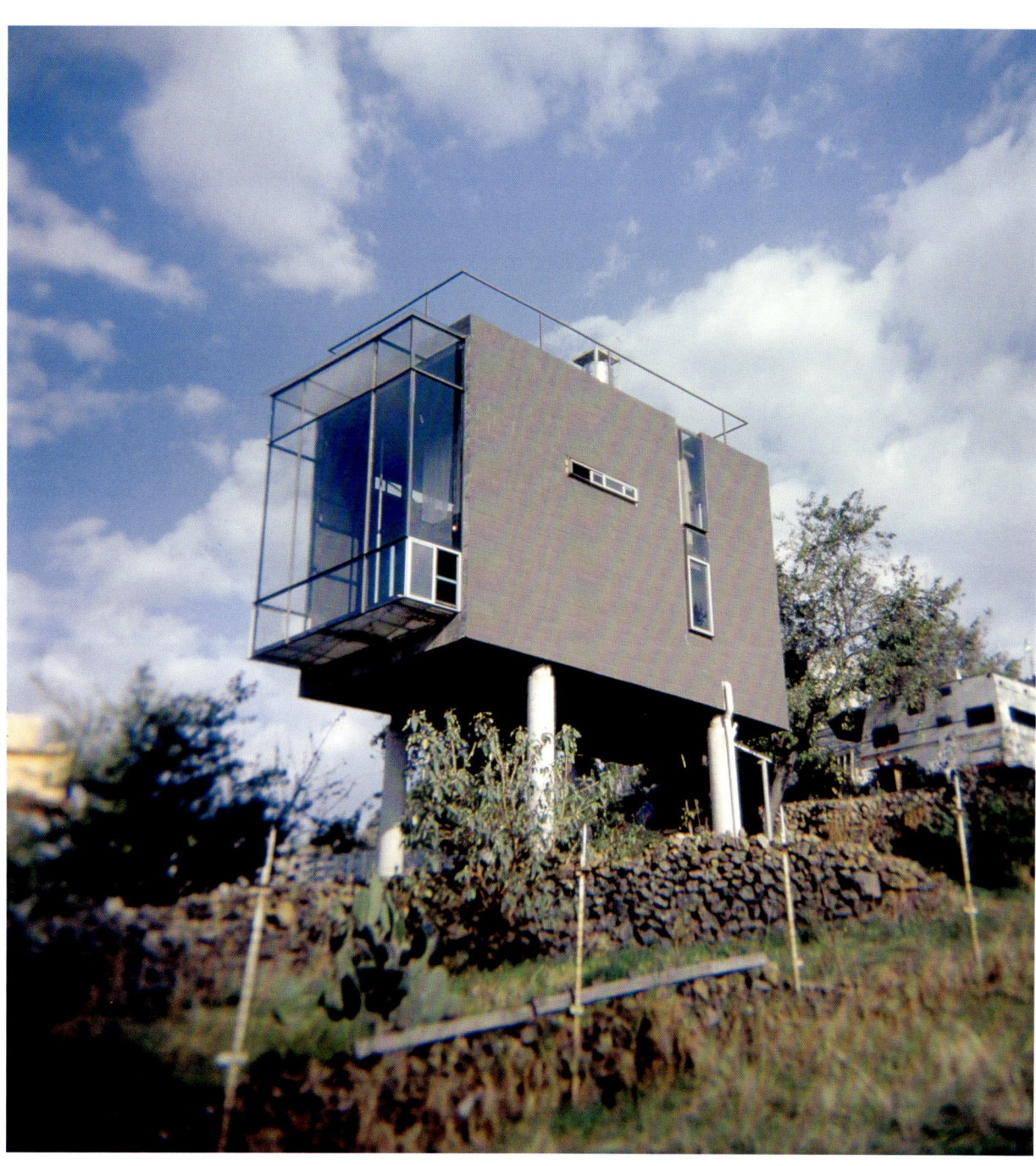

Frida Escobedo, Casa Negra, Mexico City, 2006
Photograph by José Fernando Sánchez. Courtesy the artist

I recently saw Hans Haacke's exhibition at the New Museum, in which he analyzes the relationships between power, real-estate value, and built space in New York. His research draws lines between the Shapolsky family and 142 buildings across the city, while keeping a record of each property's square meters, its conditions, its owner, et cetera. It is well known that power concentrates in very few families around the world; yet, visualizing it in such a clear way takes the subject out of the abstract. A similar analysis, but one made indoors, is Daniela Rossell's series *Ricas y famosas* (Rich and famous, 1994–2001), where she shows the interiors of immense mansions in Mexico, unveiling the tastes and personalities of women who may lack anything but money. It is a portrait of society through space and architecture from an intimate perspective.

AGR: **Haacke's piece sounds similar to what you achieved with your research project and book *Domestic Orbits* (2019), based on the fact that there are more than 2.4 million domestic workers in Mexico and that 90 percent of them are women. It is a cartographical analysis of the way the domestic sphere is configured around race, class, and gender. What triggered your interest in this subject?**

FE: Few people know that Luis Barragán's domestic worker still lives in his house, more than thirty years after Barragán's death. As part of his will, he decided she could continue living there for the rest of her life. We are talking about an iconic house built by a Pritzker Prize winner, which currently functions as a museum but has a hidden configuration: a house within a house that no one knows about and that is designed not to be discovered by visitors. Nonetheless, if you pay attention, there are hints of that invisibility everywhere. There are bells under the tables to communicate with that other zone, and there are secondary routes that allow staff to pass through the main areas without being seen.

This analysis of Casa Barragán was the first exercise. Three years later, we decided to expand our research, as these signs of invisibility can be seen in architecture on different scales. In the building where I live, there are also rooms for the service staff that are completely invisible. Walking around the city, we see massive apartment buildings with wonderful views, built by renowned architects. But what invisible architecture lies behind?

We also analyzed the house where Alfonso Cuarón's 2018 movie *Roma* was filmed, which has a little tower where the character Cleo [the family's domestic worker] lives. Another very interesting case is a building from 1957 in Polanco [a neighborhood in Mexico

City], where the service staff rooms are in a separate building a few blocks away. These are very small dwellings built around a main courtyard, where the service staff can have a private life and bring visitors if they so wish, in addition to having a spatial separation between work and leisure. That possibility has almost completely disappeared within one generation, and current domestic workers often commute up to four hours every day from the outskirts of the city to their workplaces.

AGR: **You live in a building designed by Mario Pani, one of the most widely renowned architects in Mexican history, and a representative of what was perhaps the golden age of architecture in the country. What reflections do you have from living in a space like that?**

FE: Two years ago, I went through a separation and moved into this apartment, although it was rather by chance. This is a building from 1956, a time when many buildings full of two-hundred-square-meter apartments were built. It is a space with a history, which means it

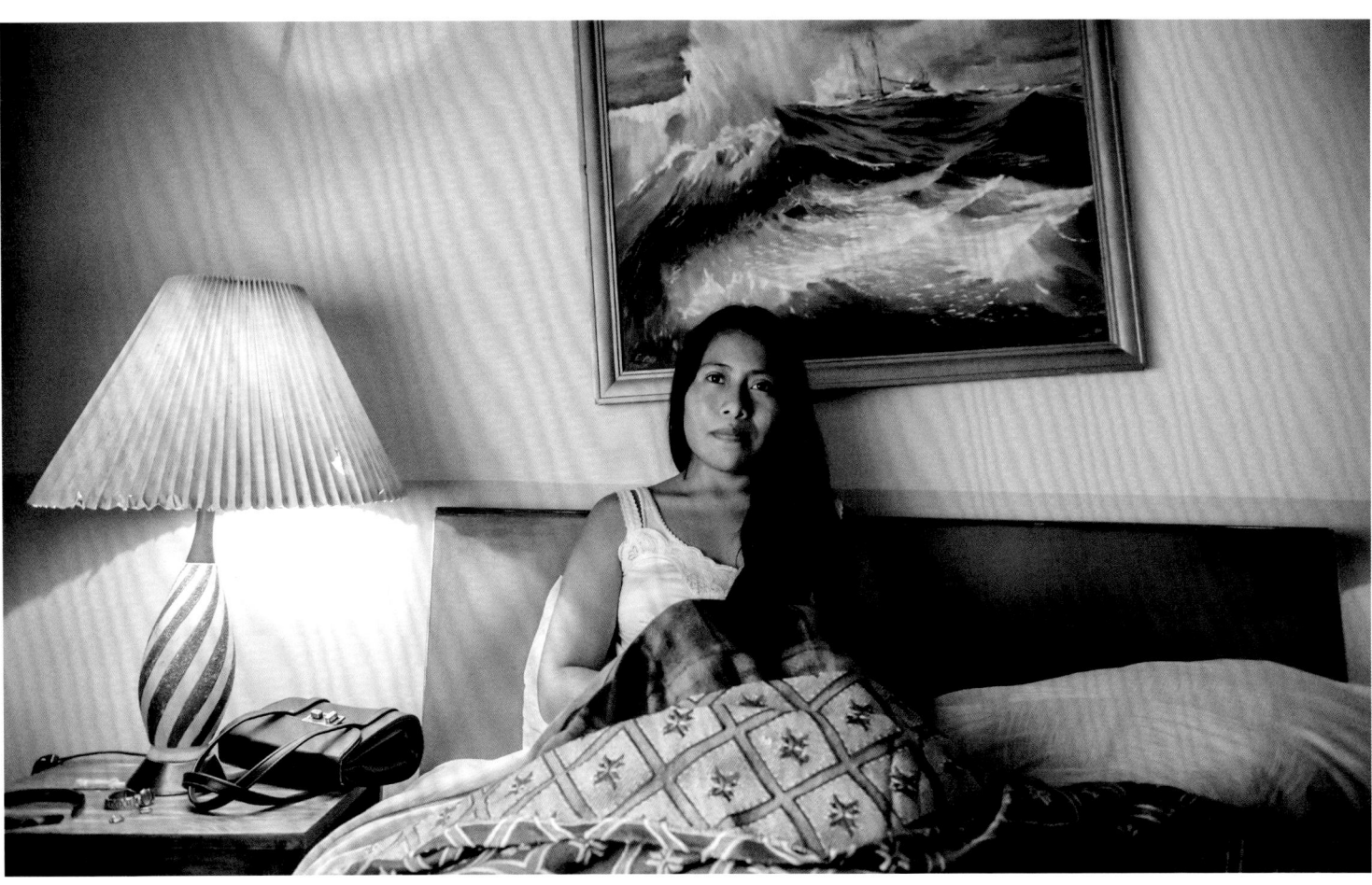

Carlos Somonte,
Still of Yalitza Aparicio
in *Roma* (Alfonso Curarón,
dir.), 2018
Courtesy Netflix

has been modified before. In the past, it was divided, but now it consists of rather open spaces. I have very few pieces of furniture: one Wassily chair that my father gave me when I first went to live by myself, and another we made at the office, which is a reinterpretation of the Donald Judd chairs, but made of volcanic rock. It's more of a joke. The table is attached to the wall, as was Barragán's, and the bookshelves surrounding the space are very low, so they can be used as seats when throwing a party. There are very few things, but I like the space to look empty, more like a dance floor. My walls are also clear. I do not like hanging pictures on the wall, as it looks way too formal to me. I prefer to lean them against bookshelves or other objects and move them around from time to time.

AGR: **From an architectural point of view, what is your idea of a home?**

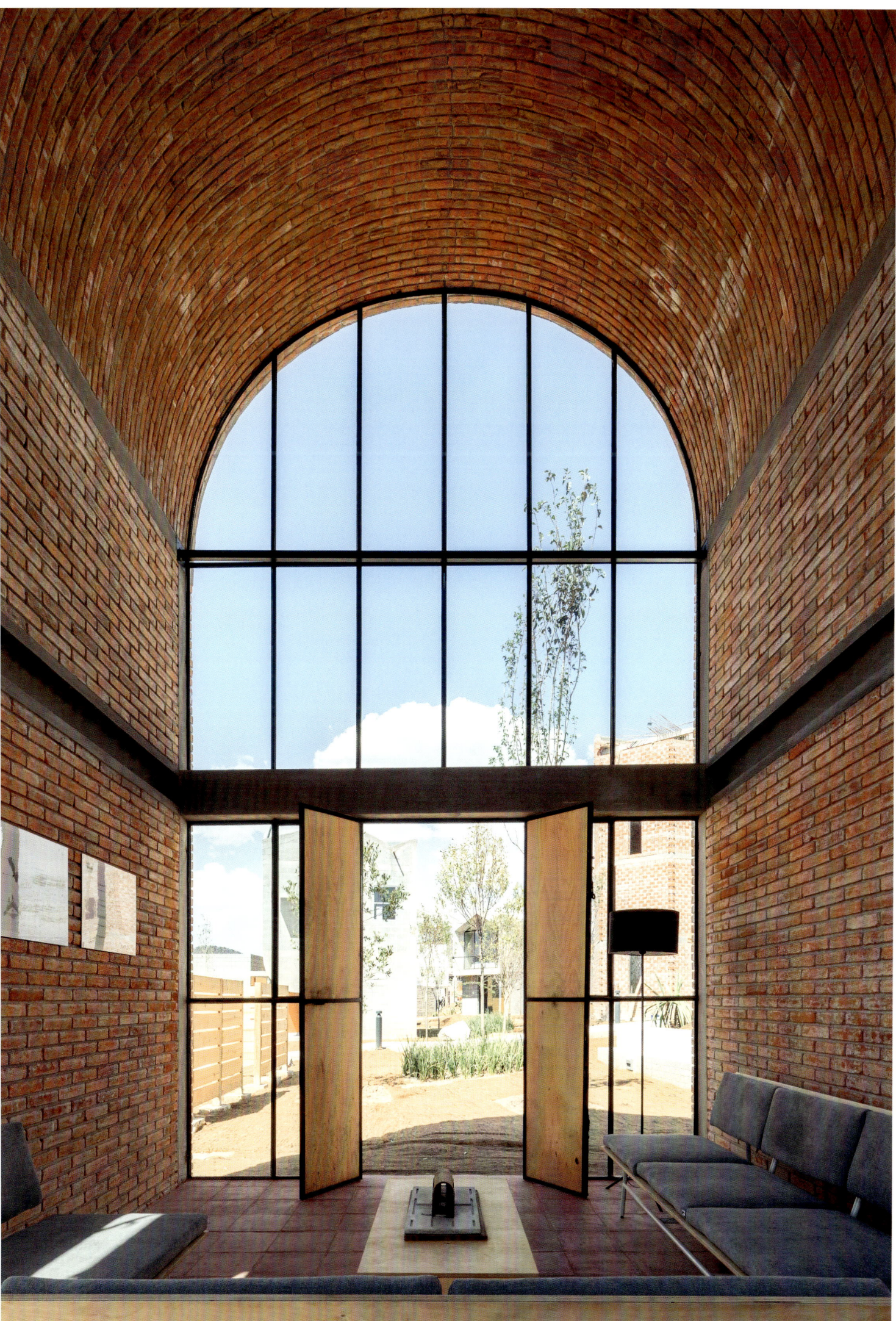

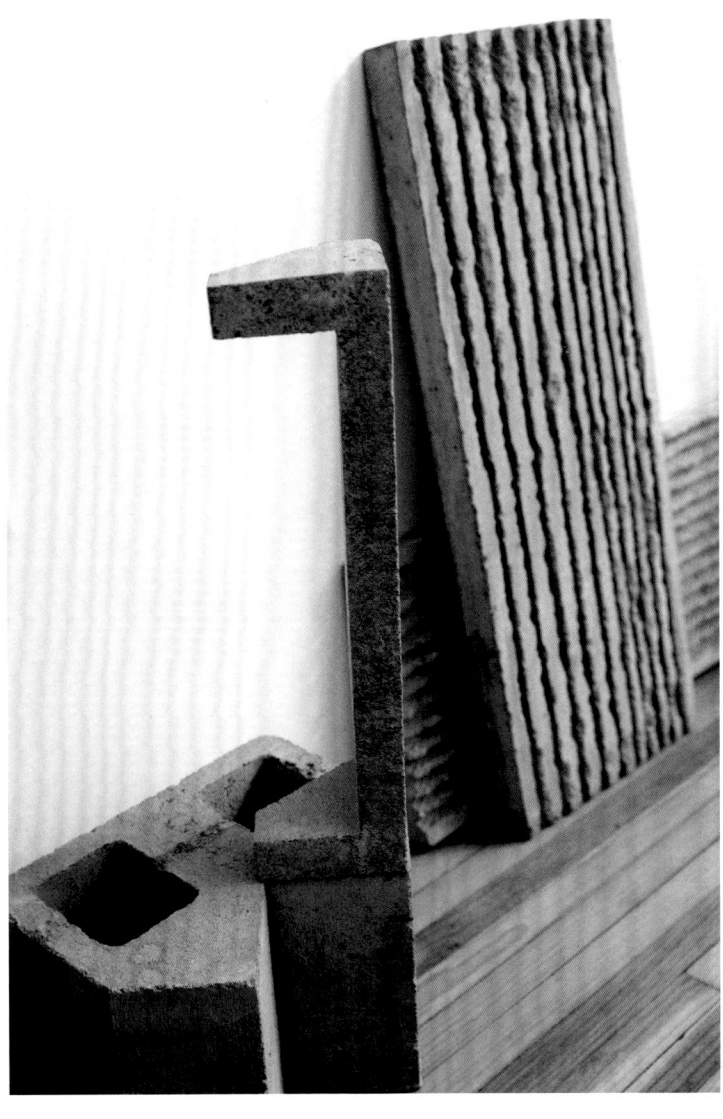

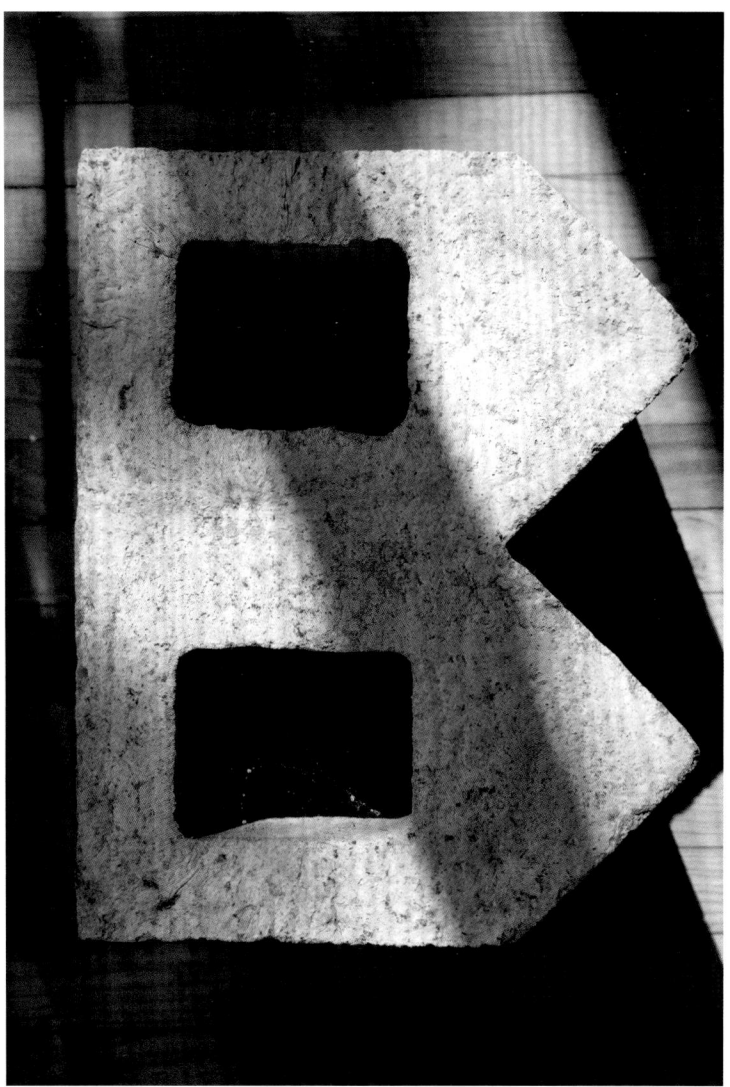

This page and opposite: Objects in Frida Escobedo's home, including concrete panel research and design models, Mexico City, 2019
Photographs by Yvonne Venegas for *Aperture*

FE: I don't think there should only be one concept of home. I think the actual problem is the will to standardize. There are many configurations of housing and family that are not considered when developing real-estate projects. They insist on selling us as many labels as possible in spaces that are increasingly small: a living room, a dining room, a kitchen, two bedrooms, two and a half bathrooms … and that nonsense walk-in closet, as if that were indeed going to increase our quality of life. Why doesn't anyone go for, say, large, flexible areas for people to transform freely?

AGR: You built a house for the Ordos 100 project (2008), organized by Ai Weiwei and Herzog & de Meuron. For this, one hundred architects from twenty-seven countries were invited to build a thousand-square-meter luxury villa in the Mongolian desert. You also designed a small house as part of a program for the Mexican government that sought low-cost housing alternatives for disadvantaged people. How did you respond to such opposite concepts?

FE: For the Ordos 100 project, the challenge was to rethink housing and come up with an experimental proposal to be developed in a rather inhospitable territory. There were guidelines to be followed—some interesting, some obvious. The idea was to create weekend houses. Each one had to have a safe, a cellar, a pool, et cetera. What caught my attention was the fact that they asked for two kitchens: one closed with storage space and the other open, like an island. After talking to the organizers, I understood that the first kitchen was for the service staff, and I realized that they would live there full-time. Therefore, in the remaining

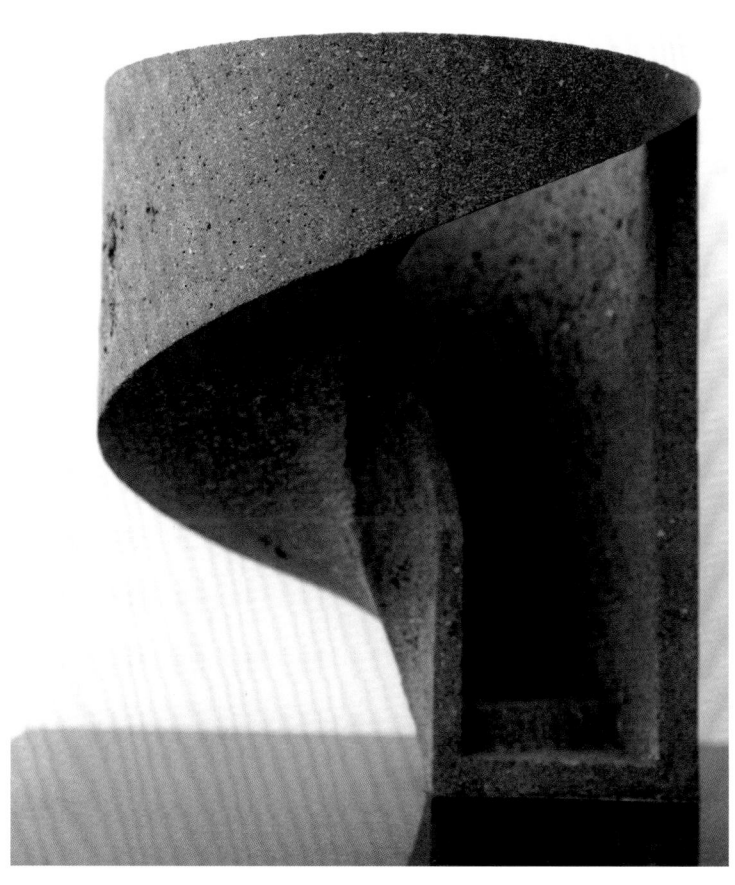

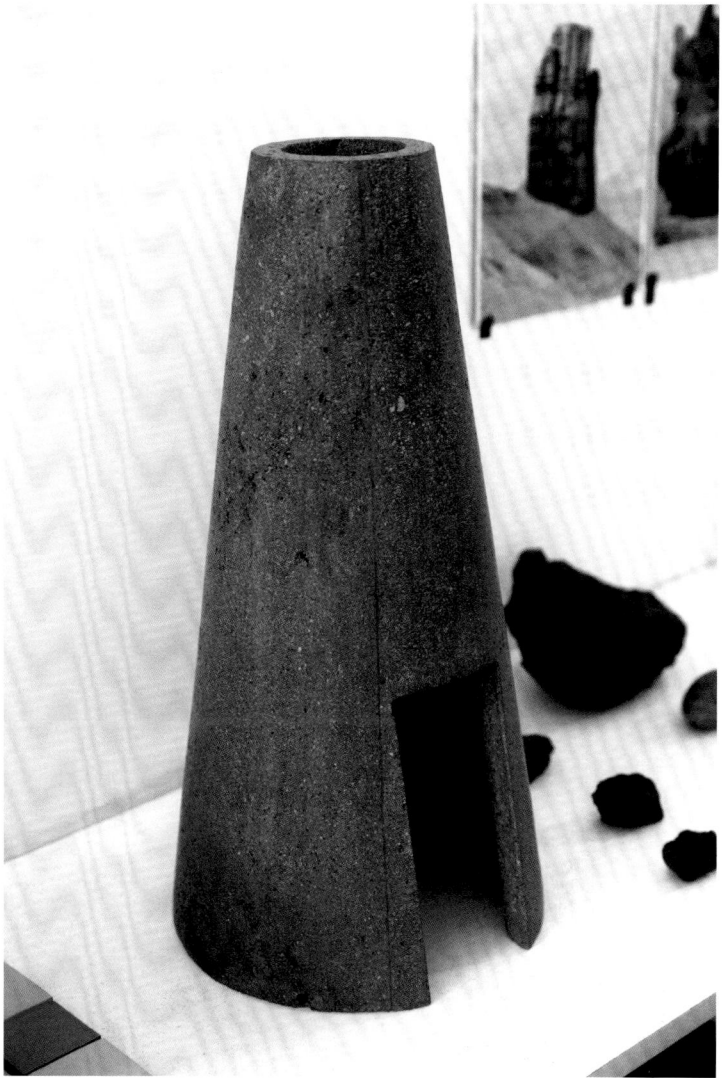

space, I designed an independent house for the cleaning staff, cooks, gardeners, et cetera, where they would have their own courtyards, linked to the main construction. For that project, enormous, outrageous houses were designed. I was the youngest among a hundred architects, and my house was the smallest one.

For the INFONAVIT (Institute of the National Fund for Workers' Housing) project (2019), the challenge was quite the opposite: designing with minimal resources and in a reduced area. I was invited, together with other architects, to design a social-housing prototype. We created one that would adapt both to a rural area and to an urban context. It is a very flexible vaulted house, which in a rural context can also be adapted as a barn. As for an urban environment, these arches integrate very well with the local architecture, as they are part of the architectural language of that city, Taxco. On a certain level, it is similar to the Casa Negra, which we discussed at the beginning, because it was an open space with a mezzanine offering easy and economical possibilities of expansion without the need for skilled labor. The idea is that instead of repeating that design ad nauseam—as has been the case with many social-housing projects, and I think it is a big mistake to believe that this configuration should be massive and standardized—families living in contiguous houses would have common, adaptable courtyards and spaces that would contribute to building communities.

AGR: **However, the housing project remained in limbo, making evident the government's lack of commitment to address the precarious condition in which a large part of the Mexican population lives.**

At first glance, a brick is a rigid industrial piece. Yet, when people appropriate it, the expressions are infinite.

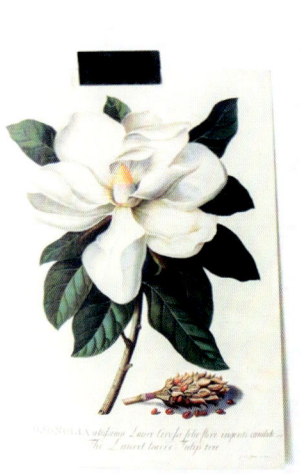

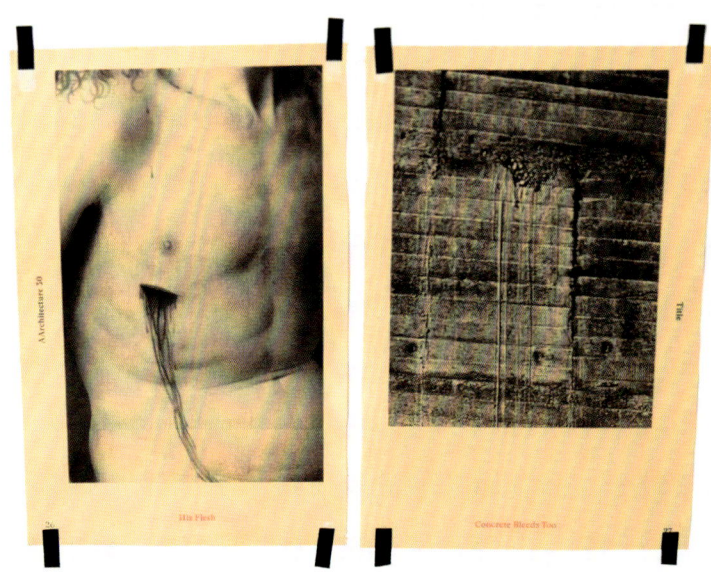

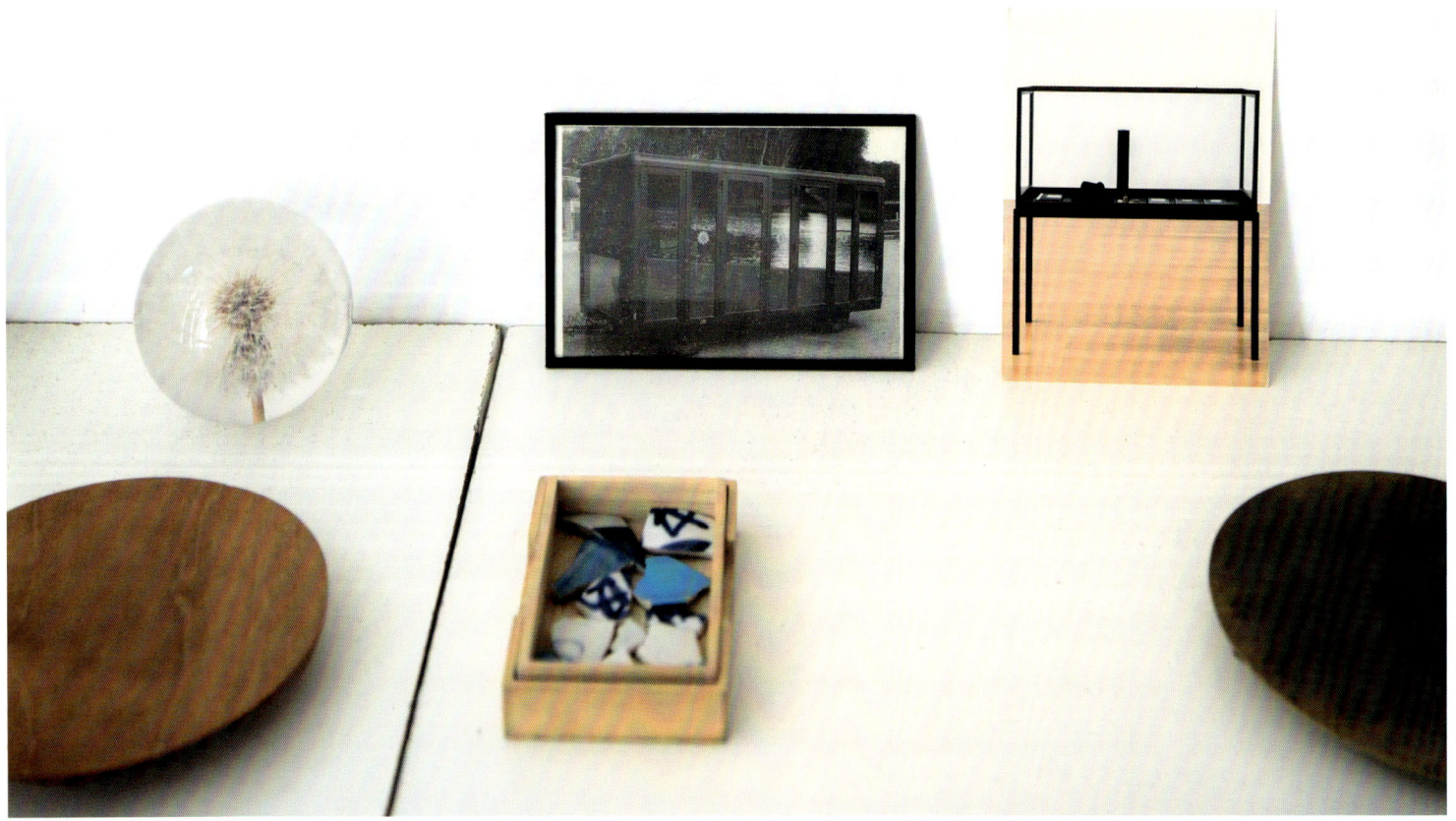

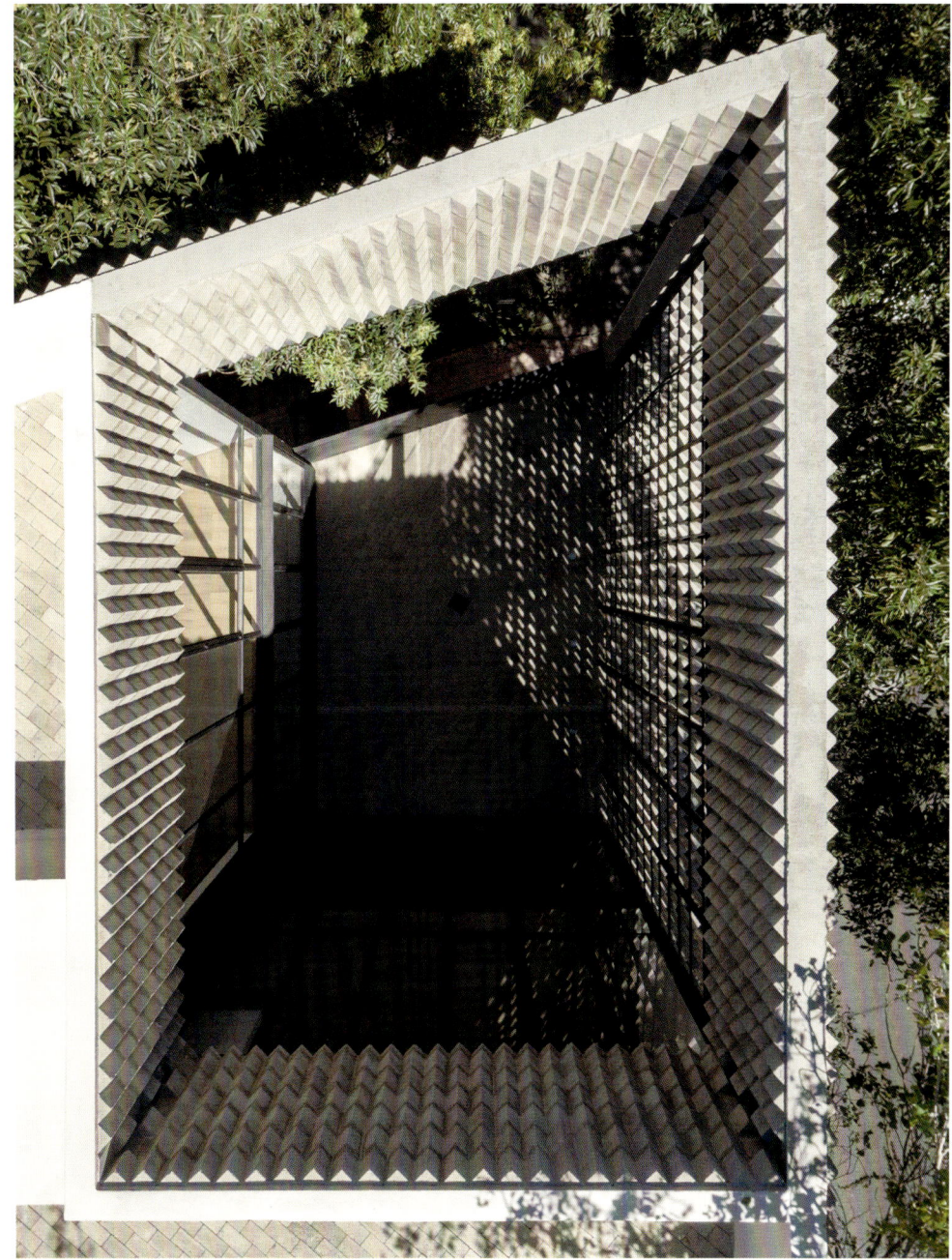

FE: As soon as we completed the project for INFONAVIT, we were told that all those prototypes, designed for different contexts, would be exhibited together in a plot intended to become a housing lab for researchers. Thus, instead of giving those houses to people who actually need them, they are in some kind of showroom. That project ended up being tremendously frustrating for me. It was a waste of resources that we cannot afford.

AGR: Many of your projects transcend the boundaries of architecture and could be read as similar to those of a visual artist. How do your references to other forms of art come into play in projects like the pavilion you created for the Museo Experimental El Eco in Mexico City, or in your installation for the Victoria and Albert Museum in London?

FE: In the case of El Eco, I was dealing with very high-level architecture—a work by Mathias Goeritz. Thus, profiting from the flexibility offered by loose bricks, I proposed guidelines to build a different space configuration for every event taking place in that courtyard: a stage for concerts, seats for a film projection, or simply a brick sculpture that kids could play with or destroy to build something new. In this case, one of my references was the concrete poetry of Ferreira Gullar, who seeks the maximum

expression with a minimal amount of words. At first glance, a brick is a rigid industrial piece. It looks like an object that does not allow much expression. Yet, when people appropriate it, the expressions are infinite.

The project for the Victoria and Albert Museum was developed in the context of the Year of Mexico in England, so the challenge was to make a pavilion in the central courtyard that made reference to Mexico. Nowadays a national pavilion is a somewhat forced idea, because everyone has windows to other countries and cultures, so we intended to enable an exchange, which seemed more interesting. We started from an investigation on land appropriations and decided to allude to the first appropriation that took place in Mexico City after the [Spanish] conquest, to recall the original city, which was a lake city full of reflections. This lake city is literally buried under the urban history of the country's capital. It is fascinating, even surreal. How did anyone come up with building a city on water? The idea involves high doses of magical realism, but somehow they managed.

Alejandra González Romo is a journalist based in Mexico City and an editor at *Gatopardo* magazine.

Translated from the Spanish by Enrique Pérez Rosiles.

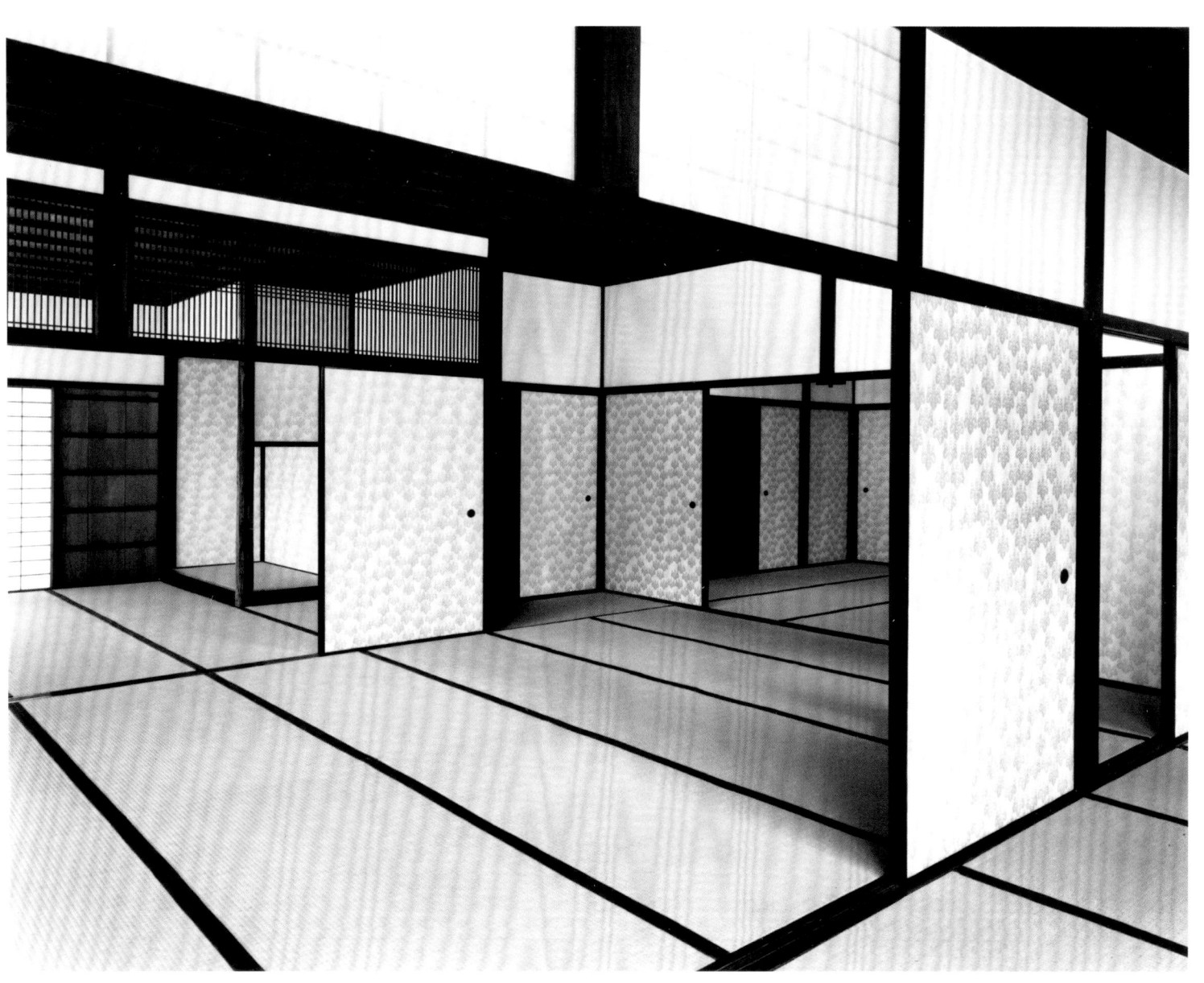

Minimal, Messy, or Melancholic?

The many faces of "home" in Japanese photography
Lena Fritsch

The English word *home* does not have a Japanese equivalent but links to various terms and concepts: *ie* and *katei* relate to the house spatially; *kazoku* (composed of the characters for *house* and *tribe*) is the immediate family and household; *furusato* defines a nostalgic image of one's home, hometown, or birthplace. Just as the Japanese language is highly situational, the idea of home also depends on the context. It is therefore not surprising that the motif of the home in Japanese photography is diverse, raising compelling questions: How do architectural photographs present the Japanese home? Are Daido Moriyama's blurry 1970s images of the village of Tono linked to a hometown vision? What kind of family home do younger photographers portray in their work?

Ie: Home as a house

Yoshio Watanabe, best known for his 1953 Ise shrine photographs, and Yasuhiro Ishimoto, who studied at the Institute of Design in Chicago before returning to Japan in 1953, were both concerned with the traditional architecture of Japanese temples, shrines, and villas. Unlike the Western idea of architecture that is durable and permanent, it has been a long custom in Japan to constantly change and re-create space, for example through the use of sliding doors and futon beds that are stored away during the day and taken out at night. In Watanabe's Japanese architecture photographs and Ishimoto's meticulously composed *Katsura Imperial Villa* series (1953–82), sliding paper doors and light tatami flooring contrast with dark wooden pillars; architectural shapes are captured as clear lines and geometric forms reminiscent of the Bauhaus (which in turn was partly inspired by a Japanese "purist" style). No detail is unplanned—forms and materials are in harmonious dialogue. The minimal, almost abstract photographic compositions convey a feeling of balance. The homes that Ishimoto and Watanabe present us with can be viewed as manifestations of the Japanese philosophy of space known as *ma*, literally "in-between." The aesthetic of the rooms (and of the photographs) comes into existence through a careful interaction between form and non-form, dark and light. The transient concept of space can be seen as following the tradition of Shinto and Buddhist culture, emphasizing the impermanence of all things.

Impermanence is also evident in a small city room in which paint is peeling off a sliding window frame. A pair of gloves, two umbrellas, and a kettle are attached to a laundry line strung across the room. It is the year 1978, and this home in Tokyo is one of many that Ishiuchi Miyako captured with her handheld camera. The dark gelatin-silver prints show some apartments with and others without their inhabitants. They were published in Ishiuchi's first photography book, *Apartment* (1978). In 1979, to her surprise, she received the renowned Kimura Ihei Award for this series. At the time, Japan was characterized by a fast-growing economy, which resulted in the area around Tokyo becoming increasingly urbanized. Residential buildings were erected rapidly and cheaply. *Apartment* documents people's simple, provisional living conditions, often in temporary homes. The photographs cannot be separated from the photographer's personal memories, as she lived in a similar apartment in Yokosuka on Tokyo Bay between the ages of six and

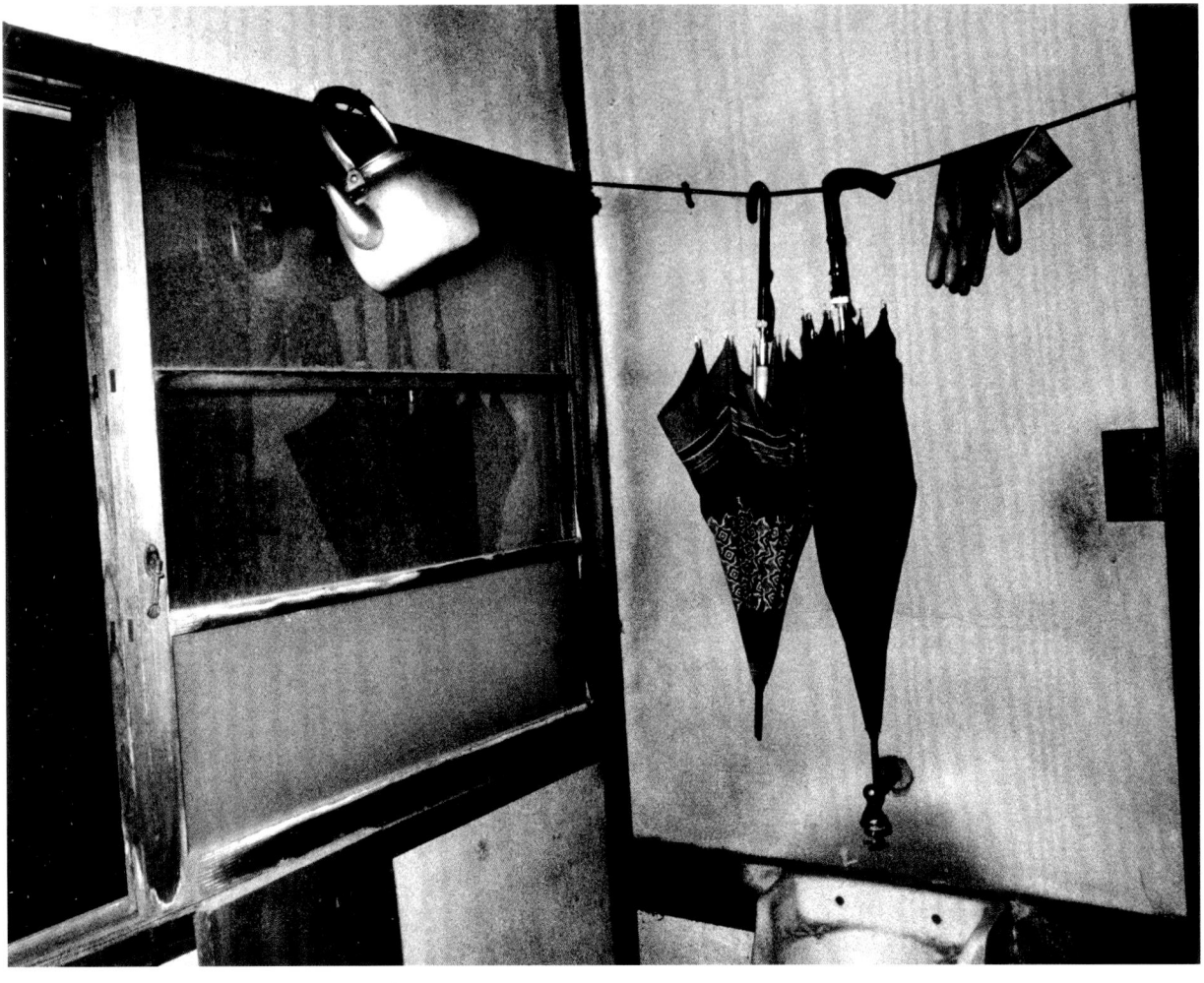

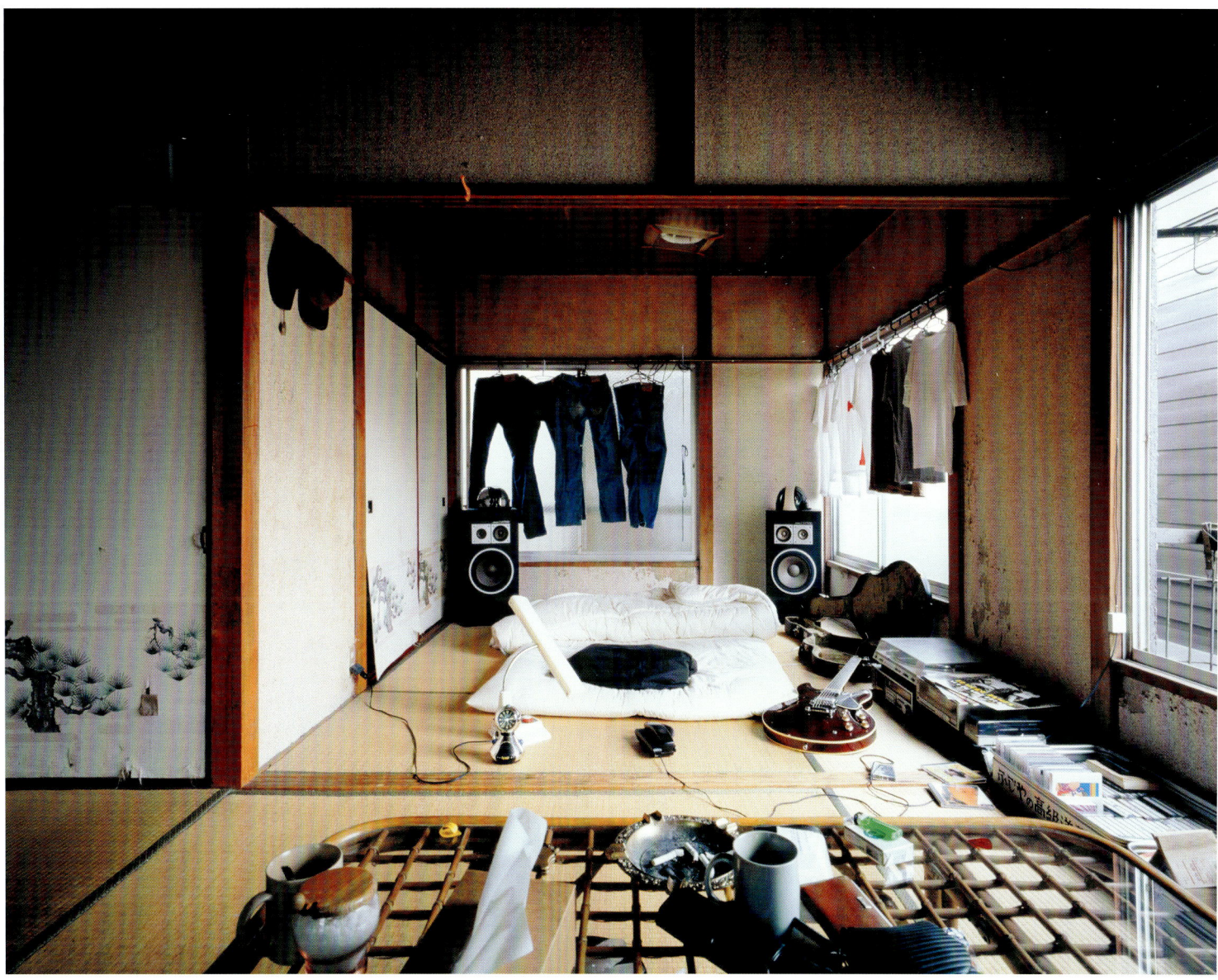

nineteen. She has repeatedly told me how she hated growing up there. The apartments symbolize her own childhood home. "I wanted to return to all the places that I associated with bad memories," she said. She has also described the apartments as being "permeated by a mix of different body smells. I have the feeling that the apartments smell thoroughly like people. These apartments are small, dark, and somewhat dirty, and nobody wants to live in them. But I sense a certain kind of reality in them—they are places that feel very human." Her *Apartment* photographs are "human" primarily because they make visible the traces of their countless former inhabitants. Walls are covered in cracks, sweat stains, and fingerprints. Objects suggest stories about their owners. As in Ishiuchi's later works depicting human bodies, clothes, or objects that people have left behind after their deaths, these poetic images tell of people, their mortality, and bittersweet remembrance.

In 1993, the photojournalist Kyoichi Tsuzuki published a small-format book, *Tokyo Style*, that also documented small homes. Compared to Ishiuchi, however, Tsuzuki is less interested in the memories captured in rooms. Rather, his photographs of approximately one hundred apartments are concerned with everyday, real interiors. In one image, an electric guitar and large speakers contrast with traditional tatami flooring. Clothes are provisionally hung on a curtain rail. Using a large-format camera, Tsuzuki carefully constructs his photographs, presenting them with short descriptions about the rooms and their interior design or key furniture pieces, offering the same viewpoint on these inexpensive studio apartments as we might see on stylish apartments designed by famous architects. His now-iconic book was a reaction against the staged photographs of designer apartments found in interior design magazines and coffee-table books. When I spoke with Tsuzuki, he laughed about such fantasies and the "flowers that are usually not there, or fruit that nobody ever eats, and the interior designer who would also be at the photo shoot." Such magazine photographs, and perhaps also the visual legacies of figures such as Ishimoto or Watanabe, have resulted in a stereotype of Japanese people living in Zen-inspired minimalist homes. "Although the great majority, around nine out of ten people in Tokyo live in tiny apartments, including members of staff that create beautiful architectural magazines, there was not a single book about their rooms," Tsuzuki said.

Furusato: Longing for home

In 1909, when the writer and ethnologist Kunio Yanagita visited the isolated village of Tono in northeastern Japan, it was mainly inhabited by peasants, and the first railroads were only starting to be constructed. Seeking to record the rural lifestyle and folk beliefs, Yanagita collected oral stories by the folklorist Kizen Sasaki The legends were published in a 1910 book titled *Tono Monogatari* (The Tales of Tono), revealing a dark world of the fantastic and reflecting a history of severe human existence. In the late 1960s and '70s, a broad interest in Japanese folklore began to emerge, and Yanagita's work was rediscovered. With the growth in prosperity, a concern with traditions found its way into people's leisure life, as evident in the increasing number of cultural centers offering

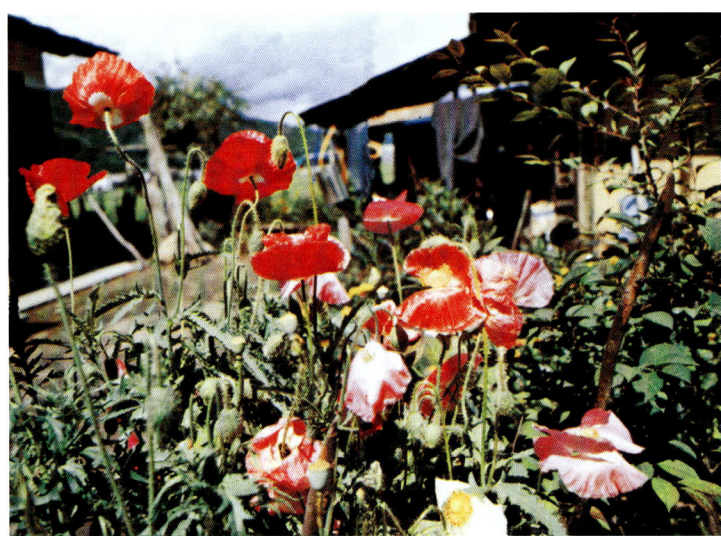

The homes that Ishimoto and Watanabe present us with can be viewed as manifestations of the Japanese philosophy of space known as *ma*, literally "in-between."

courses in all kinds of "authentic" Japanese arts. Within the contemporary challenges—enormous economic growth and internationalization on the one hand, student revolutions and protests against the 1960 Japan–United States Security Treaty on the other—nostalgic ideas of a "traditional" Japan ensured a familiar national and cultural identity. Moriyama's photography book *Tono Monogatari* (1976) and Masatoshi Naito's *Tono Monogatari* (published in 1983 but photographed between 1971 and 1982) reflect Japan's folklore boom. Moriyama's and Naito's mostly black-and-white photographs of Tono, with their stark contrasts and dark imagery, convey a sense of the mysterious. Moriyama's blurry, grainy images taken out of the train window on his journey to Tono or his cropped color photographs of flowers in someone's garden, as well as Naito's photographs of Tono at night, shot with a flash, suggest scenes that suddenly appear and then vanish again—just like indeterminate visual recollections unexpectedly surfacing from the dark realms of memory.

In Moriyama's photobook descriptions of his journey, the term *furusato* plays a major role. The modern notion of *furusato* (literally "old village") refers to one's native place and is associated with nostalgic, warm feelings. Perhaps it is best described by the philosopher Ernst Bloch's famous words about the home as a place that "shines into the childhood of all and in which no one has yet been." There is a strong temporal component to *furusato*: it is linked with an image of the past, constituting a sentimental antithesis to the present. In the 1970s, Tono became regarded as an example of *furusato*: a warmly pastoral home that functioned as a romantic counterpoint to the prosperous, fast-paced, and Westernized Japan of the present. As the folklore scholar Hermann Bausinger once said, the expansion of the term *home* tends to coincide with the dissolution of one's horizon. The loss of the war and the large-scale sociopolitical and economic changes since 1945 had surely dissolved Japan's former horizon, resulting in a fundamental severance from home. It was this alienation from home that led to Japanese artists' new concern with the idea. Moriyama writes about his wistful longing for Tono as an embodiment of *furusato*, which he defines as a "swollen utopia of countless childhood memory fragments." Both Moriyama and Naito refer to the idea of the hometown as a "primordial image" in our subconscious, using a term coined by the psychoanalyst Carl Jung that defines images from the collective unconscious, shared among all humans. Moriyama confronts his hometown utopia by interacting with the real Tono through his camera. The medium of photography helps him to overcome, at least momentarily, his melancholic search for a home. When Moriyama leaves, he is able to say, "Tono, farewell for now."

Kazoku: Home means family

Sometimes home is neither a particular place nor a distant memory. *Funabashi Story*, a series of images taken by Kazuo Kitai between 1983 and 1987, beautifully records people's mundane lives inside apartment complexes in Funabashi, a city on the outskirts of Tokyo that grew rapidly in the 1980s. One of the protagonists is a child behind transparent curtains, curiously looking out a window while the television is on. The photographs have a narrative quality, and when Kitai published them as a photobook in 1989, he added texts that describe the homes and people's domestic habits. "I decided to take photographs because I wanted to show people's lives and hear their stories," he told me, emphasizing that his viewpoint is not neutral but always aligns with the photographic subjects' position. Kitai's sincere respect for the residents is evident in his *Funabashi Story* photographs.

Yurie Nagashima, Takashi Homma, and, most recently, Motoyuki Daifu and Masaki Yamamoto have presented personal stories about their families. Nagashima first received attention in the male-dominated Japanese photography scene in 1993, as a young

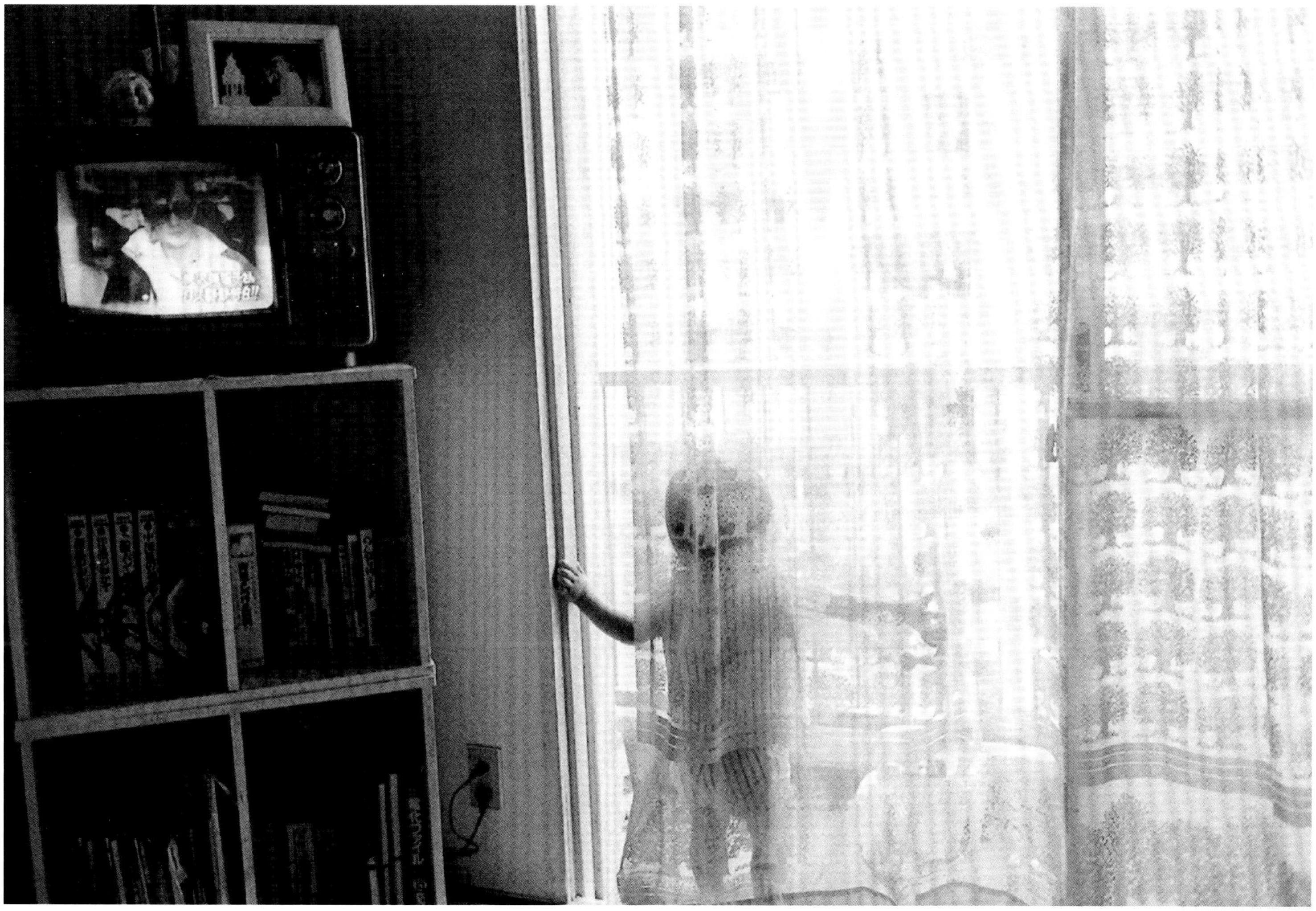

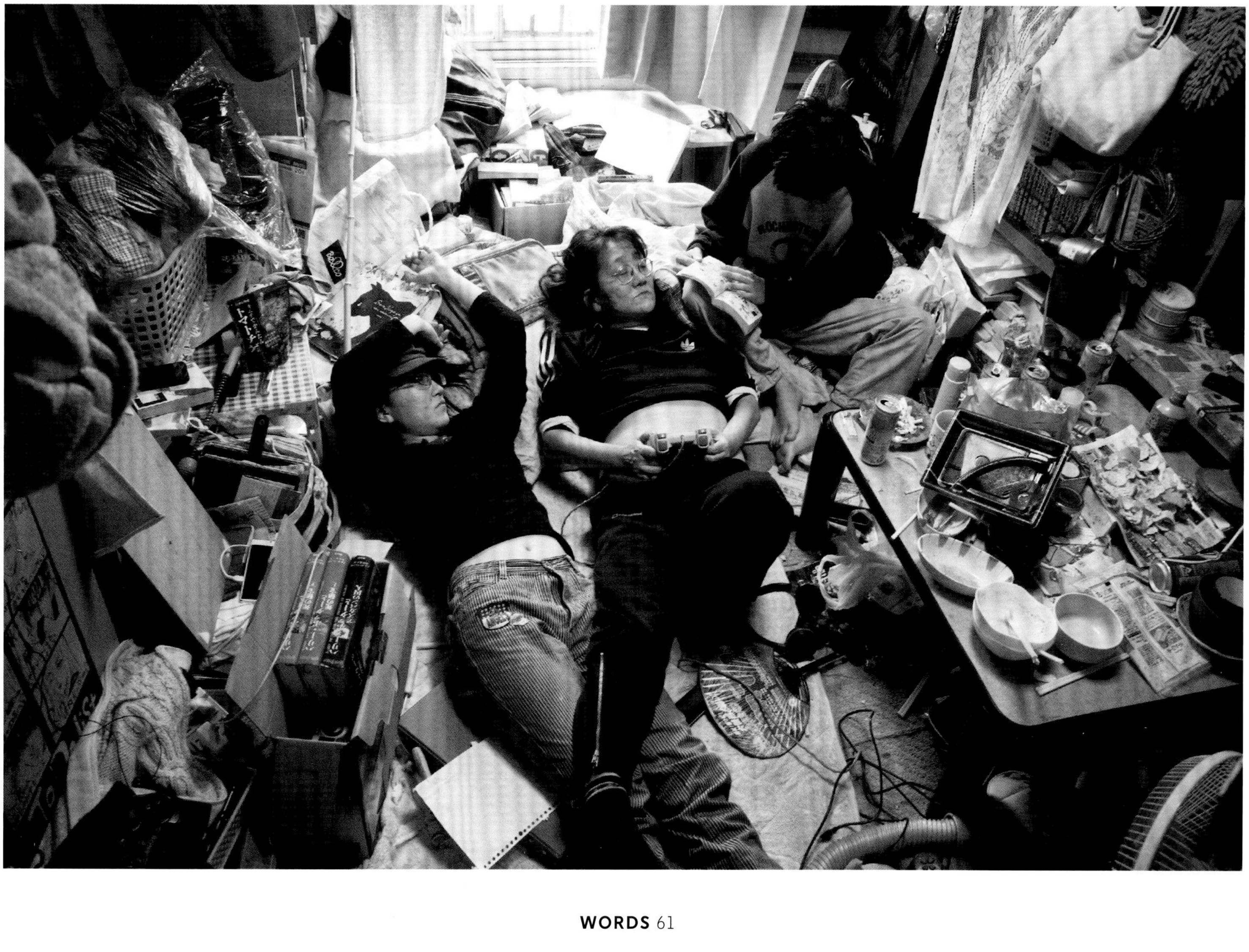

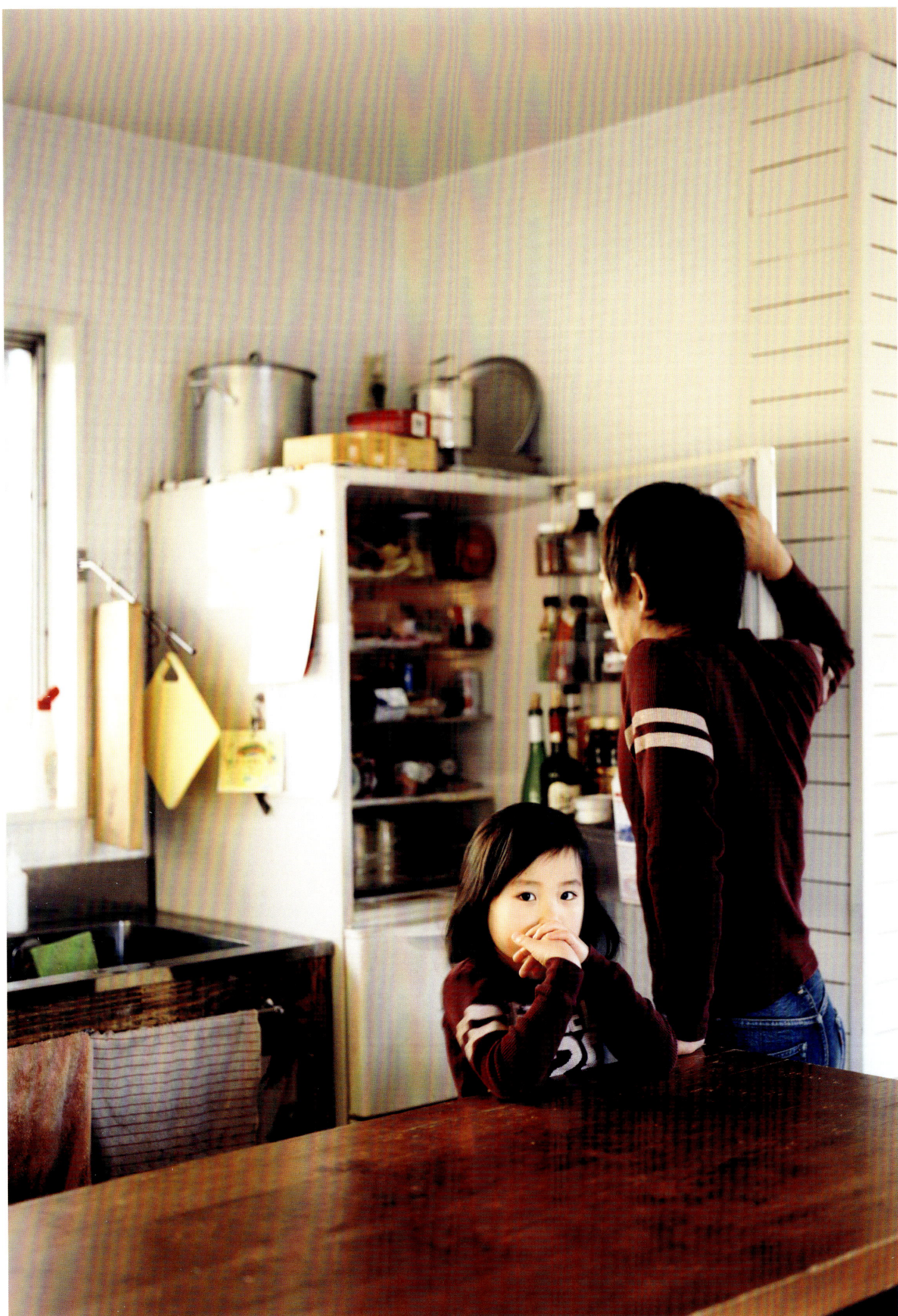

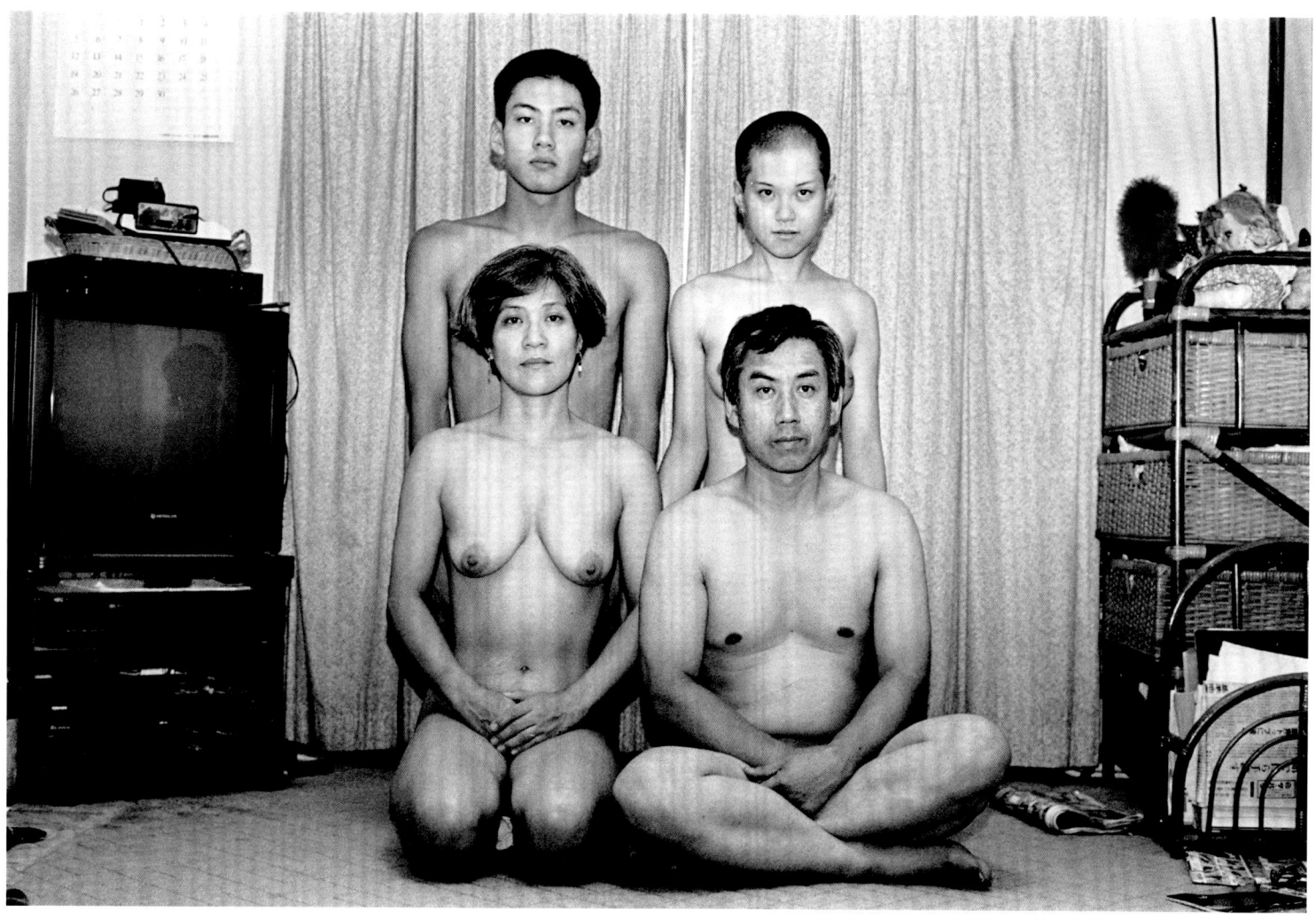

woman who portrayed herself and her family naked at home. They appear comfortably unclothed when posing for a family photograph or pursuing their daily routines. "I grew up in a free and open family environment, in quite a downtown style," she said. "My family would walk around half naked with just a towel around their bodies after taking a bath. To me, nakedness is not necessarily something sexual."

In his photobook *Tokyo and My Daughter* (2006), Homma portrays the nonglamorous and domestic, interweaving photographs of his studio with a portrait of a small dog and photographs of a young girl who appears to be exposed to the loving eyes of her proud father. We see her grow from a toddler to an elementary-school child. In one photograph, she appears wearing the same shirt as Homma, who is checking the inside of a refrigerator in the background. The girl stares directly into the camera, suggesting that she is aware of the viewer while also looking bored. The sequence of images conveys a diaristic feeling. With this book, Homma has shifted his attention from the formalistic suburban landscape to the closeness of the home space. The fact that the photographic story is fictional (the girl in the series is the photographer's friend's daughter) is not visible in the work: the book presents itself convincingly as a personal portrait of a father and a daughter's life in the city.

Homma's vision of a middle-class home contrasts with the cluttered, much more modest apartment in Kobe that Yamamoto has captured in a real and movingly intimate family portrait. Their tiny home, explored in his affectionate photobook *GUTS* (2017), is jam-packed with clothes, plates of food, cans, paper, and countless household objects. In between all this clutter, members of Yamamoto's family are lying on the floor: sleeping close together, watching television, playing video games, and enjoying each other's company. The young photographer seems to tell us that home is, above all, where one's heart is—with one's family and loved ones.

Opposite:
Takashi Homma, *Tokyo and My Daughter*, ca. 2006
© and courtesy the artist

This page:
Yurie Nagashima, *Self-Portrait (Family #26)*, 1993
© and courtesy the artist

Lena Fritsch is Curator of Modern and Contemporary Art at the Ashmolean Museum, University of Oxford, and the author of *Ravens & Red Lipstick: Japanese Photography since 1945* (2018).

Fumi Ishino
Home is Somewhere Else

Moeko Fujii

Two years ago, on his annual visit to Japan, the photographer Fumi Ishino started feeling that things were a little bit off. Perhaps it was the billboards gearing up for the 2020 Olympics. Perhaps it was the advertisements trumpeting a Cool Japan. Whatever it was, fifteen years after his move to the United States for college, he walked around neighborhoods of Tokyo with his camera, followed by a feeling that the place was suddenly neither home nor foreign. It was a feeling of *zure*, he said, of slippage, and he repeated the word softly. A feeling of *zure*, lopsidedness: a frame on the wall ever so slightly crooked.

This slight but powerful sense of unease suffuses Ishino's images, that of witnessing the familiar transform into the strange. Ishino, born in Hyogo and now residing in Los Angeles, marauds in the particulars of the placeless: what we can learn from, say, a whitewashed wall in a nameless residential town, or from the ready symbolism of the Tokyo Tower. In *Loom* (2018), Ishino's first collection of photographs taken entirely in Japan, he disrupts our habits of scouring images for markers of nationhood. "I avoided anything that hinted of Tokyo or Japan," he told me. "I wanted to obscure the sense of location." In a city stuffed with shrines and monuments to capital, Ishino wanted to capture things that weren't made to endure at all. He is interested in places that are always forgotten, the category of images that are usually shelved, in our field of vision, as unimportant. When we remember a place, what does our perception fill in on the periphery? "And, when you no longer have a place you call home," Ishino said, with a little laugh, "doesn't everything become background?"

We see a shade of white across all of his photographs in *Loom*: on exteriors, curtains, a trash can. It's cold with the blue undertones of whitewash, a hue that, exhilaratingly, doesn't yield to interpretation. I found myself alternating between examining this peculiar whiteness and being pulled to bursts of human color: a pink flower planted just at the edge of the frame, a child's imagination on a garage wall, an orange elephant, a recycling bin with brown scruff around its mouth. In my dueling impulse to fixate on the differences in the debris of people, and also on the sameness of sprawling, cut-off expanses of white, I felt the weight of my own displacements, the everyday tensions of being constructed by multiple cultures, not just one.

"I think we are always competing between wanting to travel and live in a world with no borders," Ishino says, "and the desire to call somewhere home." None of his photographs from *Loom* illustrates this more than one of a white shirt hung alone on a pole, caught mid-dry. I see the clothespins acting as competing identities and notions of nationality, tugging the cloth into a slumping, restless grace. But in its loose tautness, Ishino presents a more complicated aesthetics of suspension, a gentle balance upheld amid buffeting forces, found only from crisscrossing between worlds.

Moeko Fujii is a writer and critic living in Chiba, Japan, and New York.

All photographs from the series *Loom*, Japan, 2018
Courtesy the artist

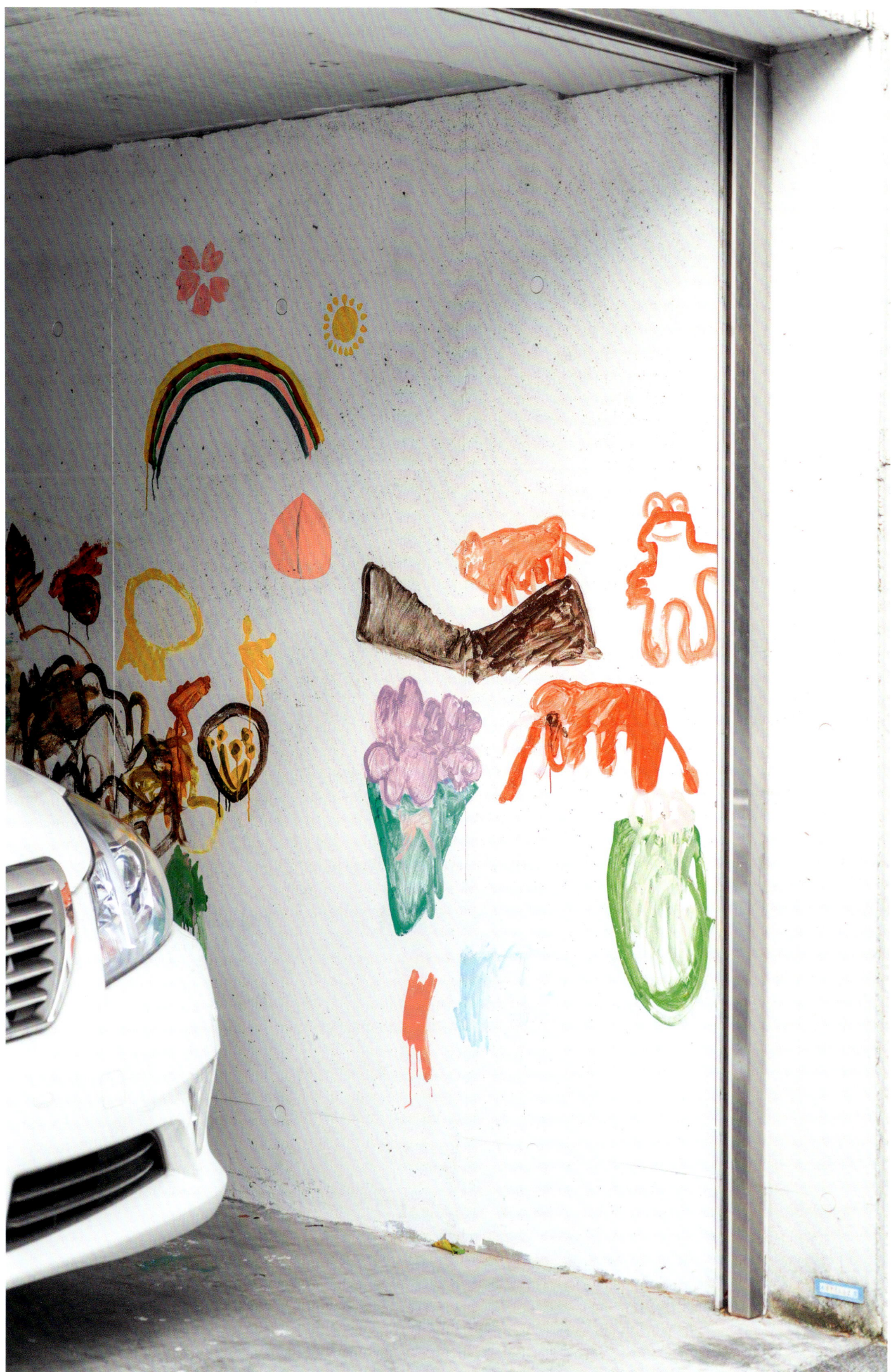

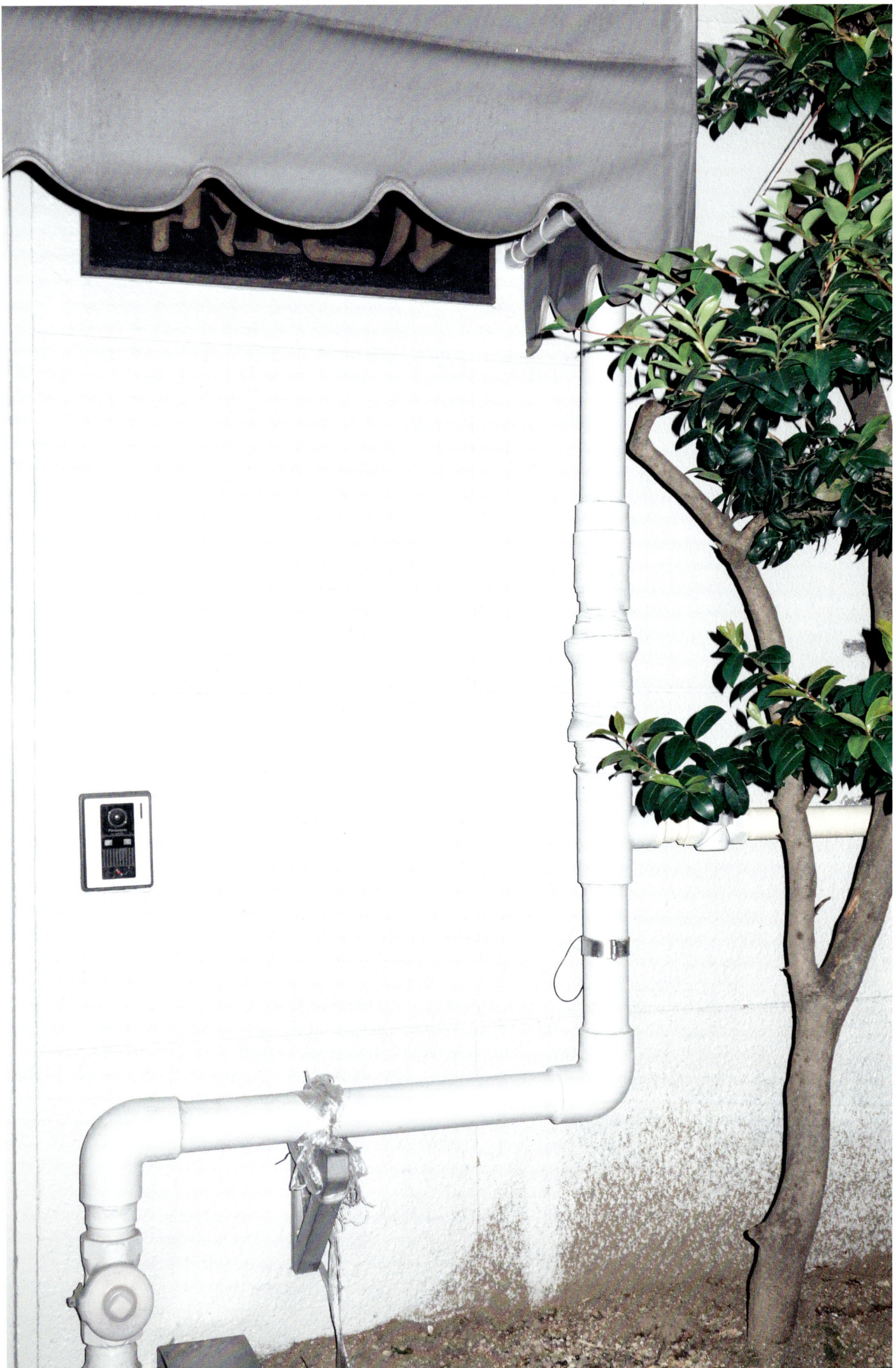

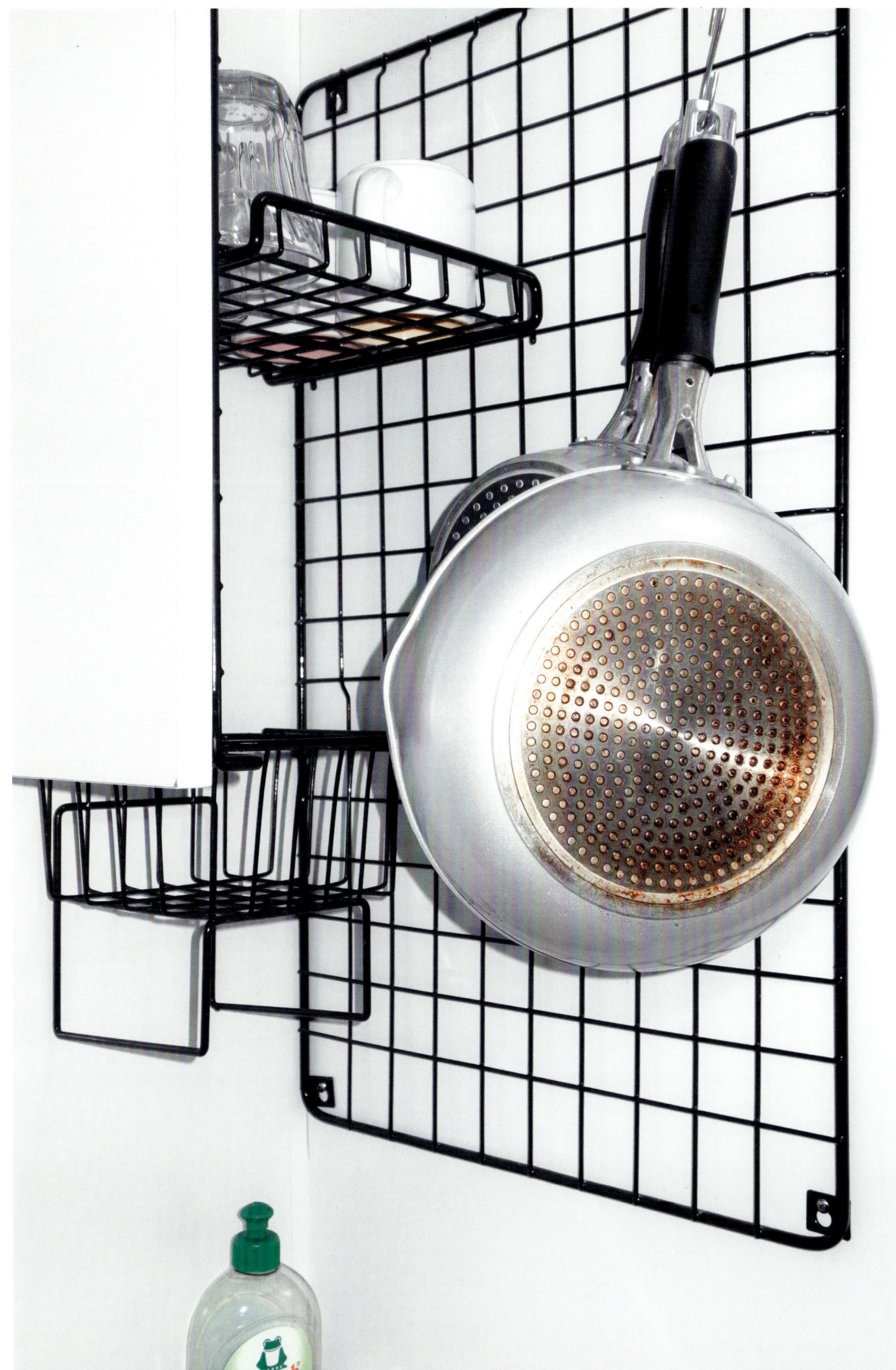

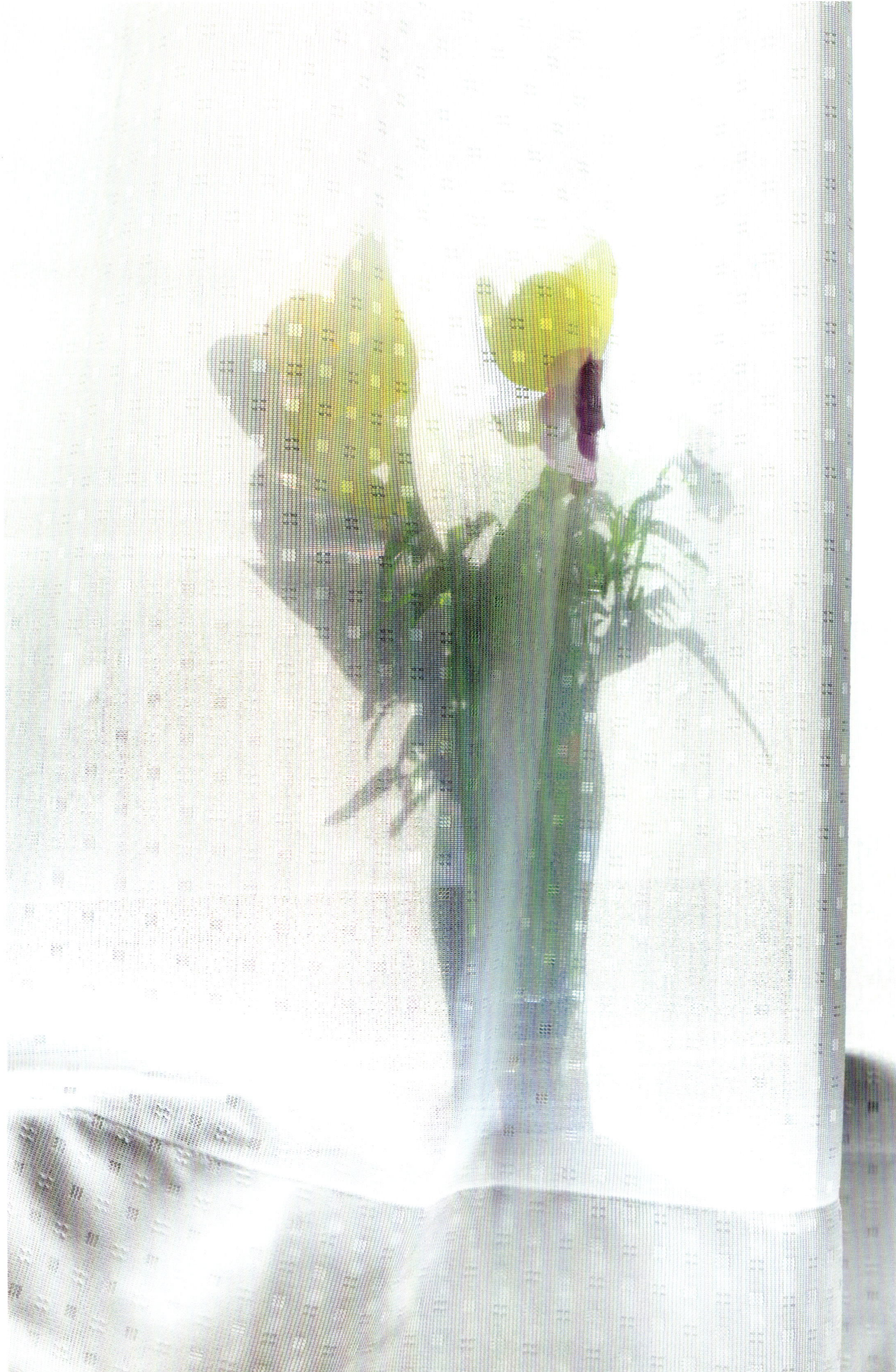

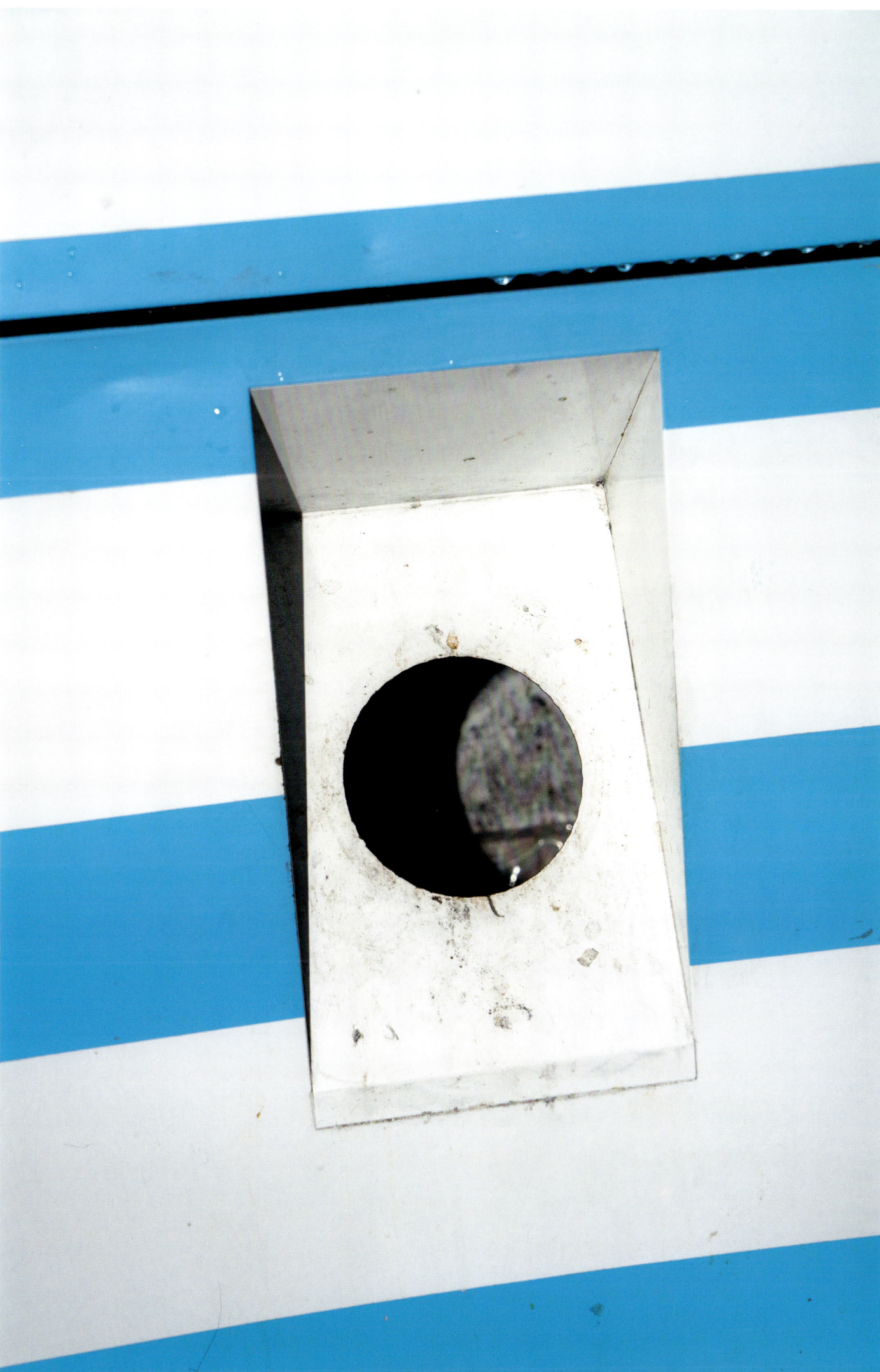

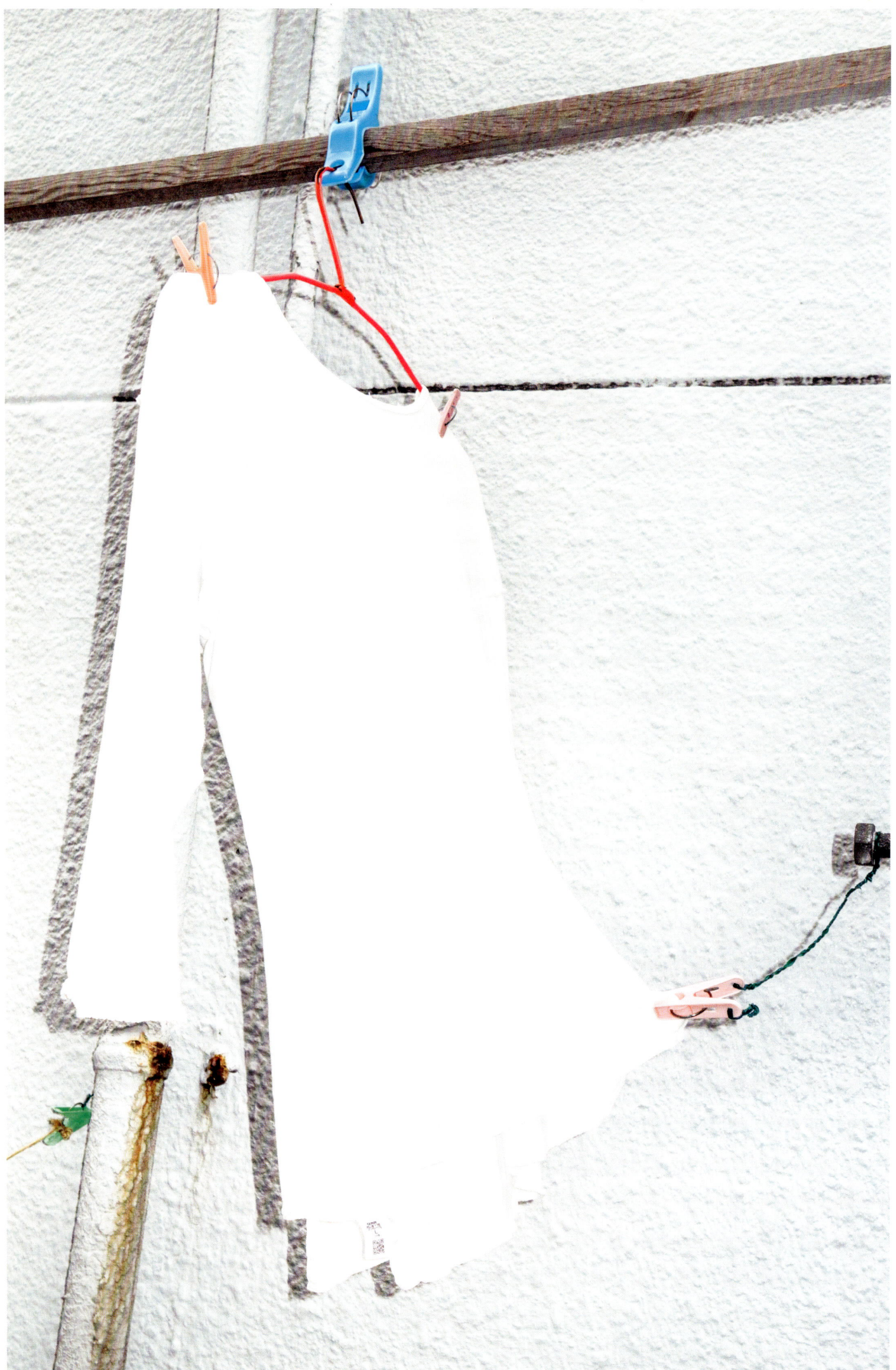

Seher Shah & Randhir Singh

The Barbican Estate

Olivia Laing

All works from the
series *Studies in Form
(The Barbican Estate –
London)*, 2018
Commissioned by the
Samdani Art Foundation for
the Dhaka Art Summit, 2018.
Courtesy the artists and
Green Art Gallery, Dubai

This isn't what I can see from my window. What I can see is a concrete planter full of geraniums and, behind it, a school playground and assorted twenty-first-century towers, one of which, at the Old Street roundabout, turns pink at sunset, a compensation for facing east. The children have just flooded out, their shouts lapping the third-floor balconies. "Where are you going?" "SIT DOWN."

Living in these buildings is a mystery. Sound moves in odd ways. At intervals, a man sings opera, his voice as resonant as if he were standing in the stairwell. The Barbican looks like a fortress, but it's actually designed on a principle of permeability. There are dozens of ways in and out—staircases, ramps, lifts, walkways, tunnels. Inside each flat, there's an ingenious row of cupboards. You put your rubbish in the bottom one, and at 8 AM it's opened from the other side and whisked away. Parcels announce their arrival via pink slips in the next cupboard up. They're reclaimed from the car-park attendants, the secret rulers of the estate.

Studies in Form is a 2018 collaboration between the artist Seher Shah and the photographer Randhir Singh, both of whom are based in New Delhi. It uses cyanotypes to explore the abstract qualities of four architectural developments around the world, among them the Barbican Estate in London, where I live. These photographs focus on the repetitive, sculptural qualities of the estate: the lipped balconies, the concrete vents that look like funnels on a ship. In these beautiful, enigmatic images, my home appears massive, elegant, austere, a little unfriendly.

What Shah and Singh have captured in their cyanotypes are the clean lines and sculptural heft of the place, the belief that utility and beauty don't always have to cancel each other out. There are lots of different ways to live, and so there are lots of different types of available accommodation. The Barbican's architects, Chamberlin, Powell and Bon, believed it was their responsibility to make each space work, no matter how small. The shipshape kitchens in the F2A studios, the kind I have, were designed by the yacht makers Brooke Marine.

The whole estate is a master class in urban planning, a fantasy of what a city could be. There are three cinemas, an arts center, bars, a tropical conservatory, restaurants, residents' gardens, and a library, but the design isn't so precious or managed that there isn't room for real people's lives. Kids do illicit parkour on the walkway. Some of the planters have been co-opted as makeshift garden allotments, bursting with onions and ruby stems of chard. On summer evenings, I often see a bat, zigzagging through the blue air in search of flies as the buildings exhale the day's accumulated heat.

The place seems so solid that it's easy to forget it only exists as a consequence of the near obliteration of the City of London. I keep a copy of *Bomb Damage Maps, 1939–1945* on my desk: a 288-page reproduction of the intricate, beautifully colored bomb-damage maps compiled by London County Council during the Blitz. Almost everything hereabouts is purple, code for "damaged beyond repair," the result of sustained bombardment on the night of December 29, 1940.

London's bomb sites were rapidly reclaimed by plants, what my friend Leo Mellor once described as a "mesmerically enfolding verdancy." Within months, the wreckage was transformed into a wilderness of rosebay willowherb, Oxford ragwort, coltsfoot, charlock, groundsel, and Thanet cress. The Barbican has kept that spirit, the commingling of the human and the wild. It's a fertile utopia, a concrete kingdom in which tomatoes, lavender, and figs all thrive.

Olivia Laing's latest collection of essays is
Funny Weather: Art in an Emergency (2020).

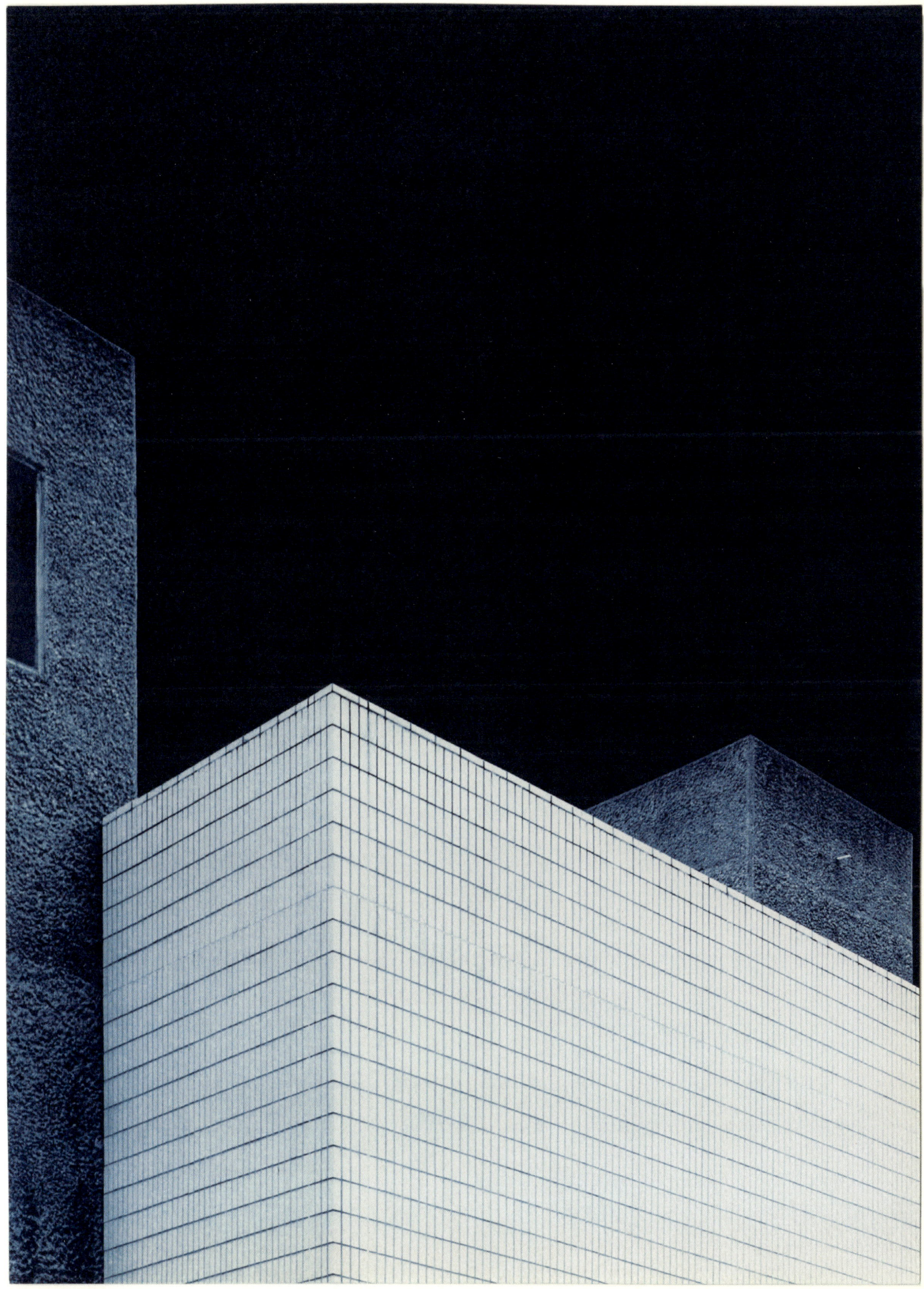

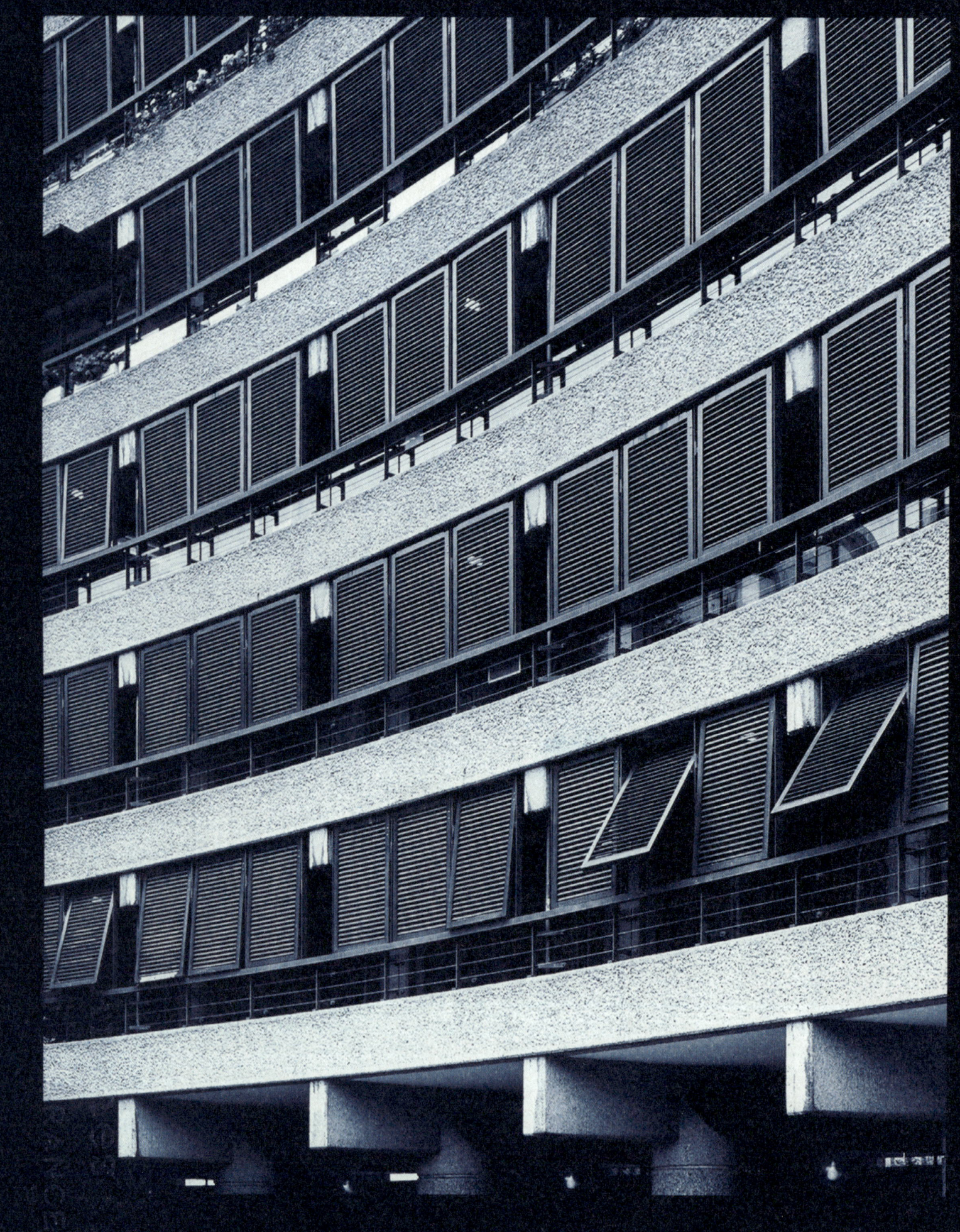

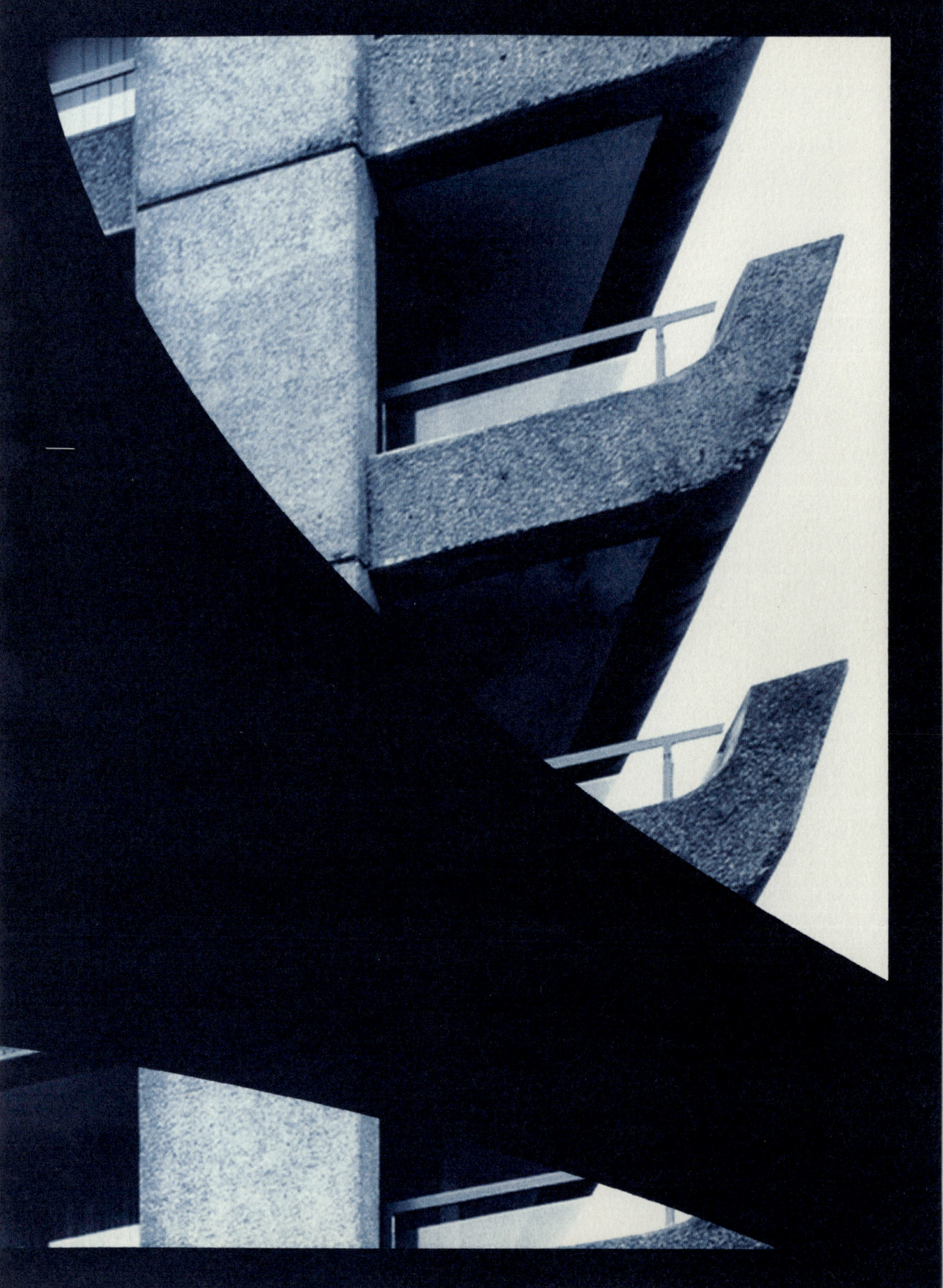

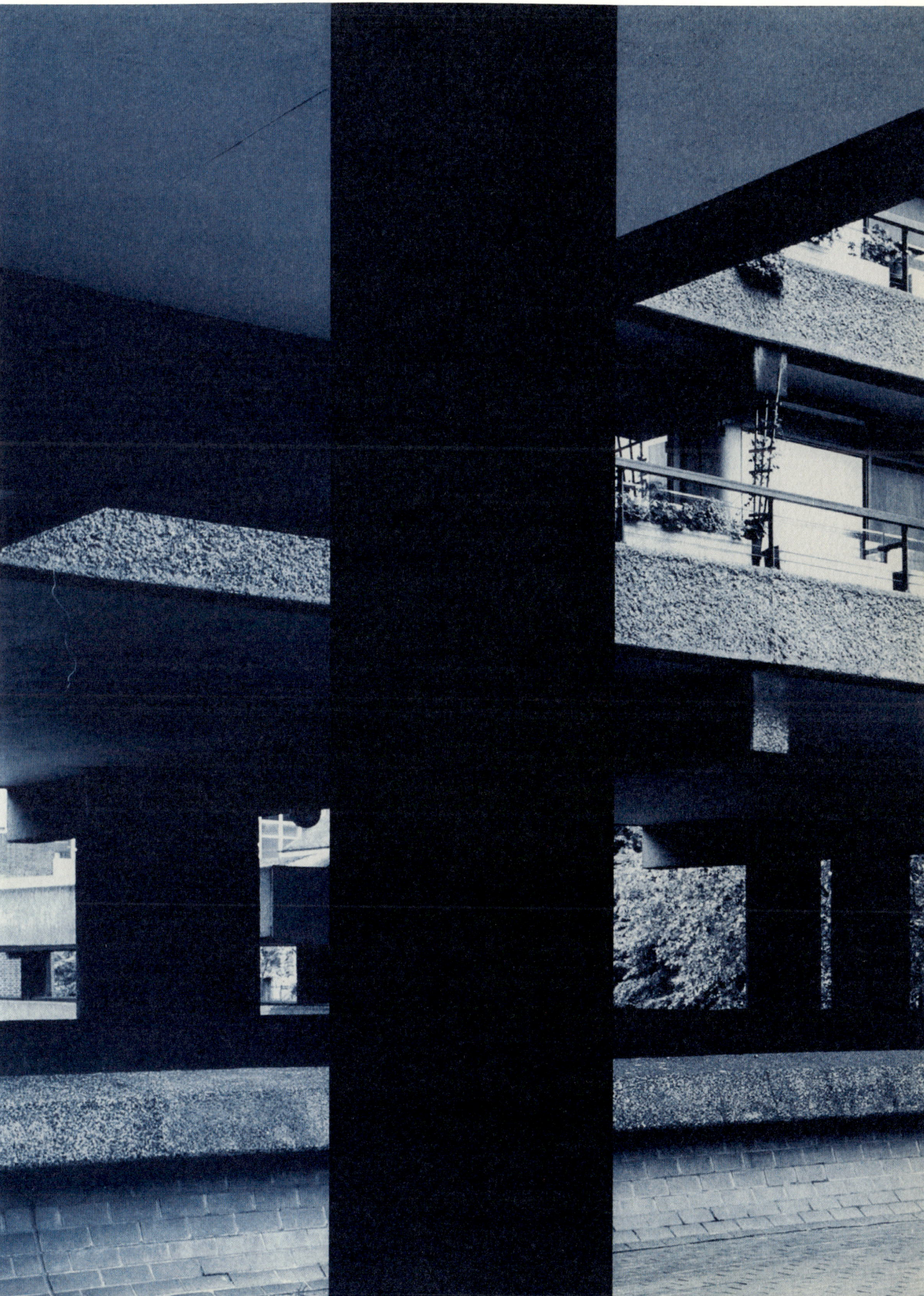

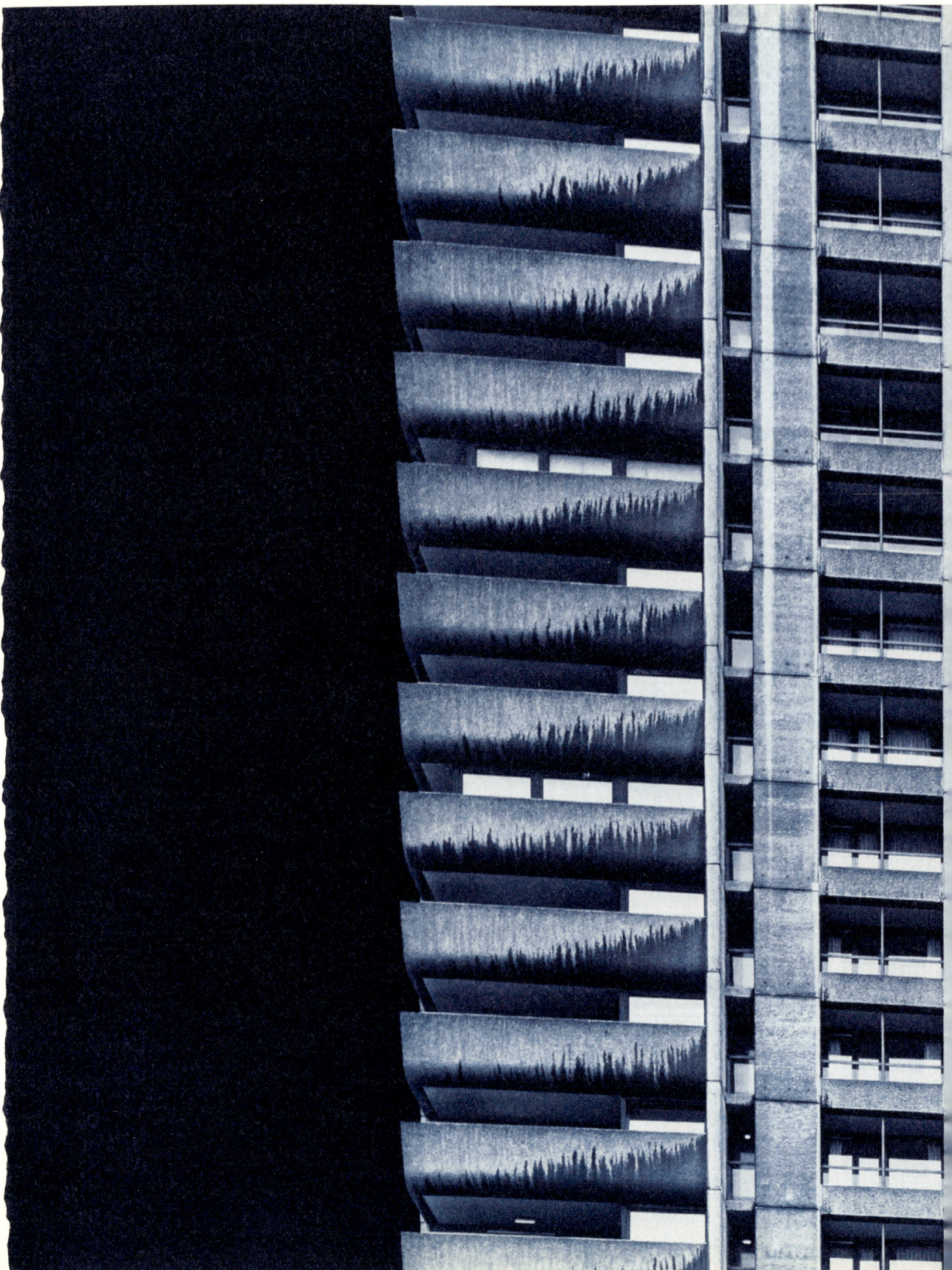

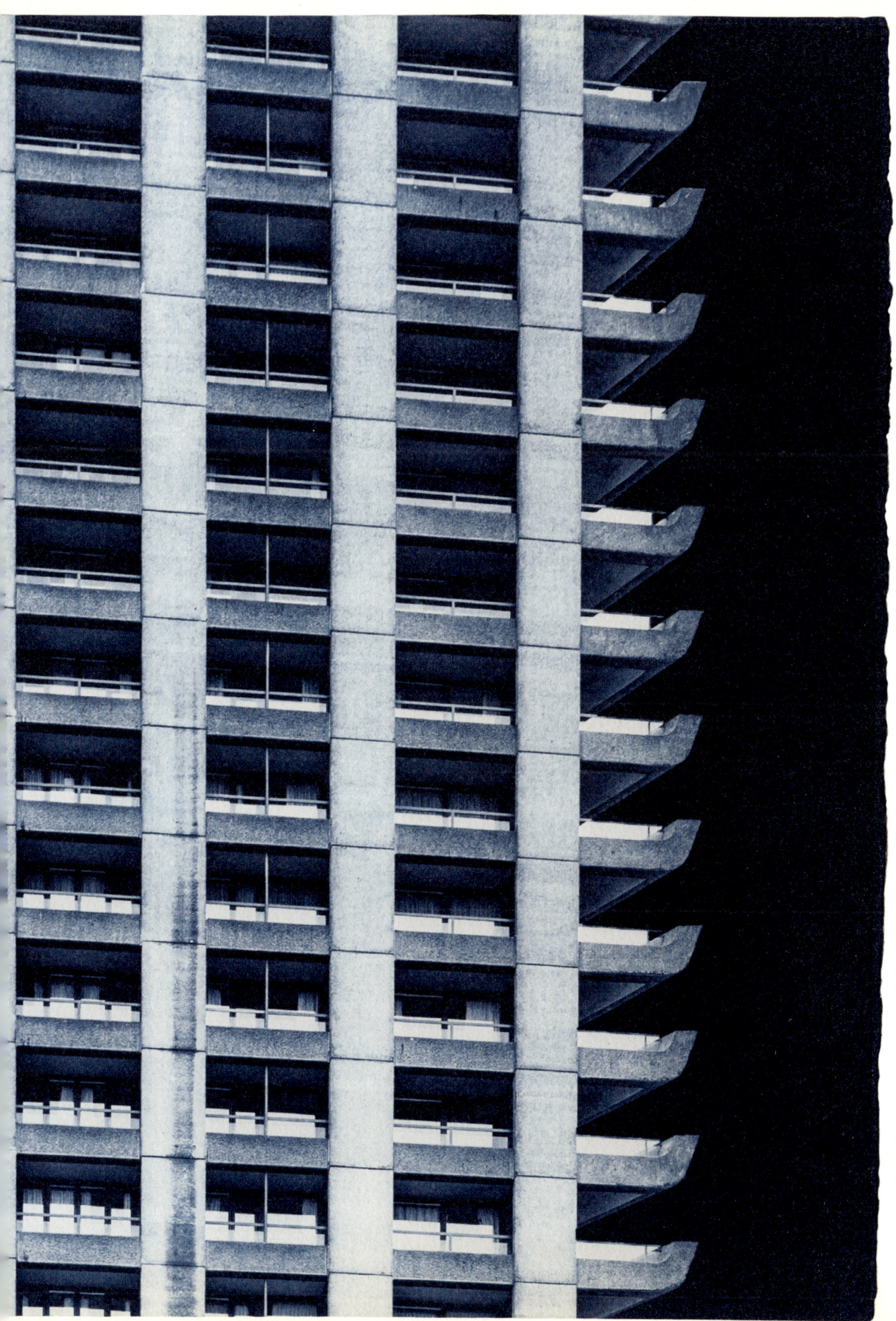

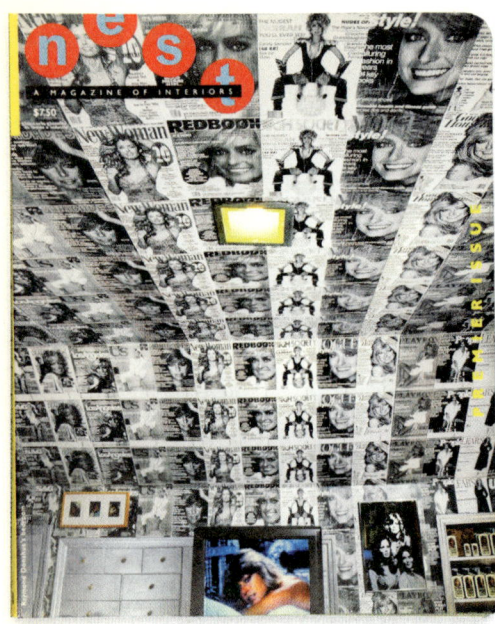

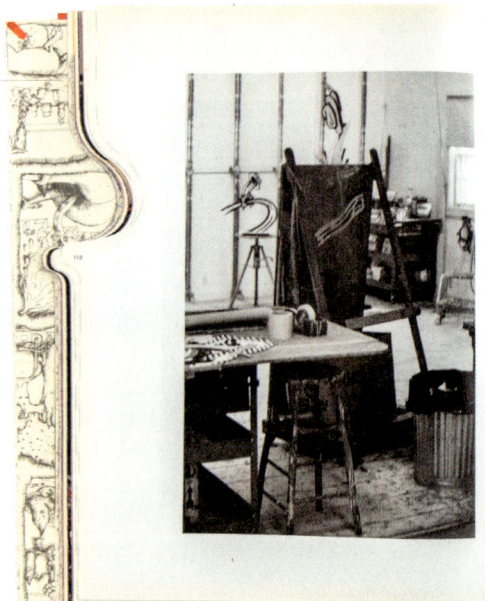

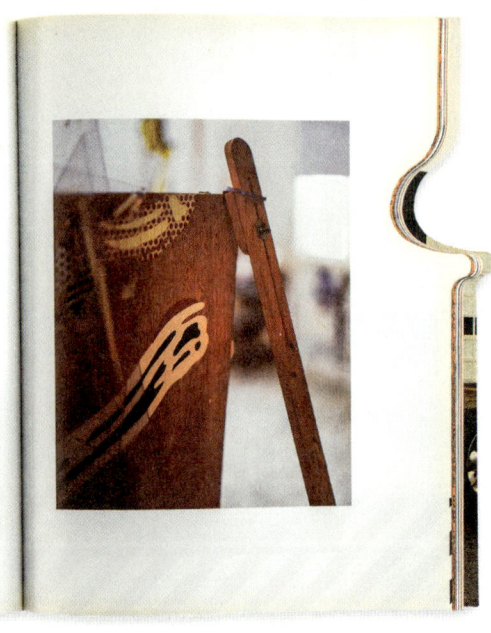

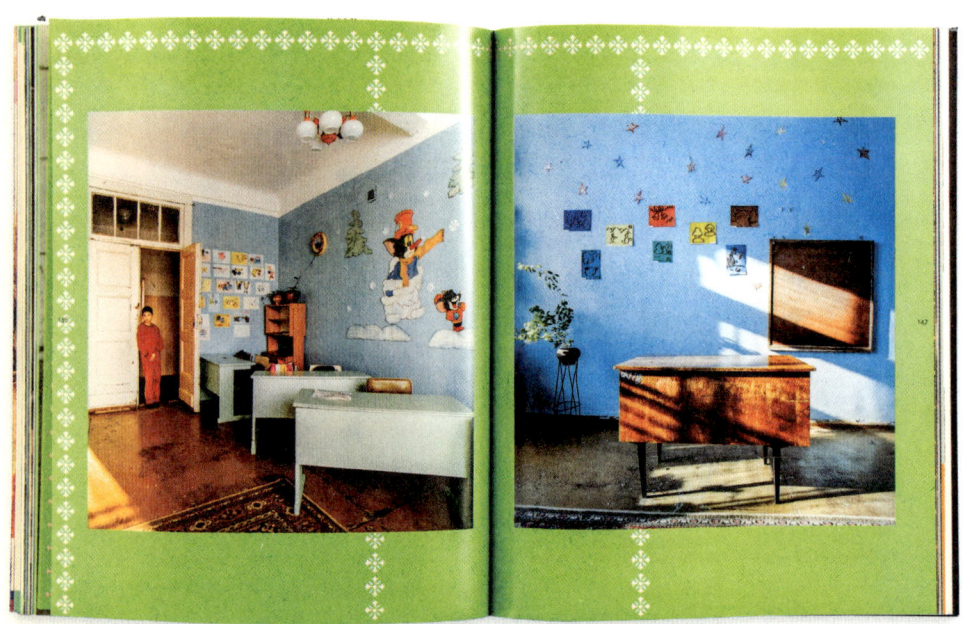

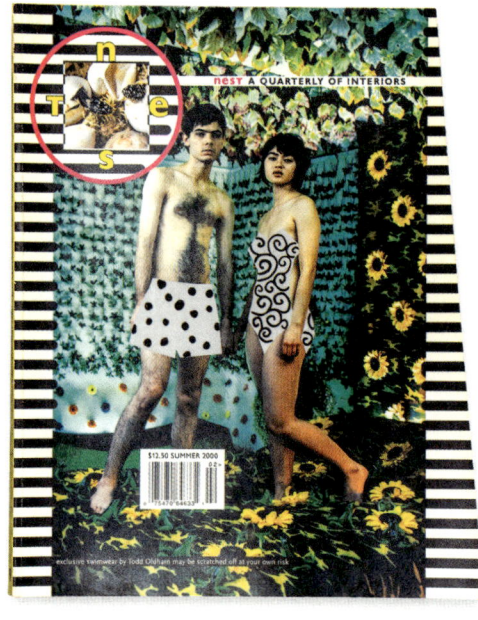

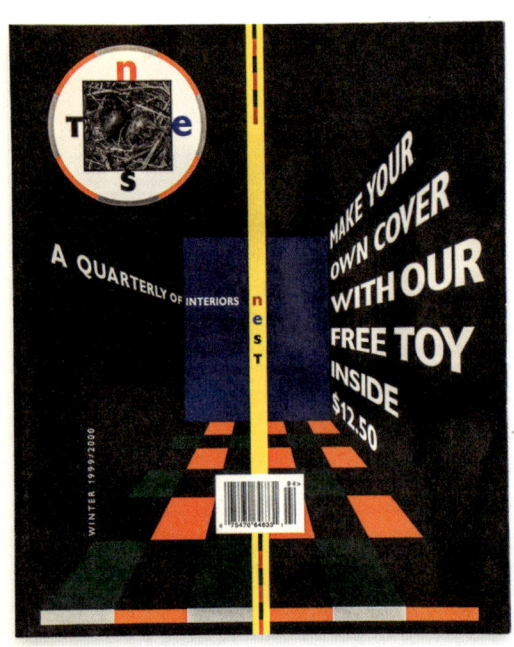

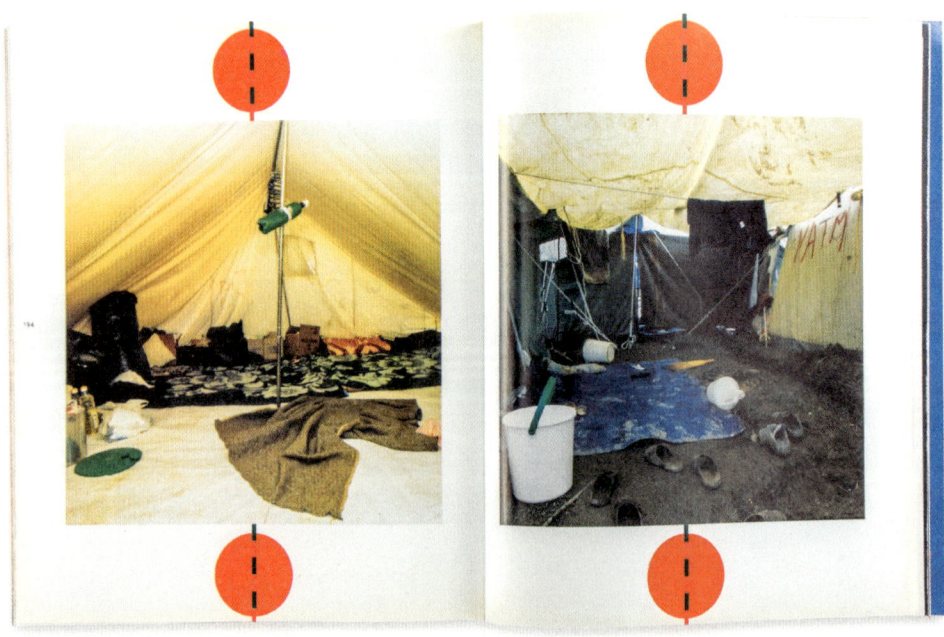

Interior Life

An irreverent, short-lived shelter magazine redefined
the idea of home.
Lou Stoppard

Opposite, clockwise
from top left:
Jason Schmidt, cover of
Nest 1, Fall 1997; David
Armstrong, spread from
Nest 16, Spring 2002;
Nathaniel Goldberg (cover
photographs) and Manny
Rubio (logo photograph),
cover of *Nest* 9, Summer
2000; Marco Di Lauro,
spread from *Nest* 7, Winter
1999–2000; *Nest* staff,
cover of *Nest* 7, Winter
1999–2000; Misty Keasler,
spread from *Nest* 18,
Fall 2002

It began with photographs of Farrah Fawcett. Raymond Donahue, a young showroom decorator for IKEA, had plastered the walls and ceiling of his bedroom in the small New Jersey bungalow he shared with his mother with black-and-white photocopies of Fawcett's magazine covers: *High Society*, *Vogue*, *Good Housekeeping*. *Nest*, a new shelter magazine, sent the photographer Jason Schmidt to capture the room, which made the cover of the debut issue, dated Fall 1997. "I love Warhol's use of repetition, so I photocopied magazine covers and made wallpaper out of them," Donahue said to the curator Valerie Steele, who conducted the accompanying interview. "*Nest* offers its own definitions in celebrating human self-invention at home," Joseph Holtzman wrote in the issue's Dear Reader letter. "Our focus will never be on focus groups. We'd love an authentic chunk of your mind, though."

Nest magazine ran quarterly for twenty-six issues. It was heady, odd, acerbic—sardonic about conformity and corporate America, yet, when it came to decorating, never overly goading or insincere. All tastes were welcome, provided they delighted, or intrigued, or tickled Holtzman, a decorator from Baltimore

Nest embraced and encouraged contradictions. One could be radically political while still having good chairs.

whose family money afforded him the opportunity to launch such an ambitious magazine.

"*Nest*—I could not resist that title. I said 'Yes' based only on that, I remember clearly," says Paola Antonelli, senior curator of the Department of Architecture and Design at the Museum of Modern Art, who profiled the Italian twentieth-century design dealer Fulvio Ferrari for *Nest*'s first issue. "It was clear he loved other human beings," she said of Holtzman. "We were all tired of exclusive, staged, rich, haughty, and glossy. We longed for intimate, messy, illicit, stolen, and generous—we wanted to find out how real people lived."

Nest was seldom cozy. Each issue clashed the refined with the banal or makeshift or extreme; a story on a luxury swimming pool could be followed by a piece on tents in Kosovo, or igloos, or the women confined to the State Correctional Facility near Grants, New Mexico.

In the debut issue, Jan Groover's photographs of the bathroom at Manhattan's Gay and Lesbian Community Services Center, painted by Keith Haring in 1989 at the height of the AIDS crisis, appeared a few pages away from David Levinthal's images of Barbie's Dream House and Derry Moore's pictures of Longleat, the home of the Marquess of Bath, who made paintings of all the women he slept with and hung them up his stairs. (Moore, a celebrated interiors photographer and the 12th Earl of Drogheda, and thus a regular at castles and manors, fulfilled Holtzman's obsession with English aristocratic taste.) The Fall 1998 issue featured a story on the Turin home where Carlo Mollino spent the last fourteen years of his life, pictured alongside his Polaroids of the prostitutes who visited him. Summer 1999 saw stories by Robert Polidori on beehive-shaped mud houses in the al-Shilo village in Syria and Mitch Epstein on the ape house at the Philadelphia Zoo. For Fall 1999–2000, Nan Goldin photographed the artist Nayland Blake in his mother's bedroom, which he'd wallpapered with over four hundred pounds

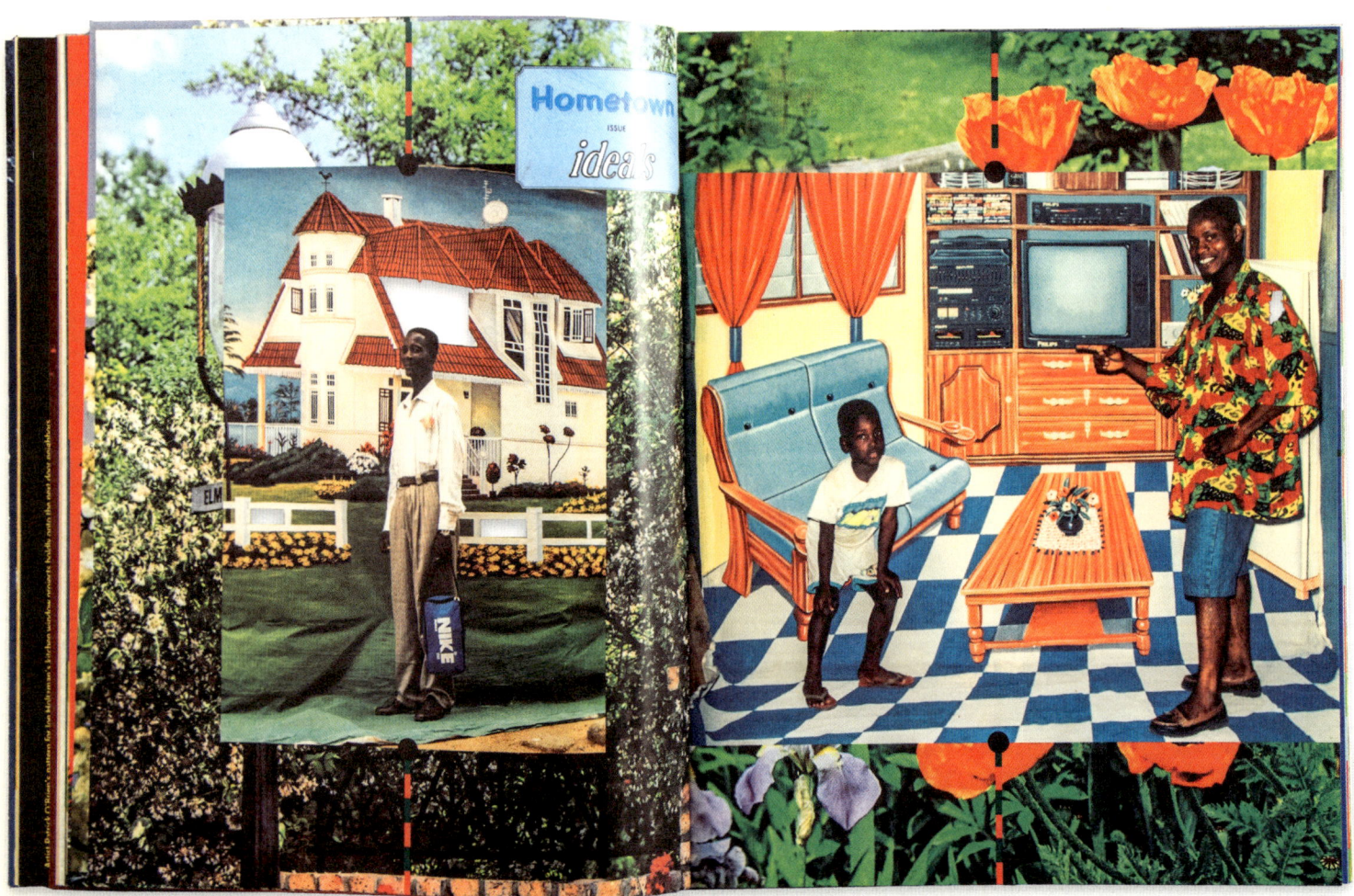

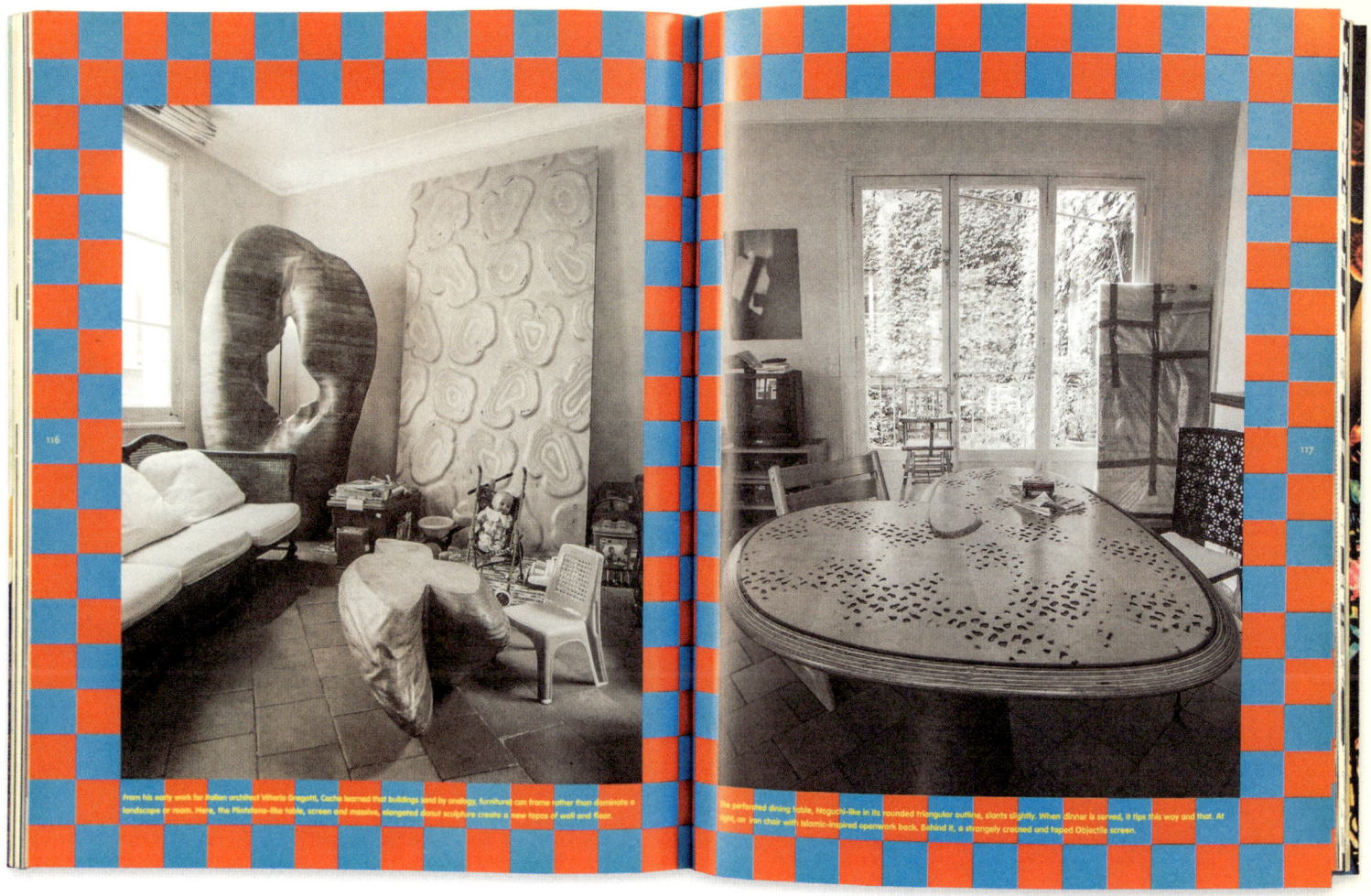

From his early work for Italian architect Vittorio Gregotti, Cacho learned that buildings (and by analogy, furniture) can frame rather than dominate a landscape or room. Here, the Flintstone-like table, screen and massive, elongated donut sculpture create a new topos of wall and floor.

The perforated dining table, Noguchi-like in its rounded triangular outline, slants slightly. When dinner is served, it tips this way and that. At right, an iron chair with Islamic-inspired openwork back. Behind it, a strongly creased and taped Objectile screen.

Antoine Bootz, spread
from *Nest* 4, Spring 1999

of gingerbread. The roll call of photographers was impressive—David Armstrong, Martin Parr, Jim Goldberg, Richard Barnes, and Terence Donovan, among others, all made work for *Nest*—yet only a handful of the image makers, such as Moore, were particularly known for classic interiors photography.

"I subscribe to a number of shelter magazines—*World of Interiors*, *House & Garden* (RIP), *Elle Decor* (before its recent decline)—but *Nest* was different," says the critic and magazine collector Vince Aletti. "When the second issue came out, I'm embarrassed to report that I wrote a fan letter to the magazine advising it to be more appealing to potential readers—not put them off with the sort of abstract design and weird graphics on the cover of the Fall 1998 issue, which no one would have recognized as a shelter mag." That issue featured a black-and-brown-striped cover and a hand-applied cutting of flocked wallpaper, the pattern of which resembled random stains, by the artist Rosemarie Trockel. "It was obvious *Nest* couldn't care less about the general audience," Aletti says. "You liked it or you left it, and most of its core readers *loved* it. I don't think I would have called it beautiful at any point, because it was not afraid to get a little ugly, and it went beyond mere beauty."

The design was "almost baroque," according to Tom Beckham, who joined *Nest* ahead of the second issue as design technician, and stayed to the end, quickly becoming graphics director. At points, it veered toward the unhinged—one issue came with four holes drilled straight through it, as if the reader was hanging a particularly hefty picture; while others arrived with scalloped edges or scratch-and-sniff patches. Photographers' images would often be placed on top of florid, graphic patterns or framed with shouty borders. The magazine was "another iteration of Joe's interior design," says Beckham.

Before launching *Nest*, Holtzman had considered starting a magazine that was severe and serious. But after *Wallpaper* launched

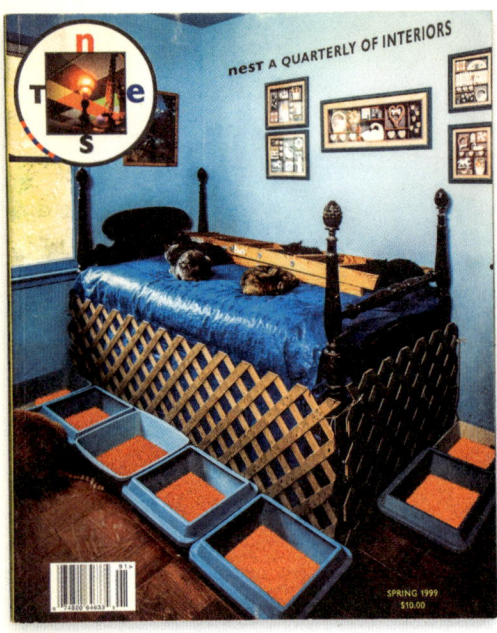

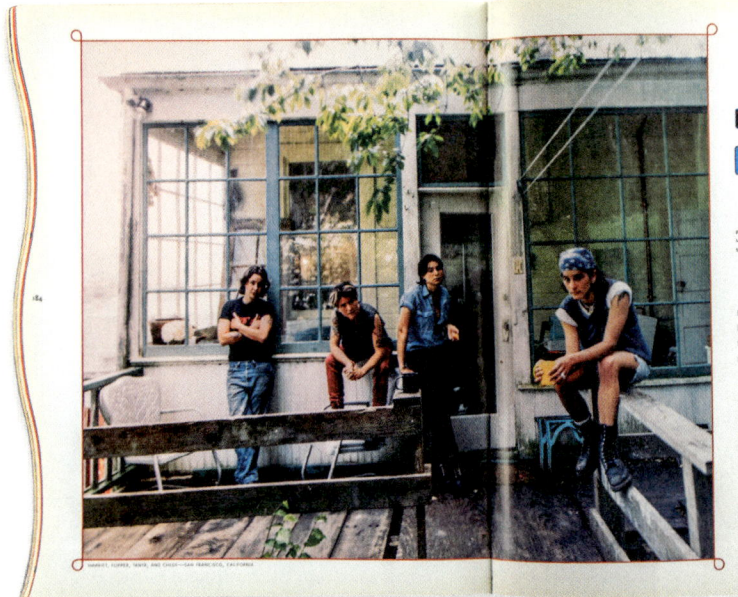

no place like home

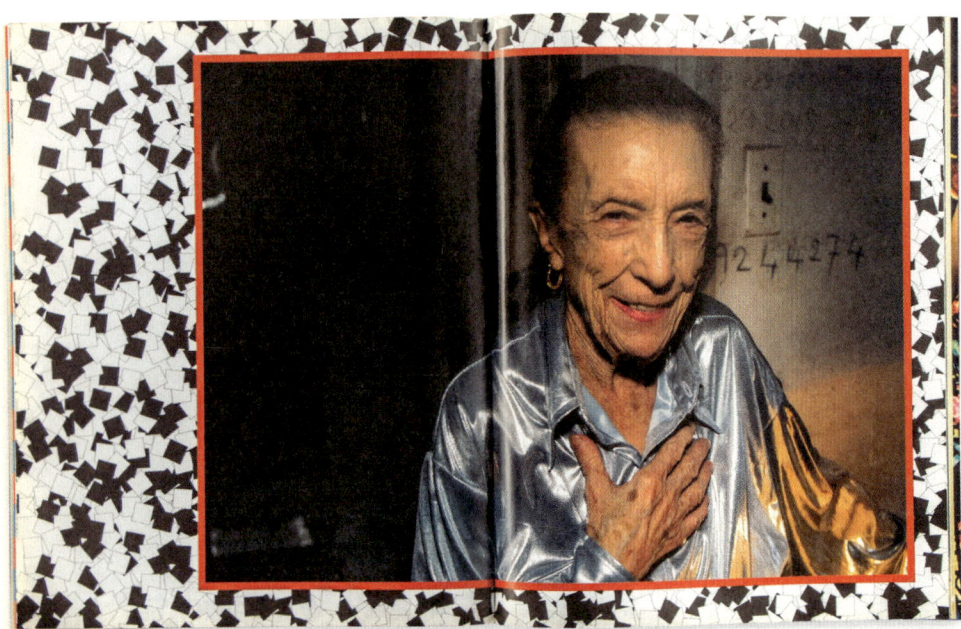

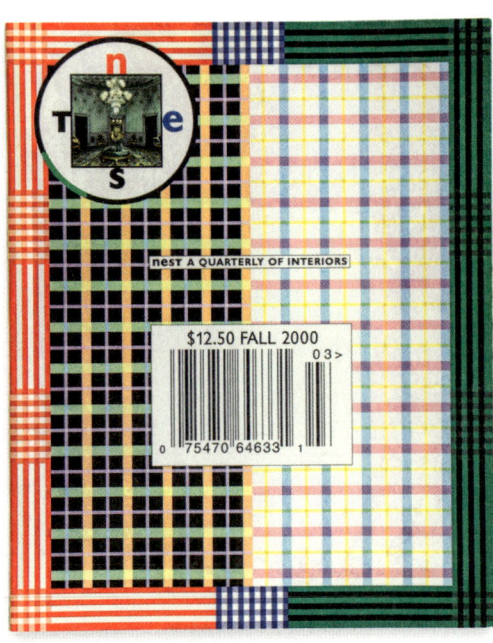

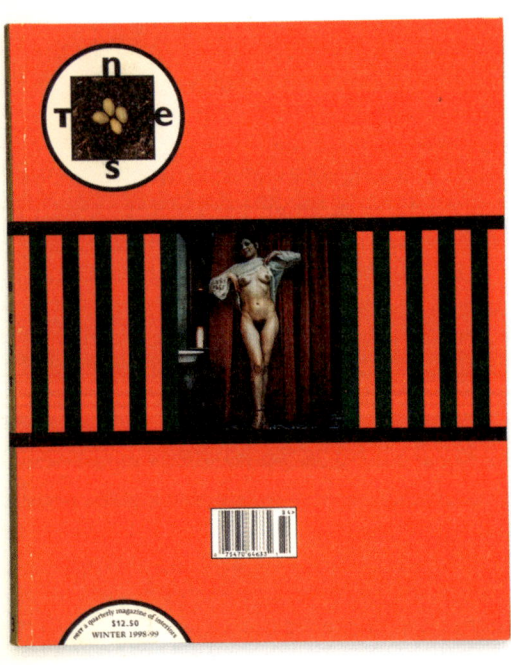

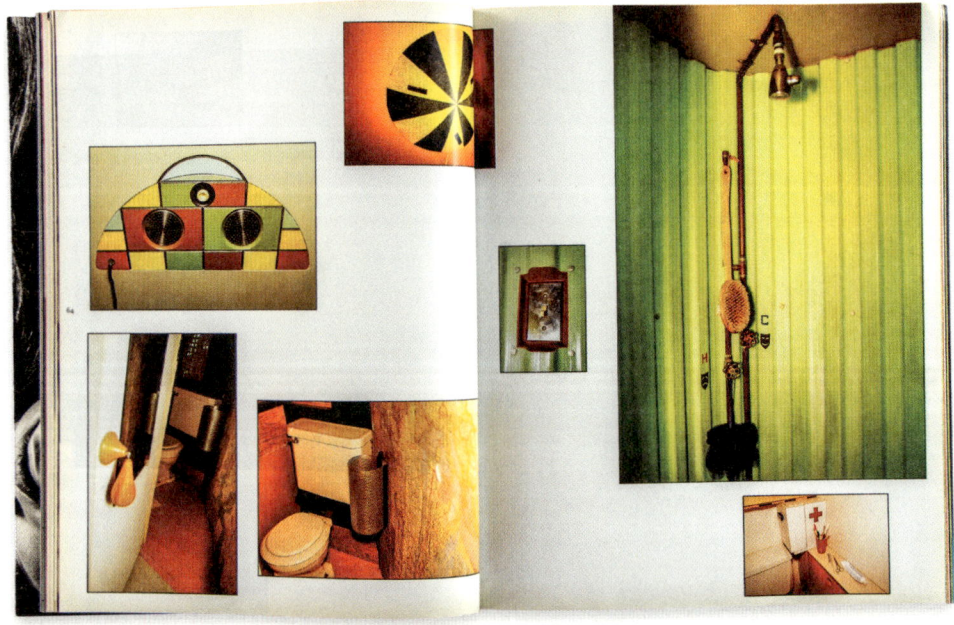

in 1996, *Nest* went in the opposite direction. Holtzman took to thumbing his nose at other, less playful titles. The Summer 1999 cover was photoshopped to resemble a comic strip; a thought bubble above the head of a handsome man, nude save for a towel and reclining in a chair, reads, "Hang me. I thought *Wallpaper* was shooting my apartment." Behind him, his decorator, clad in a fur stole, is shown thinking, "God willing, my next assignment will be for *Architectural Digest*."

"*Nest* questioned the concept of conventional beauty and redefined the importance of decoration in a world in which minimal aesthetics dominated," says Christoph Radl, creative director of *Cabana* magazine. Indeed, *Nest* came along at a relatively flaccid period within interior publications. *House & Garden*, once known for photographic commissions by the likes of Irving Penn and Horst P. Horst in the 1940s and '50s, when it was art-directed by Alexander Liberman, was floundering by the '90s; it closed in 1993 and briefly reemerged in 1995 before closing again in 2007. New launches, such as *Martha Stewart Living*, which began in 1990, were decidedly pleasant and sanitized. But *Nest* ignored the increasingly recognizable format of the tidy, symmetrical interiors photograph. "*Nest*'s photographic approach preferred individual perspectives compared to a canonical narrative of the interiors," says Radl.

"They were really looking for photographers from more of an art background than an *Architectural Digest* background, because they didn't want the spaces to be overwrought with that idea of how we view what space does and how it exists," says Catherine Opie, who shot regular stories for *Nest*. She once turned down a feature on a woman who collected vacuum cleaners. "I still kick myself," she says. "Being a part of *Nest* informed my work later on. I don't know if I would have made *700 Nimes Road*"—Opie's celebrated 2015 series about the home and possessions of Elizabeth Taylor—"without my experience of years of photographing for *Nest*, in which an environment became a portrait."

With *Nest*, the question was not just how do we decorate our homes, but also what is home. It took a conceptual approach to things like ownership, value, luxury, comfort—many of its stories seem pointedly relevant now. In one feature, Eileen Myles spent a week sleeping in a cardboard "homeless box," invented after a 1993 spike in homelessness in Rotterdam. Much airtime was given to those worried about climate change, including those who'd fashioned elaborate bunkers, and time was taken to document the living arrangements of people with mental-health illnesses or disabilities. Holtzman seemed particularly intrigued by the complex worlds of children. "The Squeeze Machine," a story in Summer 1999, focuses on eleven-year-old Matthew from Alaska, who is autistic and derives comfort from being held tightly.

"*Nest* was always political," Beckham says. One particular concern was "how being gay gets represented in culture—the idea of the gay decorator." *Nest* is "especially legendary among the gays," says Jop van Bennekom, founder of the adored gay magazine *BUTT* and, later, *Fantastic Man*. "It was a bit too opulent to me and the design was a bit too 'decorative' for my Protestant taste, but of course, there was joy that splattered from every page."

Nest is, indeed, joyful. It billed itself as ambivalent to fusty norms but celebratory about style. Impressively, given how closely the magazine revolved around Holtzman's singular vision, it was never gushing or dictatorial. Through both the sometimes haphazard, whimsical tastes of the subjects profiled and its own eclectic gaze, *Nest* embraced and encouraged contradictions. One could be radically political while still having good chairs. One could be queer while still worshipping relics of tradition. *Nest* cared enough about the march of capitalism to mock the unquestioning stuffiness of other titles, but not quite enough to turn down advertising from Calvin Klein or Diesel, or to cease from swooning at some truly extravagant pile, shot by Moore. It needled the status

quo without asking its readers to change even slightly; the best you could be, according to *Nest*, was yourself.

Though briefly courted by Si Newhouse at Condé Nast, *Nest* folded in 2004. "A Champion of the Quirky Writes Finis," read the *New York Times* announcement by Fred A. Bernstein, which recalls how *Nest* was never afraid to shock: "Holtzman wrote one of his editor's letters from what he called a 'small, well-proportioned room': in a psychiatric hospital. Furniture coverage included close-ups of electric chairs." Holtzman revealed that he'd ploughed between four million and six million dollars into *Nest*—he sold a Matisse bronze to support it. The final issue featured one of his own paintings on the cover, nodding to his new plans for life as an artist.

"We at the magazine think that we have at the very least demonstrated that a shelter magazine can march to a different drummer," Holtzman wrote in his final Dear Reader letter. He expressed hope for the future. "I do believe that the young people coming of age will make a big contribution to design and decoration. The time has come to do more than mix and manipulate the givens of our creative legacy, and I know that this generation is not afraid to stand up to the past."

Lou Stoppard is a writer and curator based in London. She is the editor of the photobook *Shirley Baker* (2019) and a forthcoming book about swimming pools in photography.

Opposite, clockwise from top left: Langdon Clay, cover of *Nest* 4, Spring 1999; Catherine Opie, spread from *Nest* 5, Summer 1999; Nicholas Buccalo (logo photograph), cover of *Nest* 10, Fall 2000; Jim Goldberg and Ethan Kaplan, spread from *Nest* 3, Winter 1998–99; Carlo Mollino, cover of *Nest* 3, Winter 1998–99; Nan Goldin, spread from *Nest* 4, Fall 2000, Spring 1999

All images from *Nest, A Quarterly of Interiors* Courtesy the collections of Vince Aletti and Donna Ghelerter

Surpris pa

Mauro Restiffe
The Tattooed Villa

Lauren Elkin

Lauren Elkin is a writer based in Paris. She is the author of *Flâneuse: Women Walk the City in Paris, New York, Tokyo, Venice, and London* (2016), and the translator, with Charlotte Mandell, of Claude Arnaud's *Jean Cocteau: A Life* (2016).

It's called the "tattooed villa." On the tip of Saint-Jean-Cap-Ferrat, on a peninsula of the French Riviera, sits the Villa Santo Sospir, once the home of the socialite Francine Weisweiller. One evening in 1950, while staying at the house, Jean Cocteau offered to draw the head of Apollo on the wall over the fireplace in the salon. Before long, Cocteau was covering the whole house in mythological frescoes, letting his whimsical yet controlled line wander where it would, across walls, doors, and even lampshades, covering some with rich, fantastical images and colors.

Over twelve years, Cocteau embellished the surfaces of the house, "tattooing" it, in his words. Photographs from the period show him balanced between two ladders, with his charcoal at the end of a long stick, like Michelangelo in a 1950s suit and tie. In Weisweiller's eight-year-old's bedroom, he painted Dionysus sleeping off a hangover. In Cocteau's own bedroom, two unicorns are fed by the god Pan, who loved both men and women. "Matisse told me that if you decorate one wall, you should do the others as well," he says in a short film called *La Villa Santo Sospir* (1952) that he made to document the process. "He was right."

The passage of time has had a deleterious effect on the frescoes, however, and so the house was closed for renovations in 2018, having previously been sold to a new owner. "It's now or never if we don't want to lose Cocteau's painting," said the lead restorer, Florence Cremer, who is overseeing a process of injecting an acrylic resin in the many areas where the fresco has come off the wall.

The Brazilian photographer Mauro Restiffe was invited to document the paintings before the restoration began. These aren't the glossy, presentational kind of photographs of the house you'll find in home-and-garden magazines; they ask us to see the drawings as more than home decor. Restiffe stayed alone in the house for a week, photographing by day and by night, trying to see the house anew every time he went wandering through it. Eventually, he says, he grew so comfortable there that it began to affect the photographs he took.

Restiffe works with analog film, mostly in black-and-white, and his images have that great grainy feeling that you also find in Cocteau's films. His camera seeks out unexpected angles as he stands in one room and captures the next, creating juxtapositions that put the walls and rooms in conversation with each other. His framing captures a lampshade, nuzzled between the drawings on two walls of the same room, or truncates a phrase calligraphed on the wall so all we catch are the words "*surpris par.*" "Picasso opened and closed all the doors," Cocteau says in his film. "All that was left to do was to paint the doors." Perhaps not quite all.

An image I particularly love shows a painting of a bouquet of posies in a square black-and-gold frame hung on a white painted door. The doorknob, made of what looks to be Murano glass, gleams like a bauble. Cocteau has outlined the door panels in black, echoing the shape of the frame; or perhaps the picture was added afterward to recall his squares. Beneath the frame, there is a scratch where the paint has come away to reveal the natural color of the wood.

Much has been made about the fact that the house has been preserved as it was, down to the notes and postcards Cocteau pinned up in his bedroom. But Restiffe's photographs are uninterested in this kind of prestige nostalgia. They capture our moment, not Cocteau's; they document a space about to be changed, but they also attest to the changing nature of all spaces, especially domestic ones, which are not meant to be preserved in amber (or in resin). This is why Restiffe's photographs are singular; they record not only Cocteau's work, but the work of time.

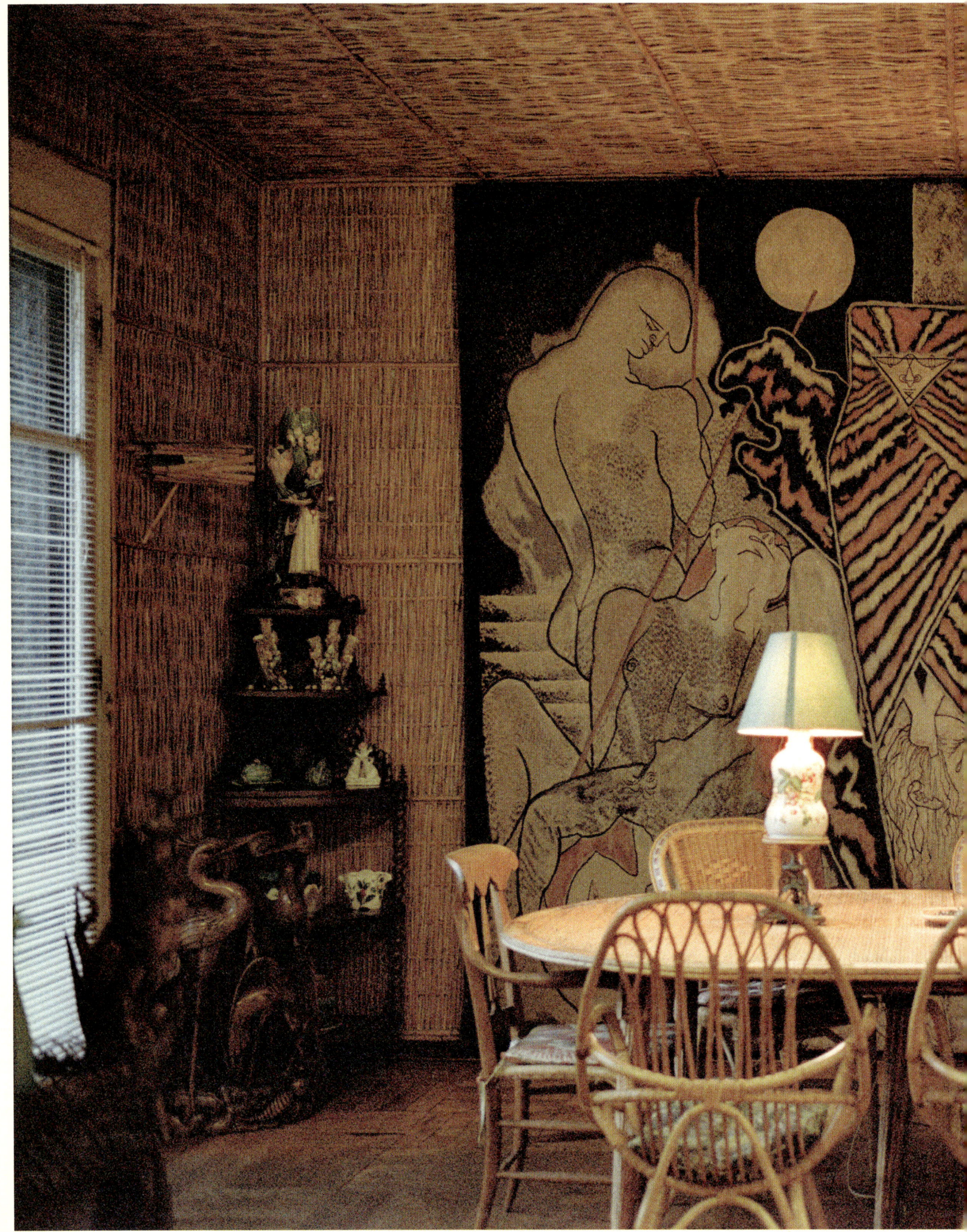

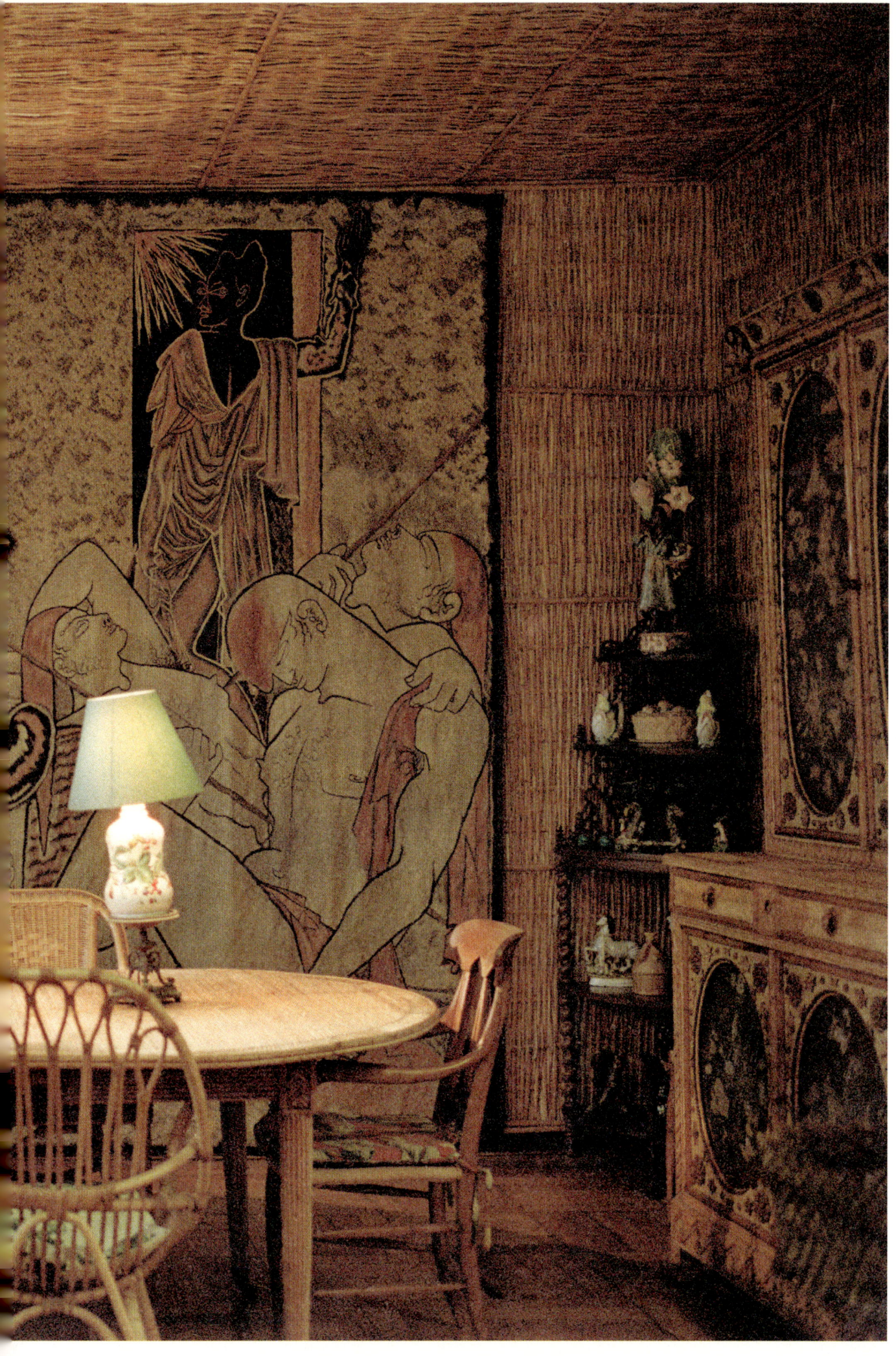

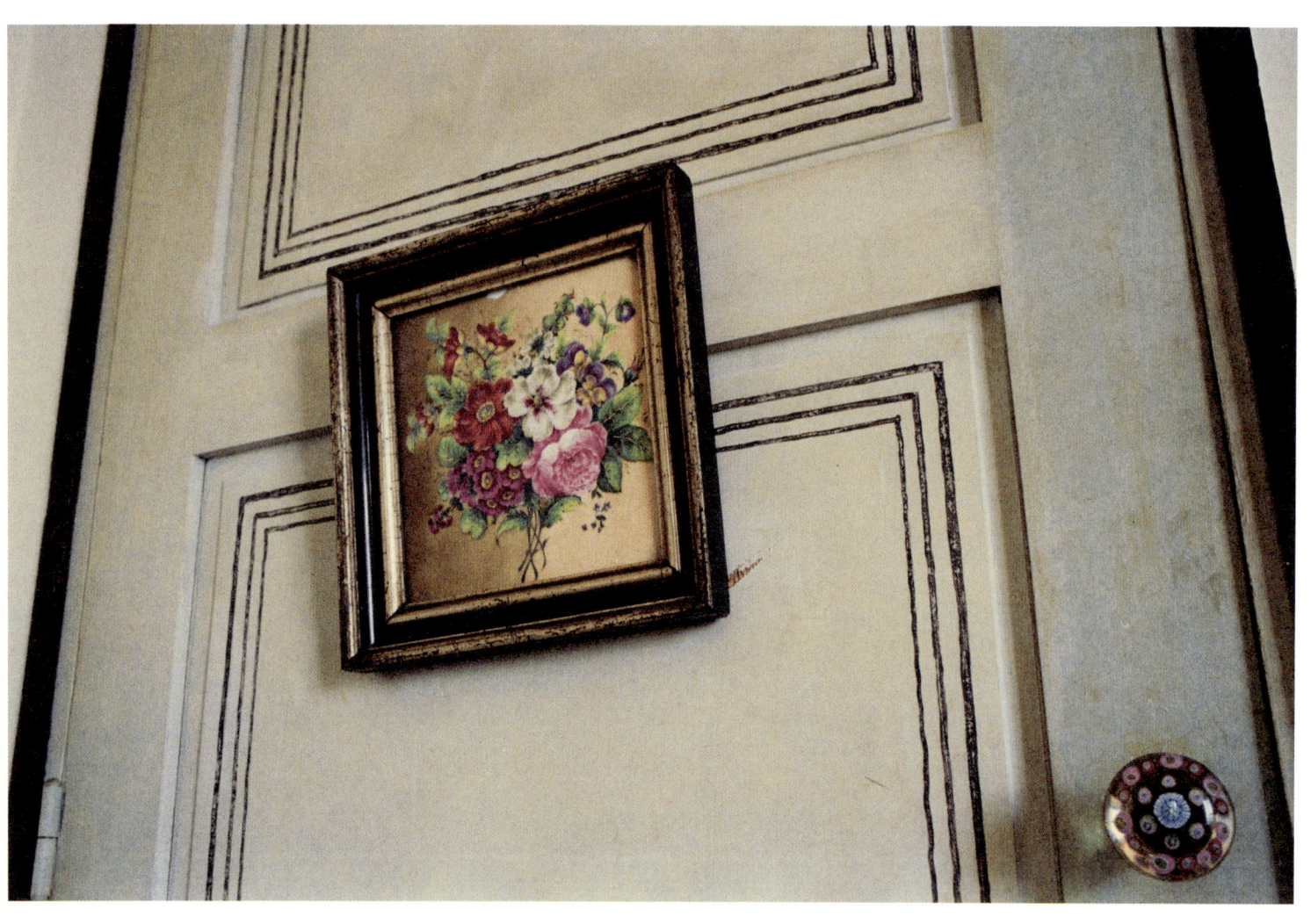

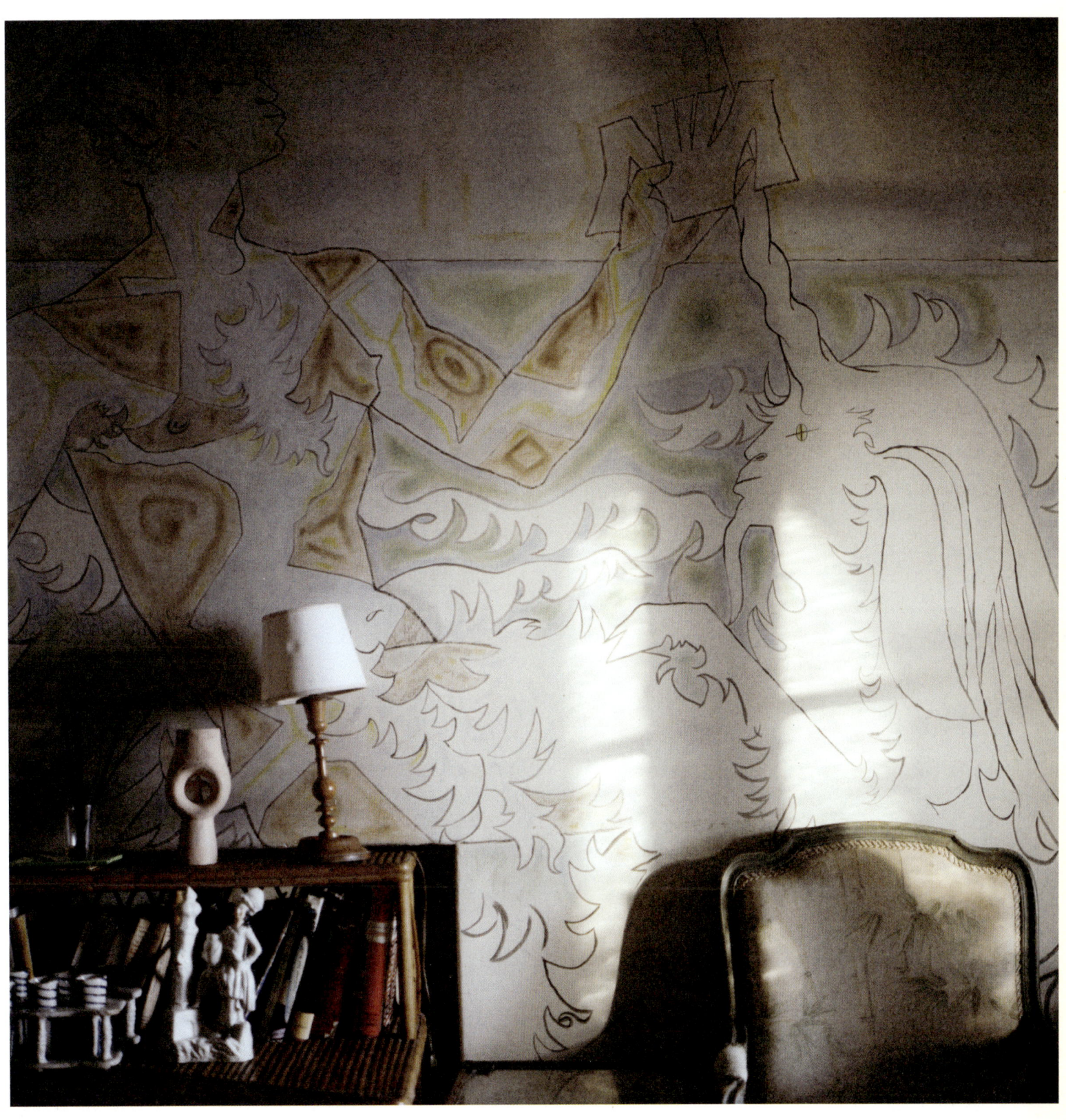

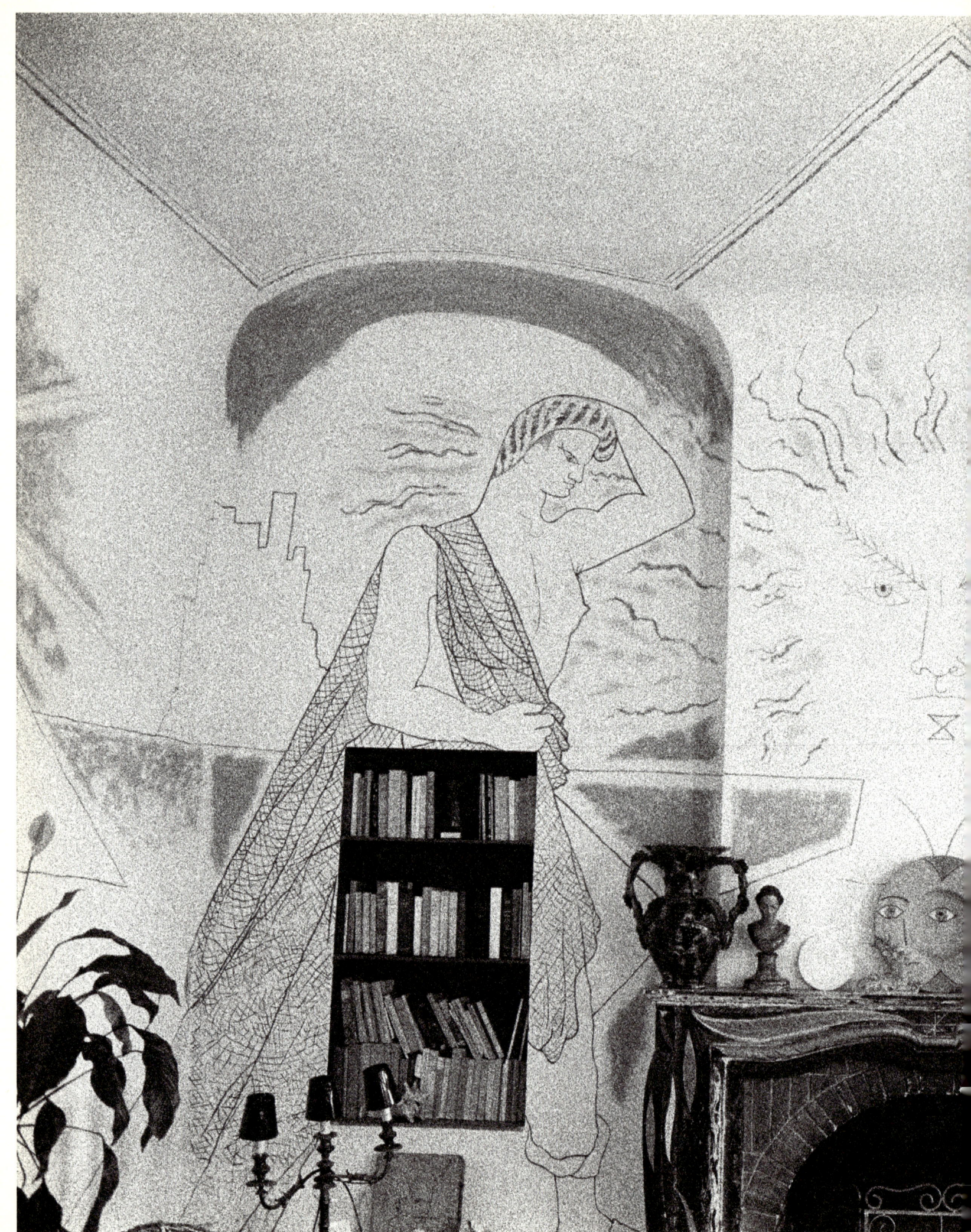

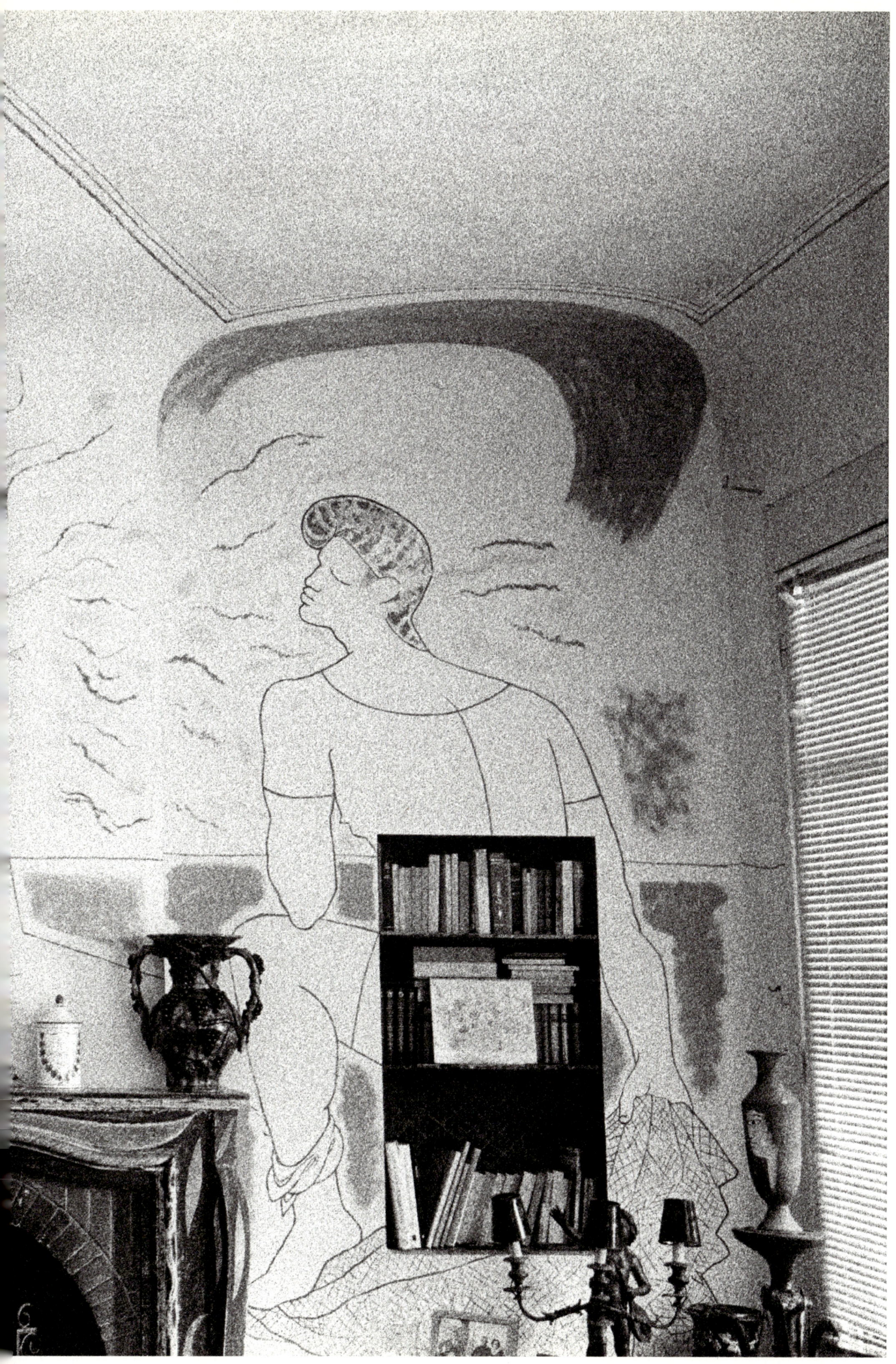

**All photographs from the
series *Santo Sospir*, 2018**
Courtesy the artist

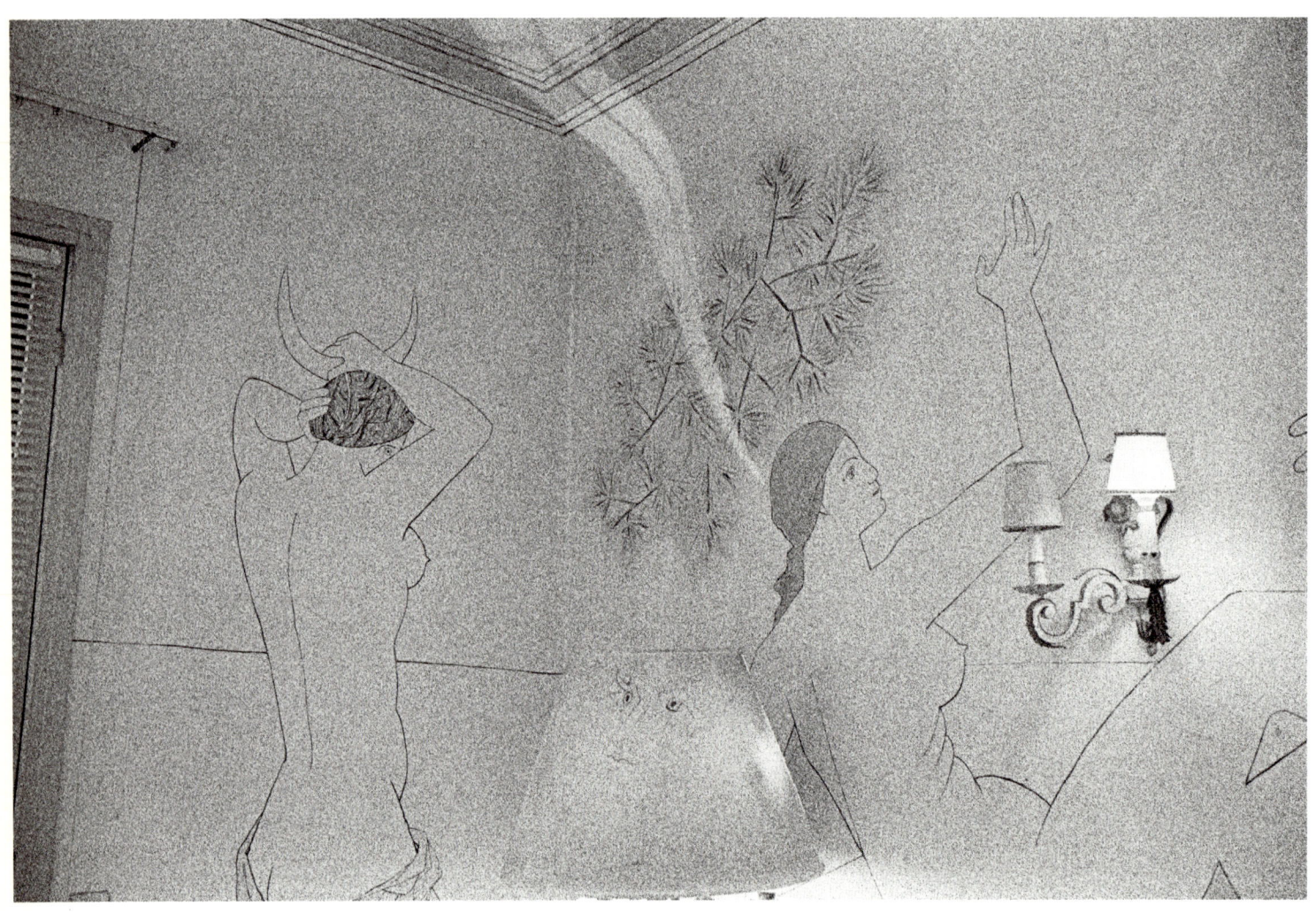

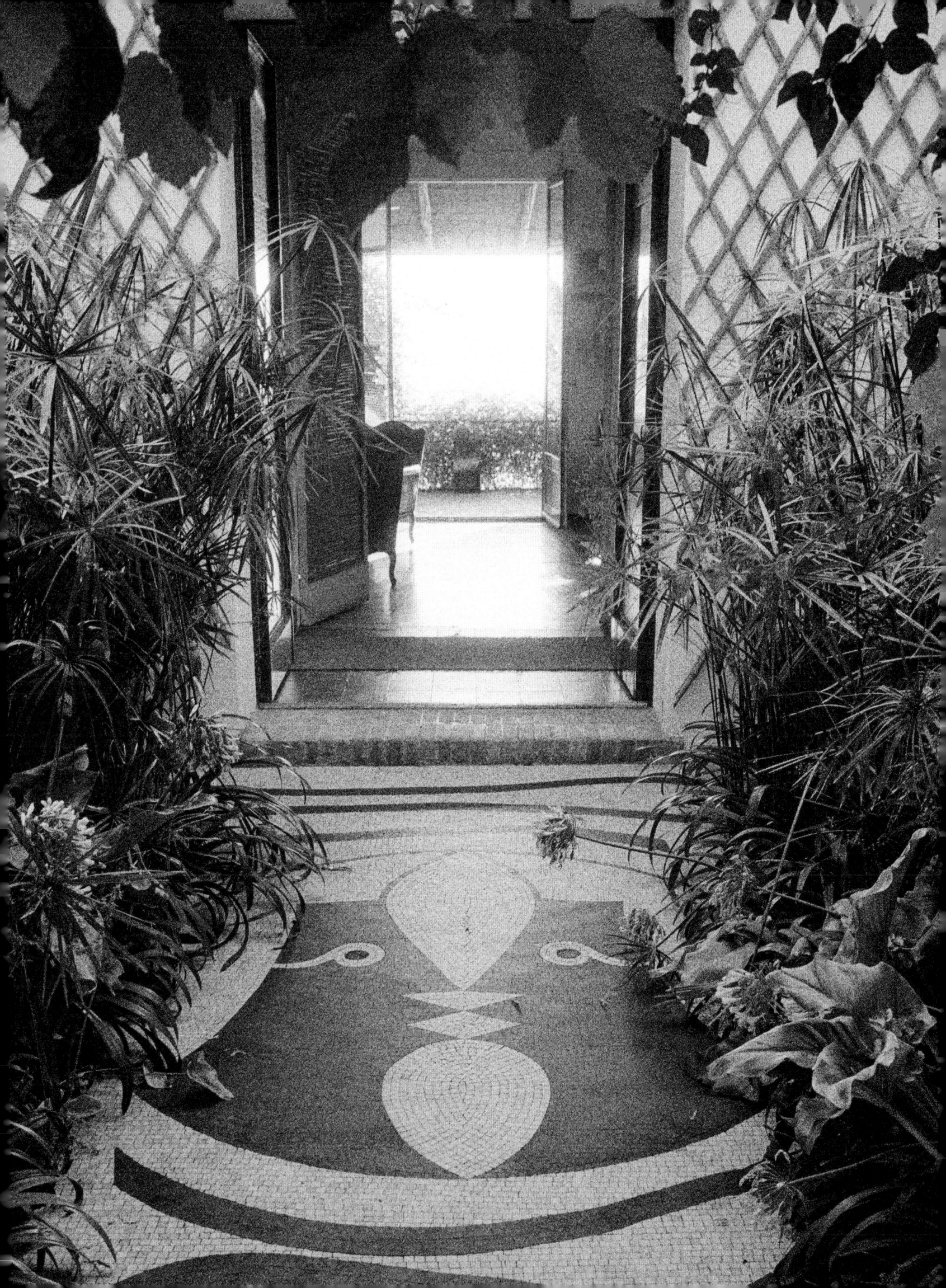

Annabelle Selldorf
"What I care about is a kind of calm, or tranquility, that creates a setting."

A Conversation with Julian Rose

Annabelle Selldorf is the art world's favorite architect. But her work is nothing if not subtle—rather than the splashy icons we have come to expect from the starchitects long chosen to design art galleries and museums, Selldorf prefers to craft what she modestly calls "functional" settings for art. Rooted in an understated modernist aesthetic, with an updated material palate and innovative geometries, Selldorf's exhibition spaces have remade the white cube for the twenty-first century. Small wonder, then, that she is frequently sought out to design the homes of high-profile art collectors, or that she has now designed major museums and galleries for over two decades, from the Neue Galerie and the Swiss Institute to David Zwirner and Hauser & Wirth.

Given her sensitivity to art, it's not surprising that Selldorf's practice is also engaged in an ongoing dialogue with artists. She has collaborated directly with contemporary artists such as the photographer Todd Eberle, and she readily acknowledges the influence of a generation of postwar photographers who examine the modern metropolis and industrial landscape—particularly Bernd and Hilla Becher, whose work hangs on the wall of her light-filled New York office just north of Union Square. That's where the architecture critic Julian Rose visited Selldorf last fall to talk about her relationship to photography, both professional and personal, and the intriguing challenges faced by architects who design homes for art.

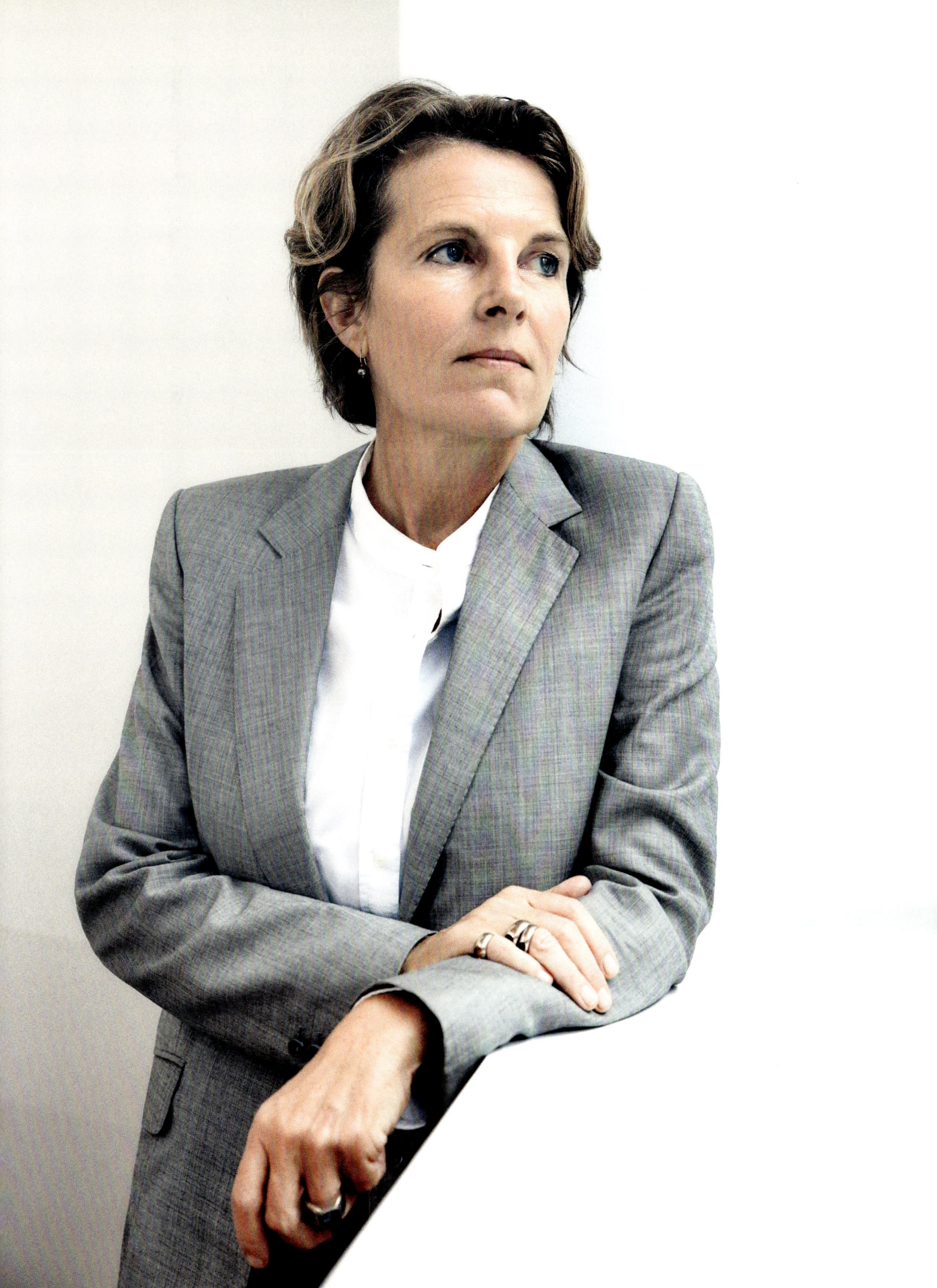

The Bechers look without drama. And the "without drama" is one of the things that I am interested in.

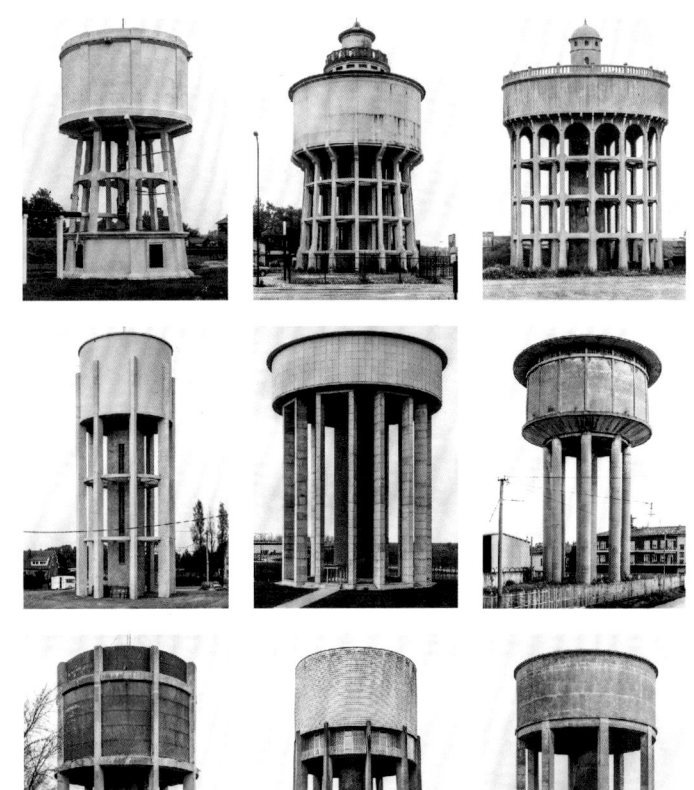

Julian Rose: Let's start with the photographs right here in your office. You have works by Bernd and Hilla Becher on the walls. I'd love to hear what they mean to you. Of course their subject is architecture, and they're gorgeous photographs, no question, but I could argue that they're critical of architecture too.

Annabelle Selldorf: They are all of that. They have a kind of face value that draws you in. It's not just what you look at, but how you look at it. The Bechers look without drama, in a way. And the "without drama" is one of the things that I am interested in, because it takes away our need for the sentimental hyperbole that accompanies practically everything people do. We always need to find hyperbole for our architects, for their work: it's "amazing," it's "incredible," and on and on.

JR: So what you're getting from those images is not so much an aesthetic per se, certainly not a style. You're talking about photography as a mode of looking, an approach to the world— a kind of methodology.

AS: Right. I don't believe I've ever had a conversation with anybody about this, but it is a process of clearing away layers that allows you to look at something straight. Mies van der Rohe once said, "One doesn't invent a new architecture every Monday morning." Rather, you develop a methodology.

JR: What other photographers are important to you?

AS: I love the work of Gabriele Basilico—he has the eye of a humanist, and, at the same time, I think it's the eye of an architect. He did a series of pictures of war-torn Beirut, and they were riveting.

JR: He did study architecture, after all, and there does seem to be a level of sensitivity—an insight into how people and buildings relate—that an architect can bring to photography.

AS: In a funny way, the Bechers don't have that because to them buildings are objects—they just categorize and anthologize. Whereas with Basilico, I always feel that his photographs are about people and how they interact with architectural environments. Whether it's images of bombed-out Beirut, or buildings in Milan, or the amazing, very moody photographs he did of the industrial park in Dunkirk, France, his work is unbelievably powerful because it has this human dimension. I'd always hoped that one day I could get him to photograph one of my projects. That's so naive and silly, but it was a measure of my admiration.

JR: In general, architectural photography is not often done by the same photographers we think of as artists in their own right. Is that something you think about in relation to your work?

AS: Absolutely. We did a book a couple of years ago, *Portfolio and Projects* (2016), and I asked my friend the photographer Todd Eberle to do the photography. I think he is one person who negotiates between the two categories. I just asked him to put together a portfolio of images of my work. He went to all these different buildings, and he took pictures.

JR: With minimal direction from you?

AS: Yes. But we've known each other for a long time. And I wanted the portfolio to be as much about his eye as it is about our buildings. In the beginning, I really wanted him to photograph in black and white, because I find that lends a particular focus. But he didn't want to do that. Early in his career, he photographed a lot in black

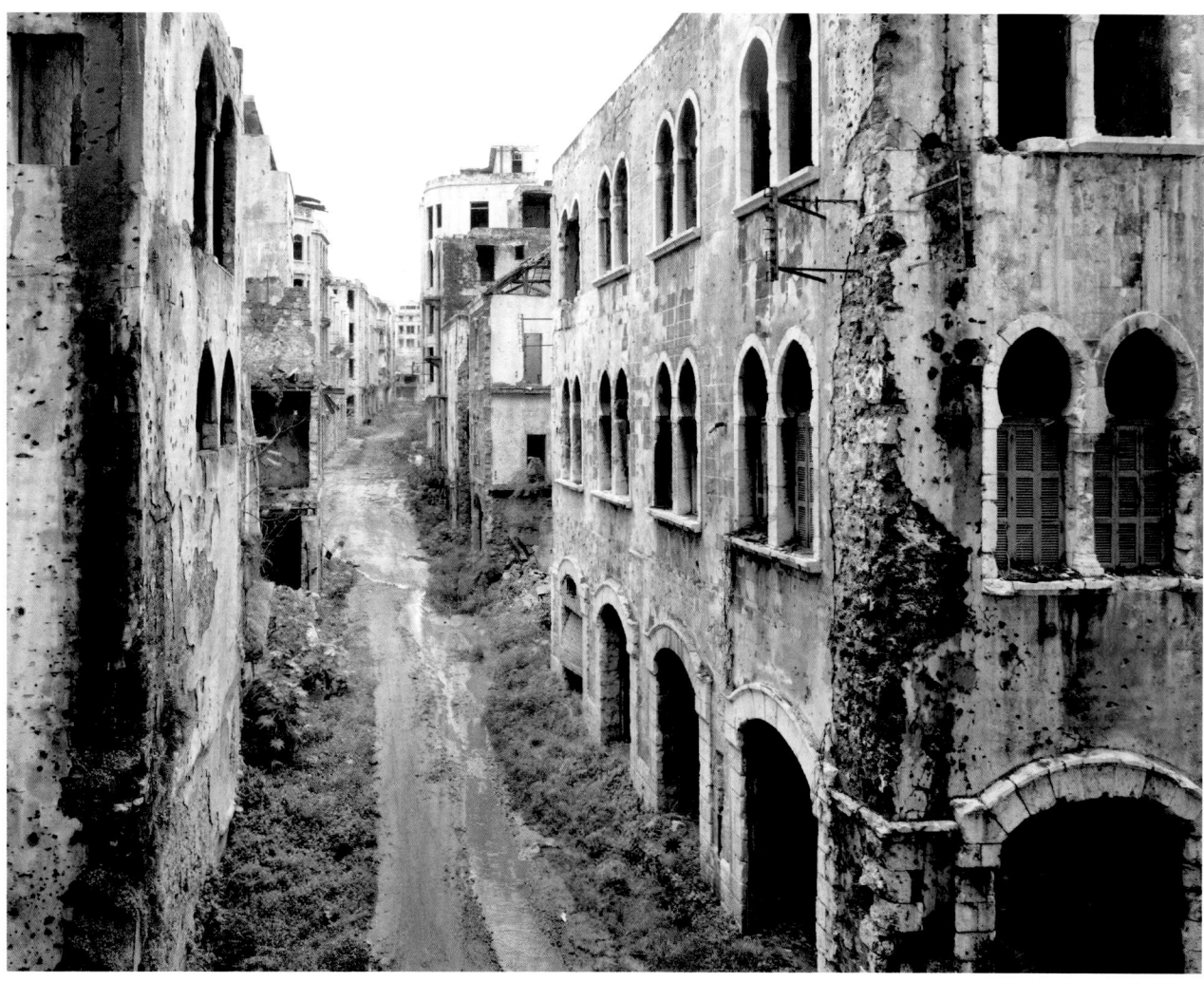

and white, but now he thinks in color. So I had to make a decision. If I was going to work with an artist, I couldn't tell him what to do.

JR: **Was it hard to let go?**

AS: Not at all.

JR: **What did you learn from seeing your work through his eyes?**

AS: He discovers the composition right away. Often the work we do comes from a utilitarian, almost wishful idea about how people will move in a space, and I start to think that this idea is guiding how the spaces should be proportioned, and all of the rest of the design. But, of course, eventually it does return to the question: what does it look like?

JR: **It's intriguing that you feel his images almost tease out the underlying intention in your designs. I think frequently it's the reverse—projects are designed for the photograph.**

AS: Absolutely. I remember from when I was a young architect people would say, "This is a three-picture job." It makes you want to weep.

JR: **Does photography play a role in your own process?**

AS: It has a lot more than I necessarily intended because of what we were just talking about. Nicholas Venezia, who works in the office in communications, is a photographer, and he has brought his sensibility to our relationship with the outside world. He has learned to understand what we do, and he channels his own talent

and his own eye to participate in our process. Sometimes when we're starting a project, I ask him to document the site, and that is so much better than relying on my own amateurish photographs— I always think that I take such great photographs, and then I look at them and I realize I'm really not very good at it after all.

JR: **I know you're also something of a collector. What is the difference between the art you work with and the art you live with?**

AS: It's an interesting question, because it has become so fashionable for people to display their personality through a collection— usually an eclectic collection that portrays them as someone eclectic. But I am not a collector. That's very important. I have a lot of things, but that's just because I'm getting old—I'm only half kidding. I have never thought of myself as a collector, but over time, I have discovered things that I respond to. I love drawings, because drawing is something that I can relate to.

JR: **It's part of your own practice as an architect.**

AS: Part of my process, yes. But sometimes I am envious of artists, like when I see a Paul Klee drawing—I can feel his immersion in the drawing process, I marvel at the exploration of color, the detail, the wit. That's the difference between an artist and an architect. An artist makes a drawing about drawing. I make a drawing because it's a step toward making something else.

JR: **It's interesting to me that we haven't discussed painting yet. Painting was really *the* preferred medium of modernist architects. Le Corbusier is the most obvious example—he actually fancied himself a painter as much as an architect—but any number of**

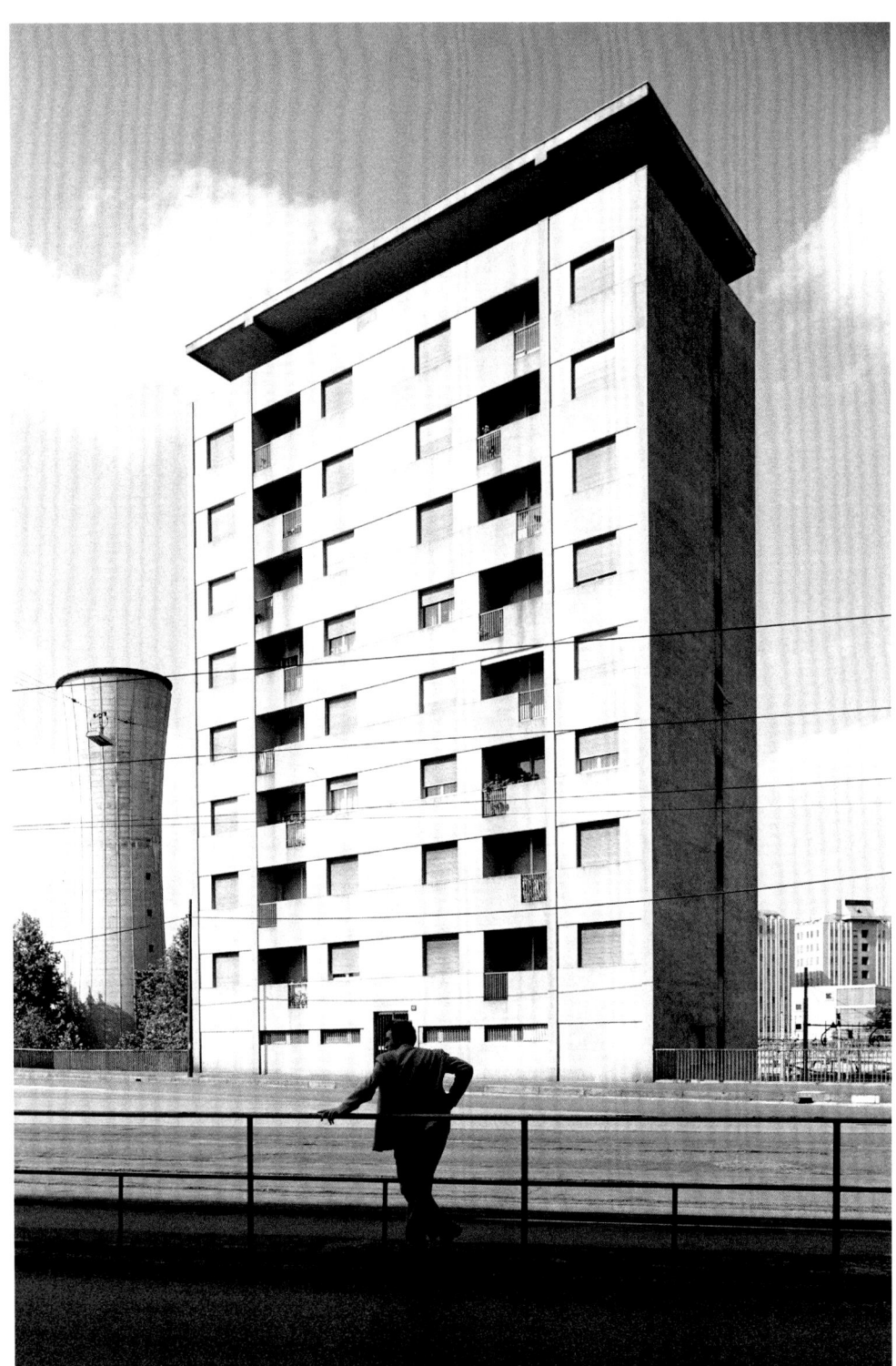

his contemporaries also cited modern painting as an important source of inspiration. Has painting's importance for architects been usurped by other media, like photography or drawing?

AS: Well, I do have some paintings too. I have two seventeenth-century Dutch still lifes that I like very much. One is a scene in the forest ground. Strictly speaking, it's not a still life because there is a salamander in it, and a fly, and a butterfly. But the painting takes you into a different world—it's an almost surrealist setting, but it has been depicted with total realism. There's something so unfamiliar and unexpected about it; it's like it opens up a new space in your brain.

JR: **You're saying that this kind of image, whether it's the Klee drawing or the Dutch painting, can transport you into a different world.**

AS: That's exactly right, and actually very different from how I tend to think about photography. Photography, more than anything else, captures a moment in time. I have a photograph that I bought from Fraenkel Gallery a long time ago. It's of one of those automated photographs from a British bombing mission during the war. The pilots documented the before and after as they flew over. I've always found this image fascinating, because it shows the crazy idea that we force change in such a brutal, sudden way, in such a violent and inhuman process.

JR: **I can see how this distinction plays into your own relationship to different kinds of art and affects what you might want to hang in your own home or your own office, but I'm curious to know if it also carries over into the spaces you design in which other people look at art. You've done a lot of houses for collectors, for example. Are there certain principles—certain ideas about what it is like to live with art—that add up to a common approach** to this kind of project? Or does each one evolve on a case-by-case basis depending on the particular client and the particular collection?

AS: I think that all our work has a kind of specificity that relies on getting to know the client. I also think that many people call themselves collectors when they are not. A lot of people have the money to buy a lot of things they like and to hang them on the wall. A collector is somebody who has a specific mind-set, somebody who pursues art with rigor and a specific intellectual disposition, who systematically fills out a thesis, if you will. Very few people do that. But it's fun to find someone who is actually putting thought into a collection, because then they think about space differently.

JR: **And I imagine that in these cases, your work can essentially become another formulation of the thesis. You're shaping the collection, perhaps not in a direct way, but you're helping to bring a particular vision to life. But this question of having a thesis—or not having one—raises the question of architecture's neutrality, which I think we should talk about in relation to your gallery architecture. It's always seemed ironic to me that the term *neutrality* has become so controversial in this context. Take the white cube, which we all know is a bit of a straw man but is still a dominant typology of exhibition architecture today. On one side, you have artists complaining that their work is always shown in a white cube. They'll say that the white cube isn't neutral at all, that it's ideological and constricting. On the other side, you have architects bristling at the fact that they're always asked to design white cubes. They'll ask why architecture needs to stay neutral. You seem to have found a way beyond this binary in your work. I don't quite know what to call the gallery typology you've invented—I wish I could come up with a good neologism.**

AS: A good hyperbole?

JR: **Exactly! But what I'm trying to get at is that your gallery spaces aren't always white, and they're not cubes either, but they still feel very sensitive, almost respectful to the art that's displayed in them.**

AS: They're not respectful. They're functional. I don't think that neutrality exists. Take the white cube: It's interesting because it's a foil, right? I don't think that's limiting. It's not inherently good or bad. Or rather, it's good only if it's good architecture, and that has to do with a host of things that have to do with proportions, with light, with the way you place a human being in the middle of it.

JR: **So would you say that you're more interested in designing a certain kind of gallery experience than a gallery aesthetic?**

AS: I tend to think that distraction is not desirable. I think that noise takes away from focus. In the most primitive way, when we design spaces for art, we facilitate concentration. We give people the opportunity to focus on what they are meant to see. I don't care whether somebody doesn't like white, or doesn't like green, for that matter. What I care about is a kind of calm, or tranquility, that creates a setting. We live in an age where everything is event-driven, and, for me, that's overwhelming.

JR: **Often this calm seems to be expressed through the details of your architecture. At David Zwirner gallery, I've always been struck by the warm wood accenting the concrete.**

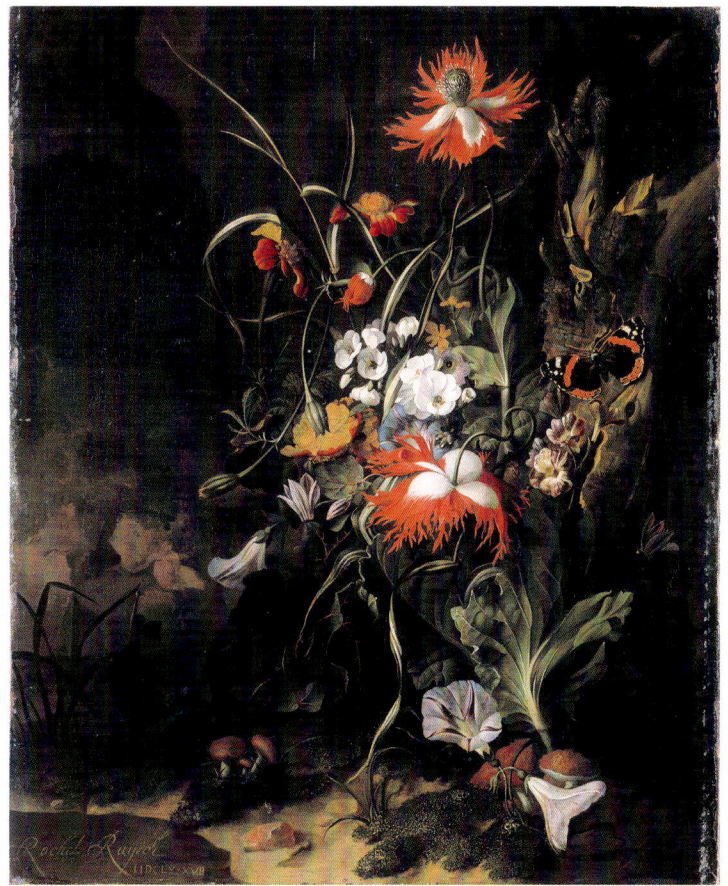

Rachel Ruysch, *A 'Forest Floor' Still Life of Flowers*, 1679–1750. Oil on canvas
© Ashmolean Museum, University of Oxford

Architecture is not about powerful images, it's about a building actually doing something.

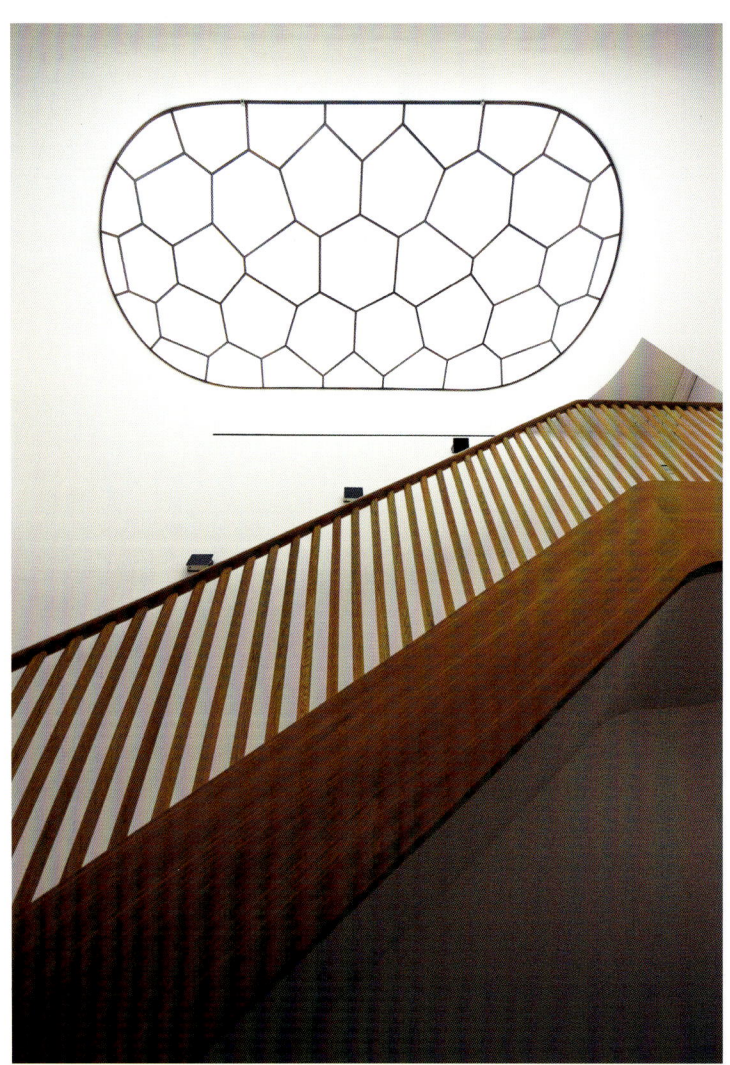

AS: Zwirner's gallery is a very good example. It's about looking at art in the best circumstances, but it doesn't deny itself a measure of personality or presence. I think it's in dialogue with the art. It's not a neutral space.

JR: It's not neutral, but also not overpowering.

AS: I want people to feel welcomed by these spaces. That's not an event-driven sentiment, for me, but more about longevity. These spaces should last. Today, we are questioning how museums function, and everyone agrees that beaux-arts museums are bad and big open spaces are good. But I think exactly how and why we've decided this are worth examining.

JR: It's definitely worth emphasizing that a neoclassical, beaux-arts museum is not inherently any more an expression of power than an ultracontemporary one. But you're also suggesting, I think, that there are fundamental continuities in the experience of art. Traditionally, museums were designed to be spaces of quiet contemplation, and we still need spaces without distraction. Maybe there is a sense in which going to a great nineteenth-century museum, say [Karl Friedrich] Schinkel's Altes Museum, is not materially different from going to any museum that has been constructed in the twenty-first century.

AS: Well, it isn't to you, and it isn't to me, because we have the confidence that comes from always being afforded that access.

JR: That's a good point.

AS: I really think that's a very, very important thing to understand. We need to ask: How do we create places that are inclusive? And if they are inclusive, they have to be inclusive of everybody, which is by necessity very complicated, because everyone is entering from a different place. How does the architecture of the museum contract or expand in ways that communicate openness?

JR: So rethinking the institution starts with the architecture, in a very fundamental sense.

AS: I think so. In a way, this gets back to photography. Today, because we are so image-driven, everybody thinks they're an expert on architecture because they've seen photographs of it. But that's not what architecture is about. Architecture is about being there. Architecture is not about powerful images, it's about a building actually doing something. When I was in architecture school, we would do field trips to visit buildings, and that was a very different experience from seeing them in photographs. And I think that is no different now.

JR: Architecture has a tortured relationship with images, though. There are so many important buildings that are known almost entirely through photographs. The most extreme example might be Mies's Barcelona Pavilion, which was built in 1929 and destroyed within a year. It was eventually rebuilt in the 1980s, but its impact on the development of modern architecture—which was enormous—was almost entirely through its circulation in the form of photographic images. Is there a tension between architecture's reliance on the image and the idea that you just expressed, that a building will always exceed an image somehow? Images can be very powerful tools in the hands of architects, but their work is also supposed to be about specificity, about a relationship to a place—precisely the things that we can't circulate, that can't be captured in a photograph.

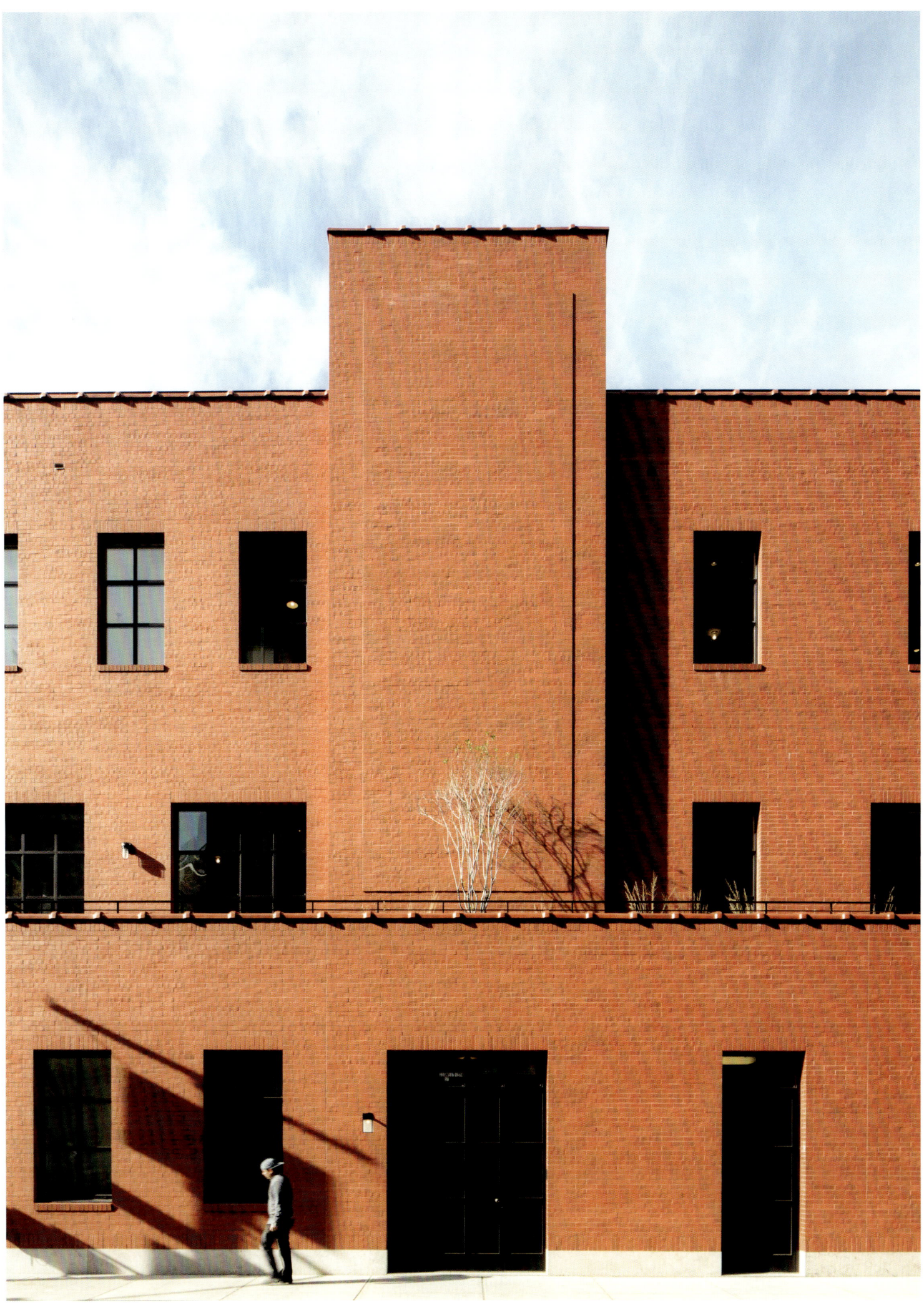

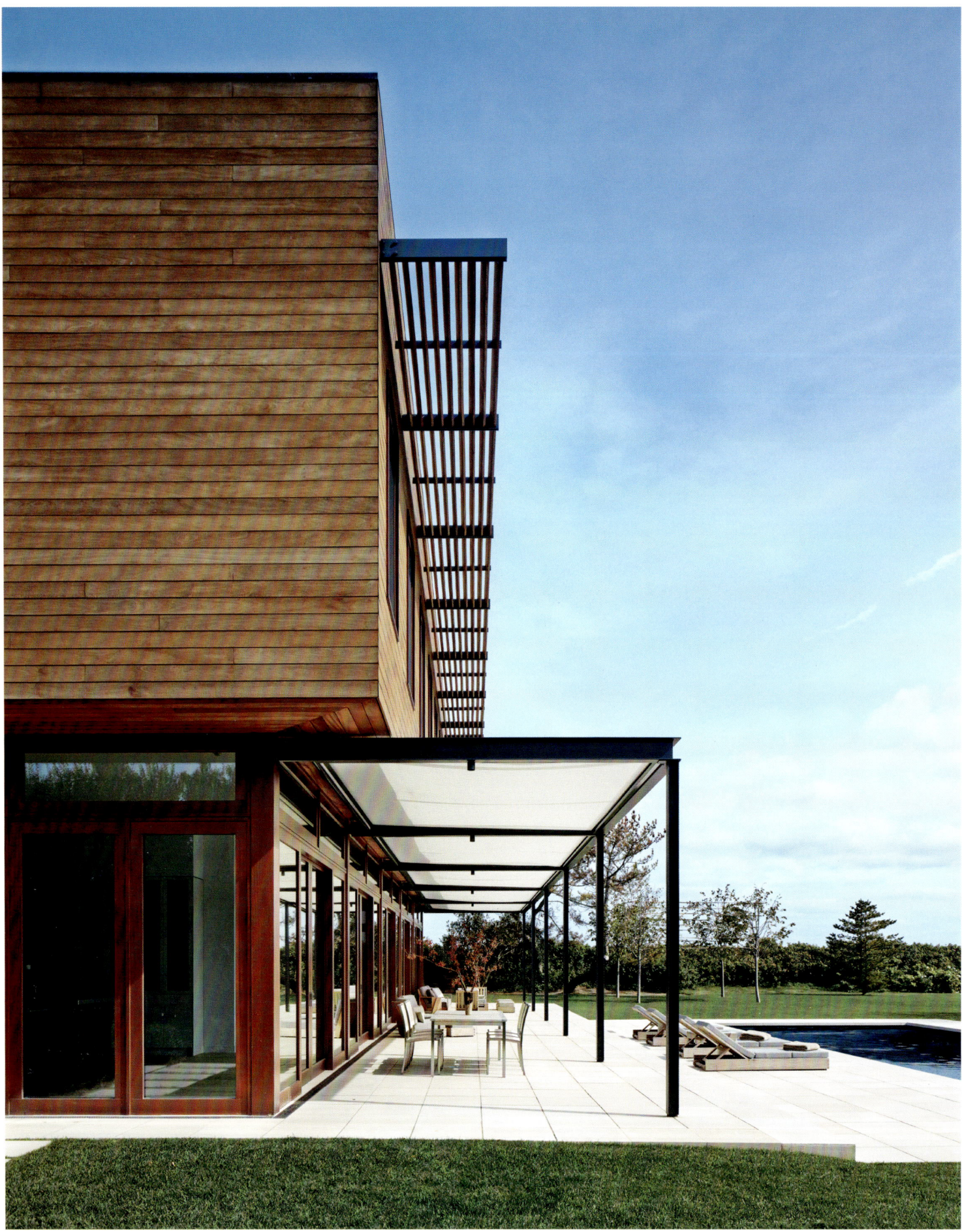

This page:
Selldorf Architects,
Skarstedt Residence,
Sagaponack, New York,
2014
Photograph by Nikolas
Koenig, 2015

Opposite, left:
Selldorf Architects,
Chelsea Townhouse,
New York, 2015
Photograph by Todd Eberle,
2015

Opposite, right:
Selldorf Architects, Neue
Galerie, New York, 2001
Photograph by Todd Eberle,
2005
All Selldorf images courtesy
Selldorf Architects

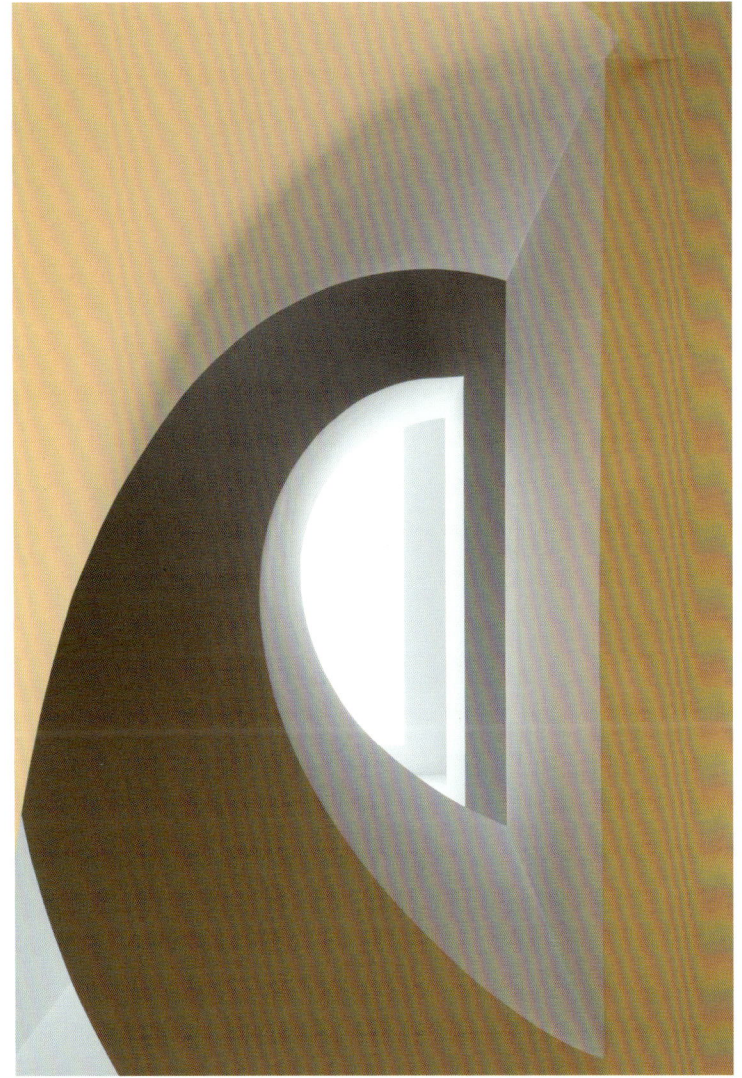

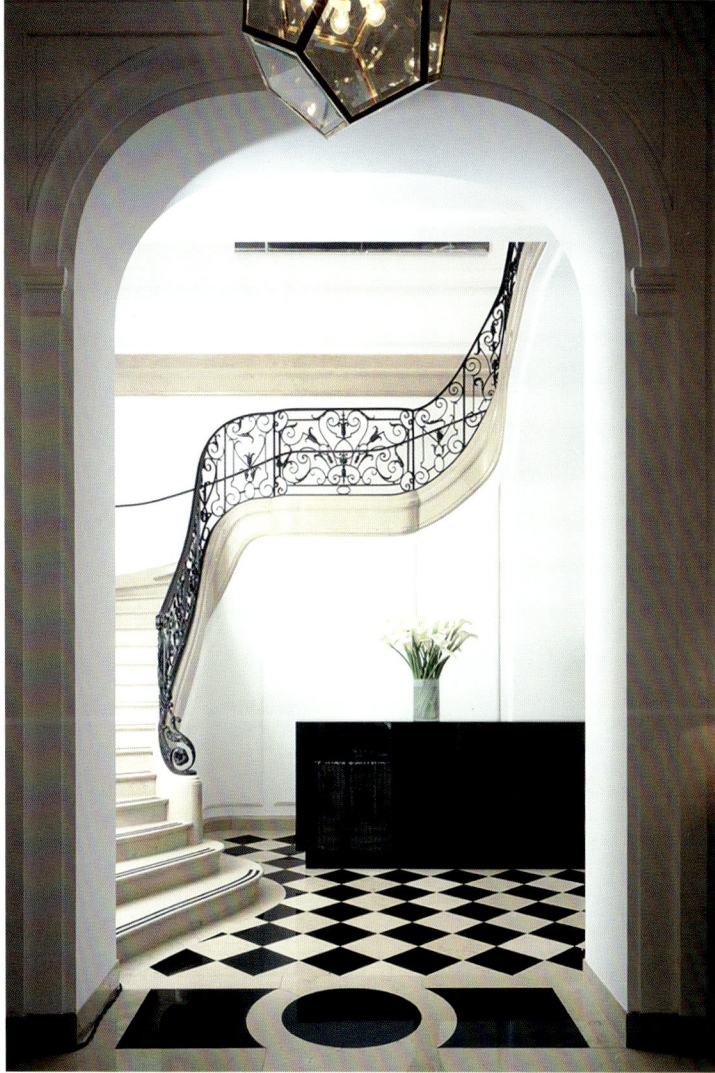

AS: There is a tension, but today I see it less in photography than in the production of renderings. Everybody wants you to show them, in advance, exactly what they're going to see when the building is finished. And because it is now possible to make renderings of such high quality that they are truly photo-realistic, that is what everyone expects. I find this incredibly depressing—it's a fake reality. I know that sometimes we do a rendering that looks exactly like the building, and after it's built, we don't have a really good photograph of that particular angle, so we continue to use the rendering because that represents it better. What I really mind about that is a kind of consumer attitude we're creating. It's like everyone is telling us, "Give it to me NOW." We just lost a competition because I didn't think of providing teaser images. I am heartbroken, because it's a job I wanted. And I didn't want this job because I was going to make amazing images; I wanted this job because it was an opportunity to do something with architecture that I haven't done before.

JR: What seems so problematic today is that often the image precedes the architecture, and the building is merely catching up. But obviously architects aren't going to stop making renderings anytime soon. Can you use images in ways that are still surprising?

AS: One interesting thing is that you cannot make a school anymore. Architects like Robert Venturi and Denise Scott Brown used images to represent a way of thinking.

JR: And that way of thinking became a broader architectural movement. It's true that the entire generation of postmodern architects was, on some level, united by a shared interest in certain kinds of images.

AS: There is no longer any interest in that kind of intellectual community. I think architects are valued only as individuals. Sometimes people ask me if I'm a modernist, and I don't even know what that means. How could I represent something like modernism by myself? The irony is that when I started my office, I was alone, and I was unbelievably intimidated by my colleagues—I really did not seek the company of other architects. Today I do. Because I think, in small ways, I can contribute to changing our conversation.

Julian Rose is an architect and critic based in New York.

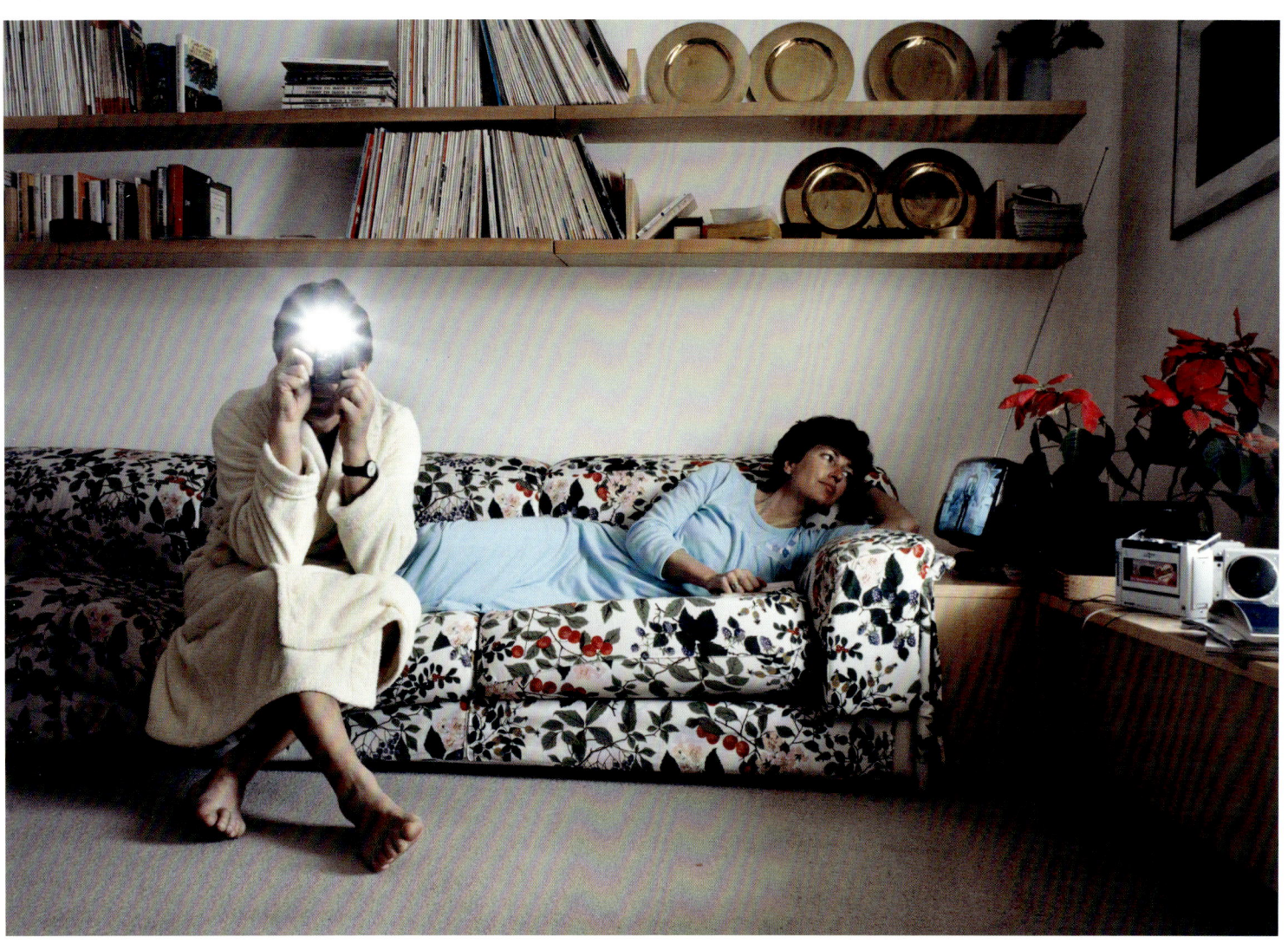

Domestic Comfort

How did an early 1990s exhibition anticipate the transformation
of family life in the U.S.?
Sara Knelman

This page:
Philip-Lorca di Corcia,
Sergio and Totti, 1985
The Museum of Modern Art,
New York/Art Resource,
New York

Opposite:
Doug DuBois, *My Sister
Lise, Christmas Eve,
Far Hills, NJ*, 1984
Courtesy the artist

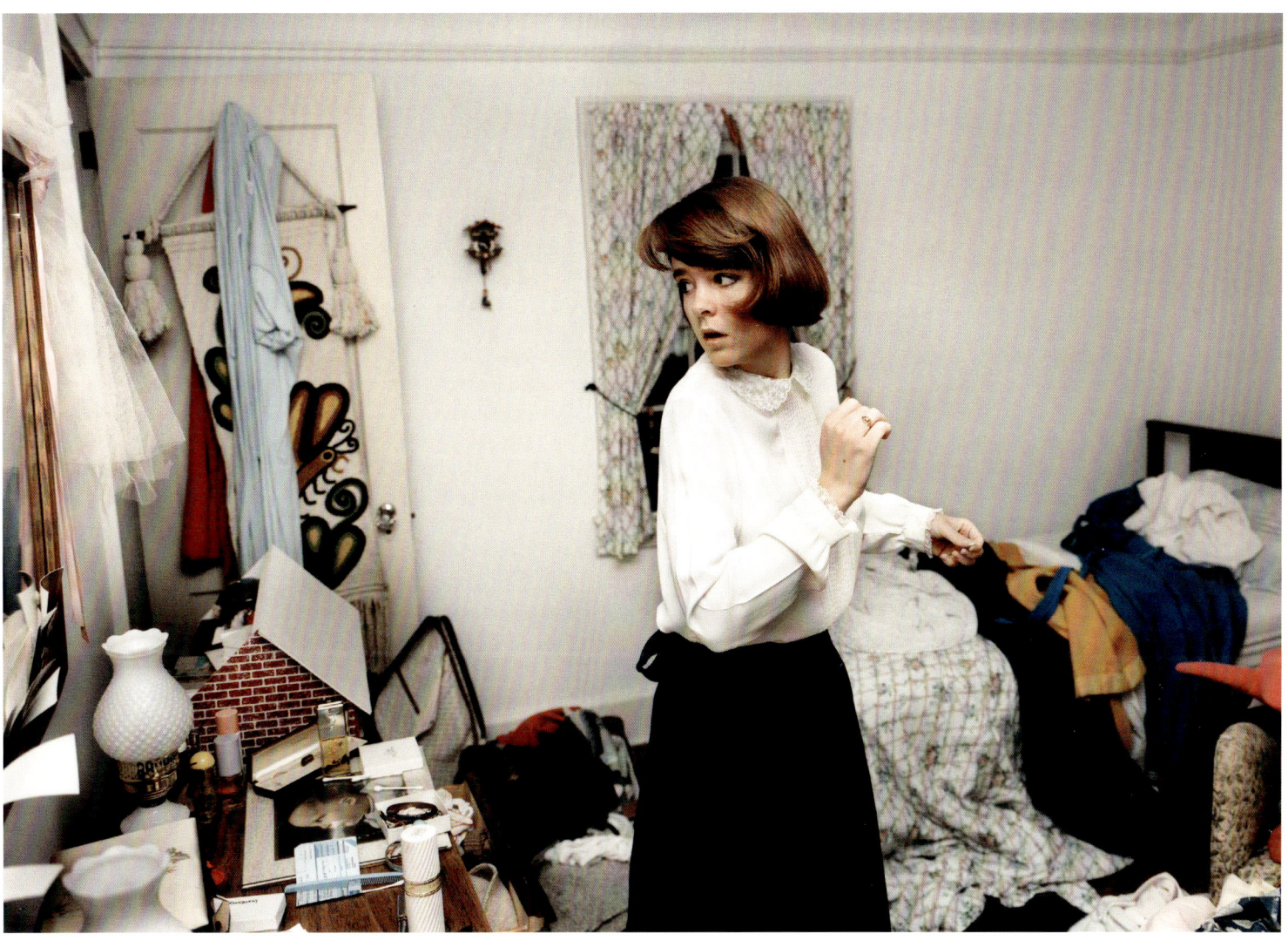

In 1991, the Department of Photography at the Museum of Modern Art in New York staged *Pleasures and Terrors of Domestic Comfort*, among its most ambitious group exhibitions since *The Family of Man* in 1955. While *The Family of Man* sought to universalize human experience by surveying journalistic images of familial bonds and rituals from around the globe, *Pleasures and Terrors* looked squarely at a narrow swathe of distinctly American life: the home and, more pointedly, its affluent surfaces. ("Comfort," after all, implies not only the rounded edges of cozy furniture, but the economic ease that affords them.) Curated by Peter Galassi, who would formally succeed John Szarkowski as head of the department during the show's run, it included over 150 images by more than seventy artists. *Pleasures and Terrors* marked a shift in interest, by both photographers and their subjects, from the politics of the wider world and even from the street outside, toward the warm, lit living rooms of American domestic life. What might we understand of this moment if we take the time to wander back through some of these homes today?

With the exception of William Eggleston's 1970s images—Eggleston being the hero then as now of recasting the mundane as monumental—most of the works in the show were made in the 1980s. After Watergate and Vietnam, after Margaret Thatcher, Ronald Reagan, and George H. W. Bush, the politics of social concern gave way to a tidal wave of late-capitalist individualism and aspiration. A culture of slogans and protests retreated inside to the solace of TV and tchotchkes. Galassi explained it this way:

> It became all too reasonable to conclude that moral conviction and political effectiveness, at least on a national scale, had parted company forever. If there is any truth in these partisan simplifications, then perhaps an effort to get one's own house in order, or at least to see it clearly, will seem less a withdrawal from responsibility than an expression of sanity.

The American dream, it seems, is alive and well, if a little frayed at the edges.

On the surface, there were the usual snapshot-worthy events in the exhibition: babies and backyards, Christmas trees and card games. The plethora of patterns and interior decor is one of the pleasures of looking back. Indeed, the show drew attention from *Elle Decor*, *House Beautiful*, and *Parenting*, which all ran lighthearted notices. The soft pinks of Laurie Simmons's *Coral Living Room with Lilies* (1983) and the typical youthful mess of Doug DuBois's *My Sister Lise, Christmas Eve, Far Hills, NJ* (1984) give us a feeling for the palettes and textures of the time, the kinds of pictures that might provoke nostalgia in a certain generation or inspire Pinterest mood boards or period cinema now. Set against the backdrops of enviable domestic spaces, the kind we might find in advertising images for perfect kitchens or in home-decorating magazines, the subtler hints of disquiet can be missed.

Yet the stark undertone and palpable discomfort in many of the images, often overlooked at the time, are unmistakable from this perspective—though one also wonders if the past always looks a little melancholy. The cinematic stagings of Philip-Lorca diCorcia and Tina Barney are dramatically forlorn, suggestive of larger narratives that never quite unfold. The young boy in diCorcia's *Brian* (1988) looks glumly at a large hunk of meat, the counter awash with piles of food and gadgets. In *Sergio and Totti* (1985) a couple in loungewear sit on a floral couch looking away from one another, one watching television, the other obscured by the camera's flash, as he—presumably Sergio—documents his own documentation. (Interestingly, the exhibition also utilized television as a promotional tool, a medium that museums had long eschewed. A three-minute spot for a short-lived PBS culture show called *The Edge* broadcast an unnarrated montage of images from the exhibition interspersed with audio clips from popular TV shows and Hollywood movies of the era, making an implicit connection between popular dramatizations of domestic life and those displayed in the MoMA exhibition.)

Barney's *Sunday New York Times* (1982) shows a big family orbiting a table, the newspaper spread across it, in a warm-yellow room. A woman in the corner holds a baby and scowls ineffectually at a man in the foreground intently reading the news, oblivious to the baby bottle beside him and the chaos that surrounds. Similarly, *The Landscape* (1988) depicts a group sharing space but distinctly lost in their own worlds, the youngest a blur of blonde curls in the foreground. Though they are crowded together in the center of the frame, each person, even the dog, looks away. A gilt-framed painting echoes the blues and greens outside a bay window in the room beyond, layering natural and contrived landscapes. However enviable the real estate or ornamentation, otherwise gracious rooms are also filled with less tangible things—loneliness, resentment, desire, and uncertainty.

If the show is remarkable in its expression of such subtlety of feeling, this comes in part from the work of the many women photographers included (about half), whose projects look unflinchingly at the subjects of motherhood, domestic labor, and the wider expectations of girls and women near the close of the twentieth century. The show brought together poetic documents of intimacy in the work of Sally Mann, Marilyn Nance, and Jo Ann Walters, whose thirty-year project, only just published in 2018, began with the image of a family in a Connecticut backyard included in *Pleasures and Terrors*. In many photographs, like Barney's, or those of Mary Frey, women appear conspicuously as mothers and wives, often the less powerful figures in the frame. As if in challenge to them, selections from Carrie Mae Weems's *The Kitchen Table Series* (1990) and Cindy Sherman's *Untitled Film Stills* (1977–80) sought to reconsider these expectations from the inside out. In these projects, placed side by side in the catalog, Weems holds her cards close to her chest and looks sidelong at her male companion, while Sherman crouches to collect her fallen groceries, gazing intently beyond the frame. Who are we, in your eyes, they each ask, and who do we want to be?

The emphasis on female practices is significant, though it's also curiously glossed over in the catalog essay. Indeed, Galassi writes that "photographers, like businessmen, generally have maintained a barrier between work and home." Such a statement ignores the fact of domestic labor, the business of keeping house, long a cultural expectation of women and one that extended to maintaining a photographic record of the family. The photographers Rosy Martin and Jo Spence have suggested in their extraordinary work on the culture and aesthetics of the family album that, as a genre, it is beholden to a set of conventions and expectations. "Family snaps," they write, "hardly give any indication of the contradictions, power struggles or desires inherent at all levels of family life, or in the intersection of that life with the structures which make up a patriarchal society with sexual, racial and class divisions." In retrospect, *Pleasures and Terrors* is striking not only as a powerful expression of the significance of the domestic sphere, but as an opening up of its complicated dynamics, often through the eyes of women working in the wake of second-wave feminism and ushering in the third.

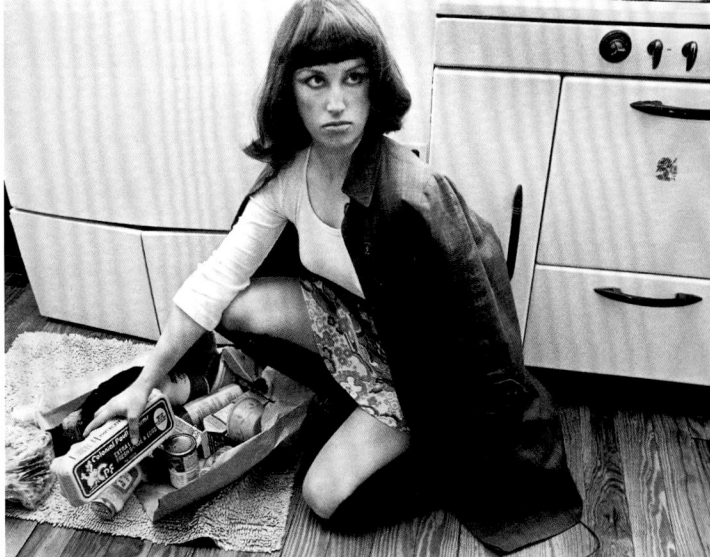

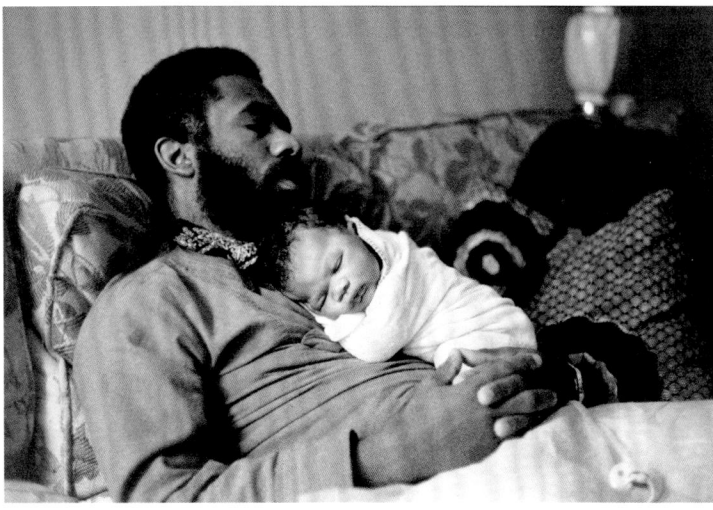

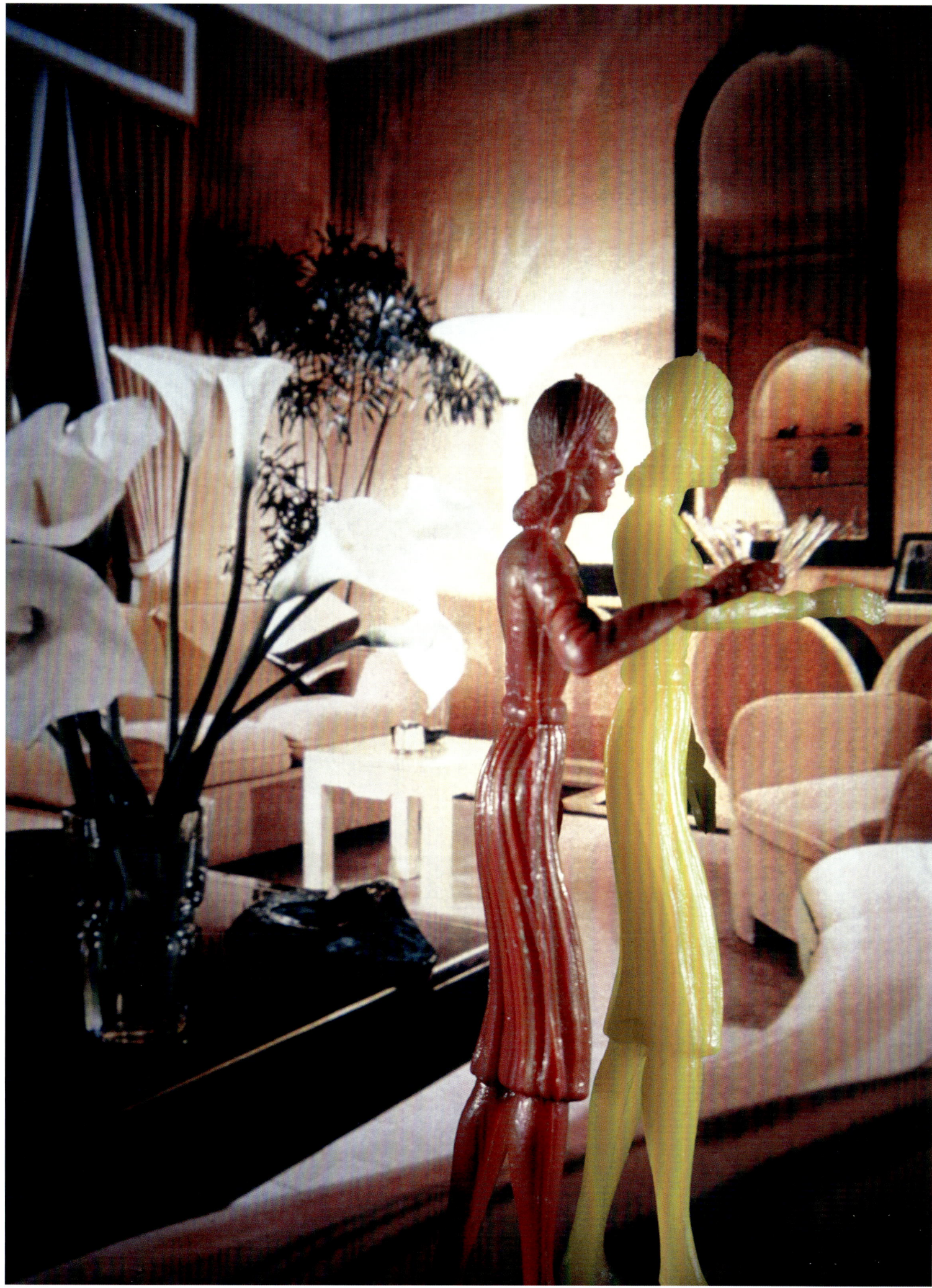

The exhibition was important not only for opening up new photographic territory, but for legitimizing the subject of everyday life.

Pleasures and Terrors also had a number of clear gaps, some acknowledged openly at the time, others more starkly visible from a distance. Galassi makes brief note of some omissions, writing that "a great deal is missing. Racially, ethnically, and economically the pictures are far from representative of contemporary America." He fails to account for these gaps, however, other than to group them together with what he calls "the journalistic favorites of domestic trouble—homelessness, drug abuse, child abuse, violence," suggesting such subjects belong to a realm that is somehow in opposition to or outside the bounds of art. This division is disturbing, a circuitous excuse releasing the museum from any sense of social responsibility. With the exception of images by Weems and Nance, most display white, heteronormative figures. Carol Squires wrote at the time that Weems's image "raises a variety of questions, not least among them whether a black female photographer has ever been shown before by MoMA's photography department." And most omit the violence, physical or psychological, that is often wrought in the home. The exception was Nan Goldin's slideshow *The Ballad of Sexual Dependency* (1986), which contains a more complex idea of family and of the brutality of desire—though it screened only once, for an extra cost of eight dollars. Like the omission of the nuclear explosion in *The Family of Man*, there is a void at the center of the exhibition's contents that hollows out both critical and moral perspectives.

This problem is inherently one of self-reflection and is hinted at, even if obliquely, in the sheer number of images that contain mirrors, or, in the case of diCorcia's *Sergio and Totti*, the camera's flash. A trick of domestic decor and a trope of self-reflection, mirrors enact a visual deceit and enable vanity. In hindsight, the show's failings made clear the willful blindness to a diversity of perspectives and lifestyles, a circumstance that began to be redressed by artists,

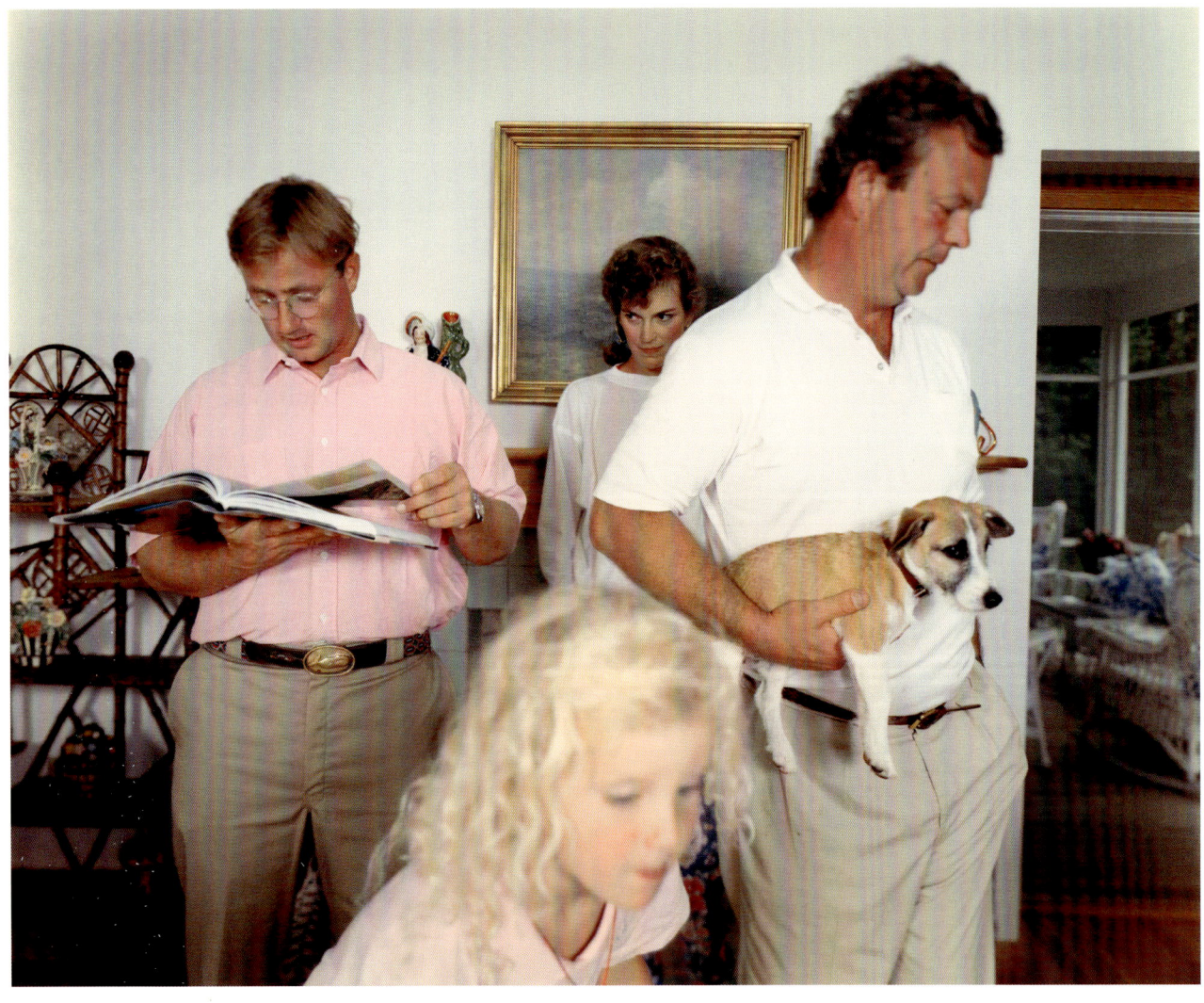

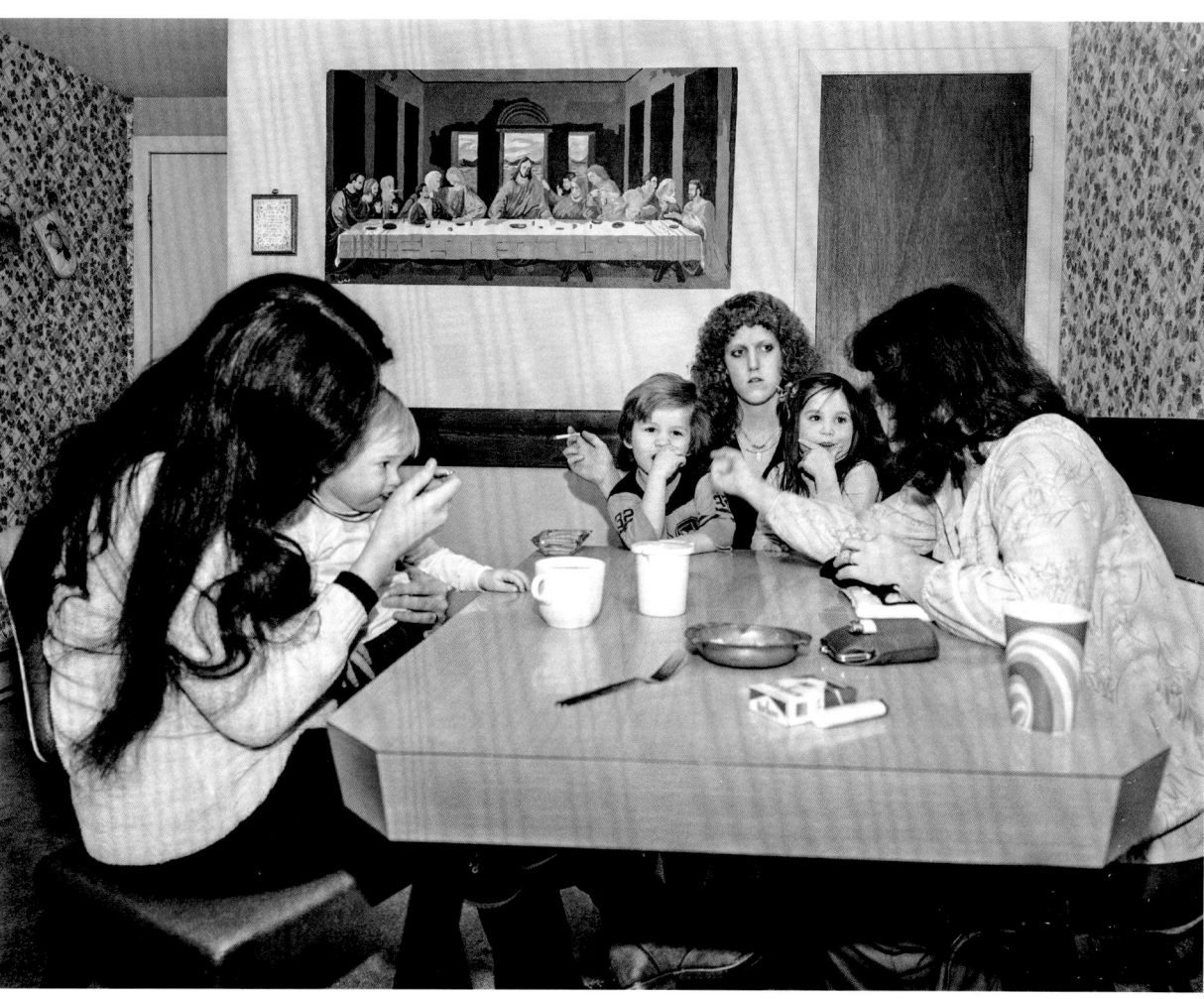

Mary Frey, *Women at Coffee Break*, 1979–83, from the series *Domestic Rituals*
© the artist/Foley Gallery, New York

including Catherine Opie and Alec Soth, who have credited *Pleasures and Terrors* as a catalyst for their work. Opie drove an RV around the country to make her series *Domestic* (1998), which pictures everyday lesbian domestic life in America, in response to *Pleasures* and as part of a conversation with Galassi. Soth, who was a college student when he saw the exhibition, has credited it with making "domestic life seem like a worthwhile subject for photographers," a subject he's pursued, loosely, in his varied pictures of American life, including *Broken Manual*, which documents the desire to abandon the comforts of home in favor of a reclusive existence off the grid.

Curators were equally attuned to the significance of *Pleasures and Terrors*, and a number of exhibitions looking at domesticity and everyday life sprung up in its wake, most notably *Snapshots: The Photography of Everyday Life* at the San Francisco Museum of Modern Art in 1998, *Who's Looking at the Family?* at the Barbican in 1994, and, over a decade later, the similarly oppositional photography exhibition *Cruel and Tender: The Real in the Twentieth-Century Photograph* at Tate Modern in 2003. *Pleasures and Terrors* is notable as the first encompassing exploration of the translation of the "snapshot aesthetic" into formal, monumental museum photography (and, it should be said, for the rise of an art market that would support such works—pictures made as much *of* the subjects as *for* their big empty walls). Galassi also understood intuitively the way that it would connect with wider audiences.

At a time when museums had to adapt to survive, the relevance of photography as a document of everyday life became crucial. *Pleasures and Terrors* was important not only for opening up new photographic territory for future generations, but for legitimizing the subject of everyday life within the history of the medium, and within the parameters of the public art museum. And as an extension, *Pleasures and Terrors* also preluded the deluge of images that would define social media within a decade.

The ambiguity of pleasure is played out endlessly in the contradictions of our enjoyment and our pathological projection of enjoyment, and in the dissolution of the boundaries between private and public.

Galassi seems to have found a poetic name in a riff on the title of Aaron Siskind's 1954 series *The Pleasures and Terrors of Levitation* (Siskind died in February 1991, as the show was being planned). The photographs depict bodies suspended dramatically in midair, perhaps floating, perhaps falling, their beauty complicated by the uncertainty of their peril or safety. Though Siskind's images are neither domestically themed nor included in the exhibition, the tension between aesthetic pleasure and lurking threat evident within them is an apt analog for the themes of Galassi's show.

Myopic as it was, *Pleasures and Terrors* opened up a conversation about what it might mean to be American, not from a view of patriotism or warfaring, but from an internal perspective of private life. It can be retrospectively understood as a fulcrum for its historical moment, connecting back to Edward Steichen's imperialist vision of a collective view of human experience in *The Family of Man* and to John Szarkowski's predilection for poetic subjectivity. But it also pointed out the problems of those histories and looked forward to the future, toward the demise of privacy, the loneliness of late capitalism, and the significance of image and identity culture in shaping our perceptions of gender, class, and race. Pleasures and terrors, the show suggests, are like holograms, embedded within one another, twisting and changing according to the slant of light.

Sara Knelman is an educator, curator, and writer living in Toronto.

Ezra Stoller Modern Times

Mimi Zeiger

Ezra Stoller photographed postwar U.S. architecture with the rigor of a true believer. His images—published widely in numerous trade magazines as well as in *House Beautiful* and *House & Garden*—presented modernism not as an avant-garde or utopian vision, but as a movement in situ, one born fully formed like Athena from Zeus's skull. Yet a global war and an ocean unequivocally separate early twentieth-century experiments undertaken at the Bauhaus and by Le Corbusier from the postwar embrace of modern architecture by corporate leaders and the cultural elite in the United States.

In Stoller's crisp, black-and-white prints, boxy-shouldered skyscrapers like Ludwig Mies van der Rohe's Seagram Building (1958) or Skidmore, Owings & Merrill's building for Union Carbide (1960), both in New York, proudly rise above the city grid—steel and glass curtain walls towering over masonry edifices. These were depicted as the heroes of a new age. Stoller, always precise about natural light and time of day, photographed Mies's structure at dusk; every floor is illuminated, and the building seems to glow with industry. His image of New York's Solomon R. Guggenheim Museum (1959), taken looking straight up into the cylindrical belly of the building, freezes Frank Lloyd Wright's experiential design of spiraling ramps into an iconic composition—modernism's dynamism temporarily tamed.

While civic and commercial architecture have come to define both Stoller's oeuvre and the heroism of the modern movement in the United States, his archive is full of transparencies showing residential buildings. Throughout his career, he photographed homes designed by architects he was friends with, and those he admired, from Paul Rudolph and Marcel Breuer to Alvar Aalto and Eero Saarinen. Indeed, one of his earliest published images is of the A. C. Koch House (1936) in Cambridge, Massachusetts, designed by the architects Carl Koch and Edward Durell Stone, who taught the evening architecture classes Stoller attended at New York University in the mid-1930s. (He would graduate a few years later with a degree in industrial design and an established photography practice.)

Pierluigi Serraino, author of the recent volume *Ezra Stoller: A Photographic History of Modern American Architecture* (2019), and Erica Stoller, Stoller's daughter and director of Esto Photographics, Inc., the company her father founded, both claim that the photographer didn't change his approach according to building type. "He was extremely studied, each composition was a painting," says Serraino. Stoller would visit each site and meticulously take notes about the building and the light before setting up a single shot. "His goal was to understand something and explain it," says his daughter. "He spent a lot of time figuring out the architecture. He believed his pictures were telling the truth."

However, the drive toward veracity registers differently when looking at houses and not at the swooping monumentality of Saarinen's TWA Terminal (1962) or the repetitive efficiency of IBM's corporate campus (1958) in Rochester, Minnesota. When modernism is performed at the scale of the home, it is personal. Each home signifies a break with the past, a new way to live, the postwar American dream. The architectural photography of Julius Shulman most immediately comes to mind when thinking about mid-century modern residential architecture. His images sell a California lifestyle of improbable vistas and turquoise swimming pools. Stoller's vérité presents the modern home as attainable, not aspirational. And although Stoller, like Shulman, photographed on the West Coast, most of his commissions were along the Eastern Seaboard, capturing pockets of modernism around Cambridge; Rye, New York; New Canaan, Connecticut; and Sarasota, Florida. That difference in geography, cultural and topographic, points away from the drama of palm trees and blue sky. A forest of tree trunks with bare branches surrounds the Baker Residence (1951) by Minoru Yamasaki, while the interior is full of lush houseplants. A spindly bush nearly dominates Stoller's photograph of Breuer's Gilbert Tompkins House (1946), its branches offering a compositional counterpoint to the austerity of the architect's geometries.

In many ways, Stoller's own bootstrapped life encapsulated the American dream he so carefully depicted. The child of Jewish immigrants from Poland, he had an upbringing marked by uncertainty. His father was blacklisted due to union activism, and his mother suffered from depression. The family moved from New York to Chicago and back again, and he went to school in New Jersey, the Bronx, and Manhattan. Success (and his eventual position as gatekeeper) was built through countless magazine and firm assignments and the ability to capture a unity within a space, public or private, even if in real life that cohesion wasn't quite there.

Such alchemical skill led the architect Philip Johnson to quip that architects wanted their projects "Stollerized." In 1981, around the time Stoller was winding down his decades-long career, the *New York Times* architecture critic Ada Louise Huxtable questioned the very truths of architectural photography central to Stoller's work. "How much is real and how much is

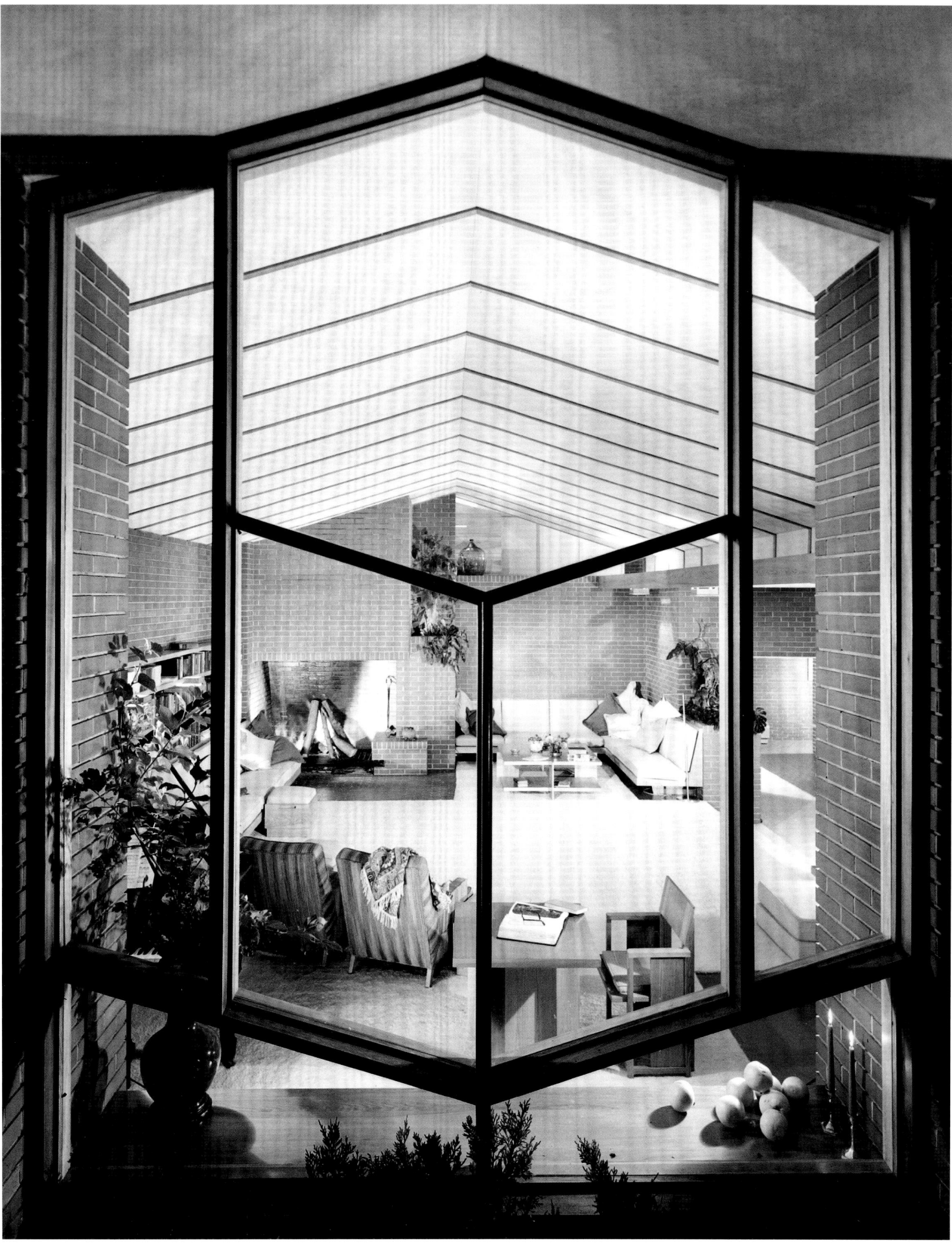

Frank Lloyd Wright,
Mossberg House, South
Bend, Indiana, 1952

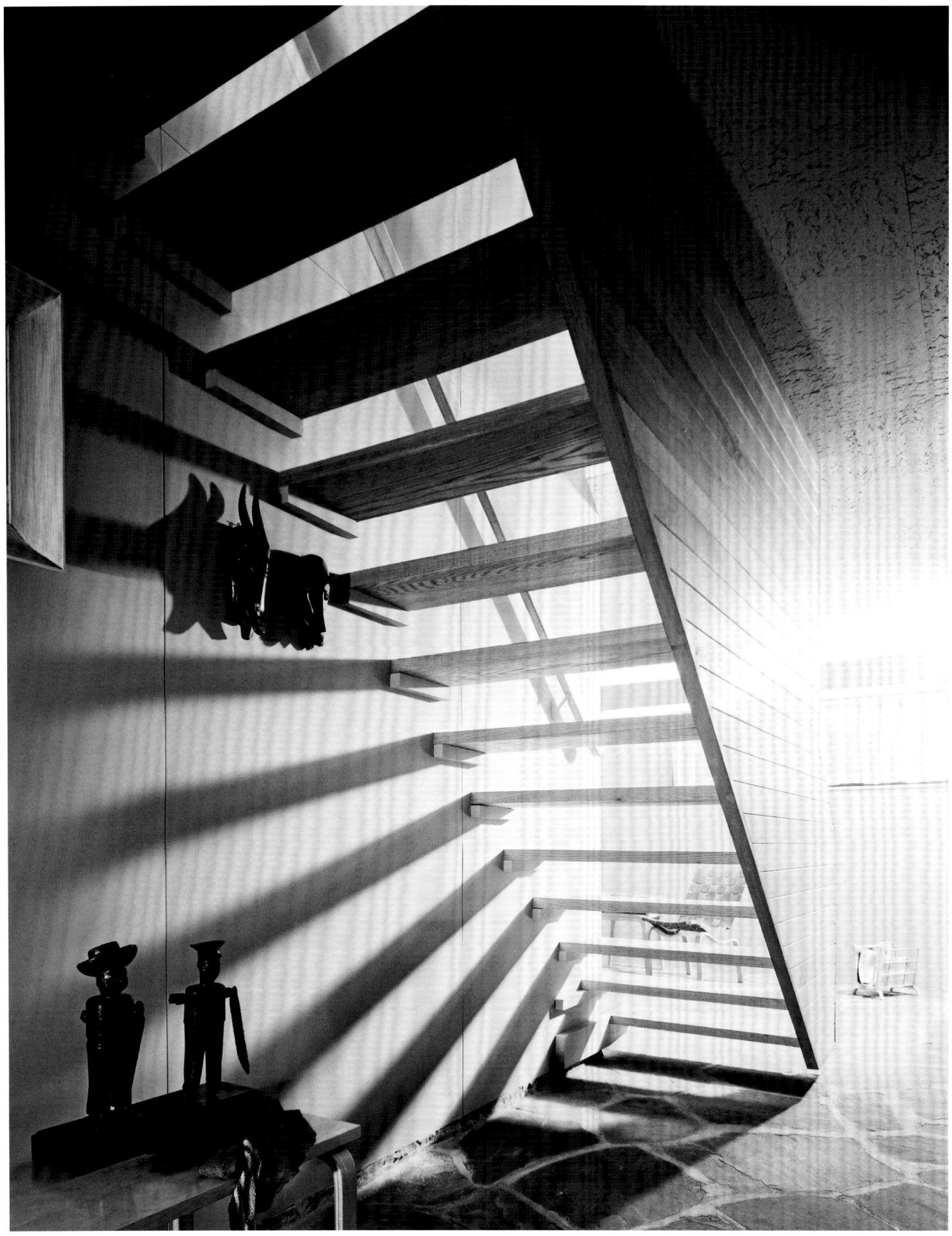

Marcel Breuer, Gilbert
Tompkins House, Hewlett
Harbor, New York, 1947

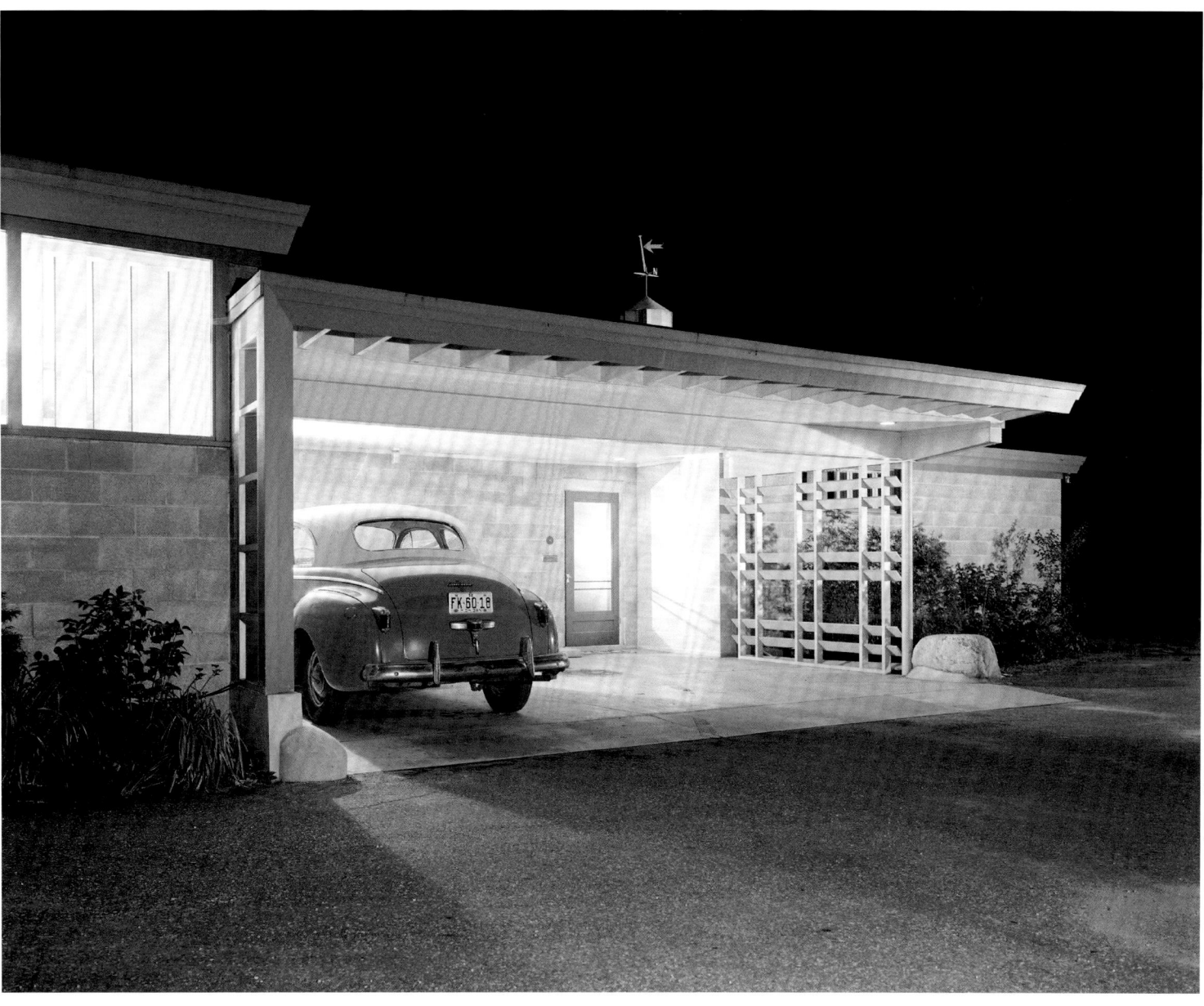

Harry Weese, Brenner
House, Champaign,
Illinois, 1952

'edited' reality?" she wrote. "At what point do the actual and the ideological merge?"

A series from 1949 underscores Huxtable's query. That year, Stoller photographed his own home in Rye. He had worked closely with the architects Abraham Geller and George Nemeny on the low-slung design clad in vertical timber. The double-height living room, pictured with Eames plywood lounge chairs, a fire in the hearth, and late-afternoon sun casting long shadows across the floor, peddles a modernism that is warm and cozy. In an image of the kitchen, Stoller's wife, Helen, stands at the stove as two of his children, Erica and Evan, sit at the counter eating from cereal bowls. Erica is in pigtails. In a color version of this photograph, Helen is wearing a bright-red dress and is posed against the white stove and blue countertops. This is the dream manifested.

"The late '40s was the American moment," says Erica Stoller. "He had a perfection in mind, especially if you grew up in rental apartments. This is the ideal life cleaned up and controlled." Her childhood coincided with the exponential growth of her father's practice, a time when he was capturing the modernist possibilities of other houses, corporate campuses, and high-rises. She recalls that he was always on the road and rarely at home: "The ideal life wasn't always so ideal."

Mimi Zeiger is a critic, editor, and curator based in Los Angeles. She was the cocurator of the U.S. Pavilion for the 2018 Venice Architecture Biennale.

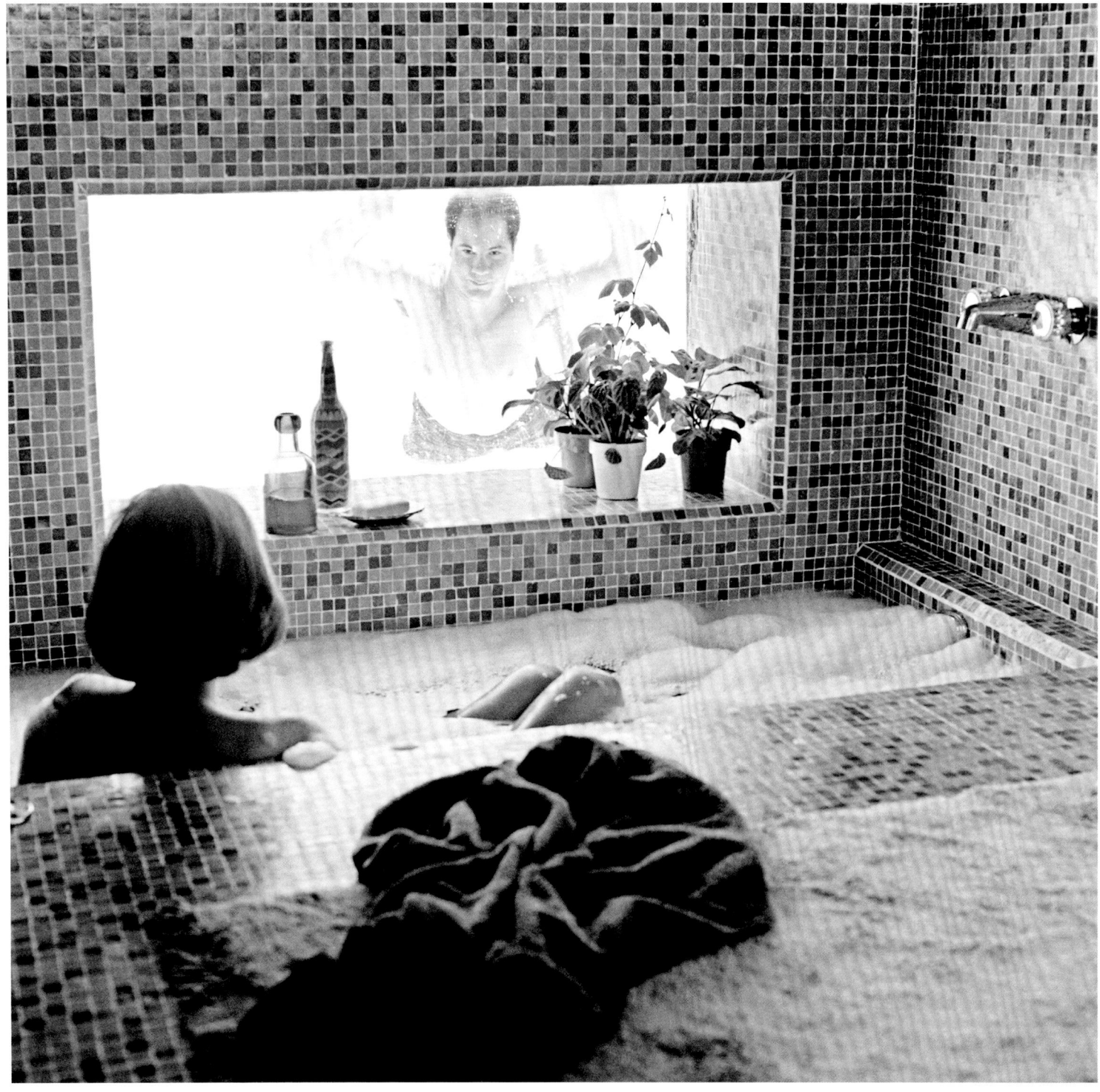

Arthur Erickson, David
Graham House, Vancouver,
British Columbia, Canada,
1967

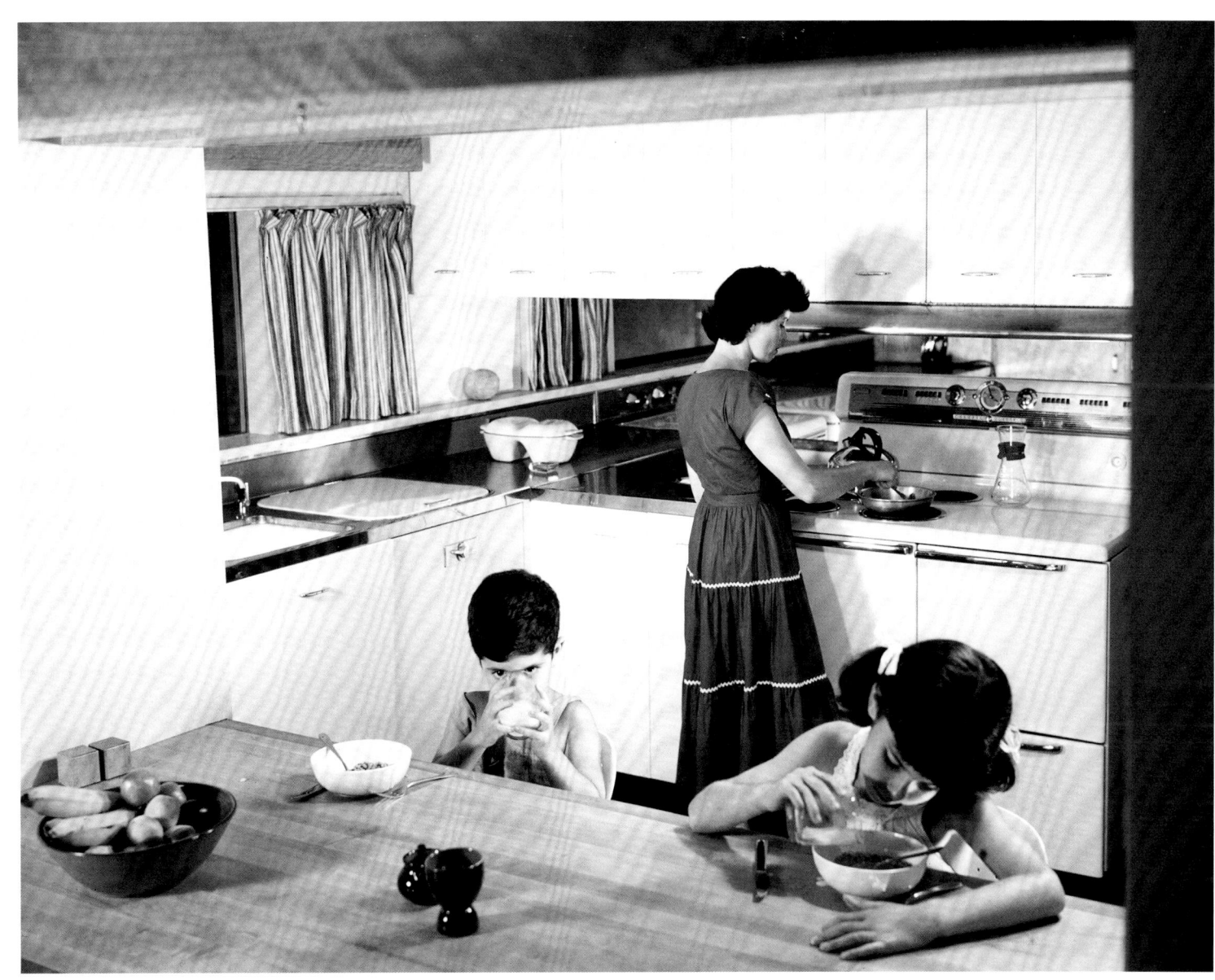

Helen Stoller with children,
Erica and Evan, at the
Stoller House, designed
by Nemeny and Geller,
Rye, New York, 1949

Overleaf:
Carson, Lundin & Shaw,
Shaw House, Long Island,
New York, 1959
All photographs © Ezra
Stoller/Esto

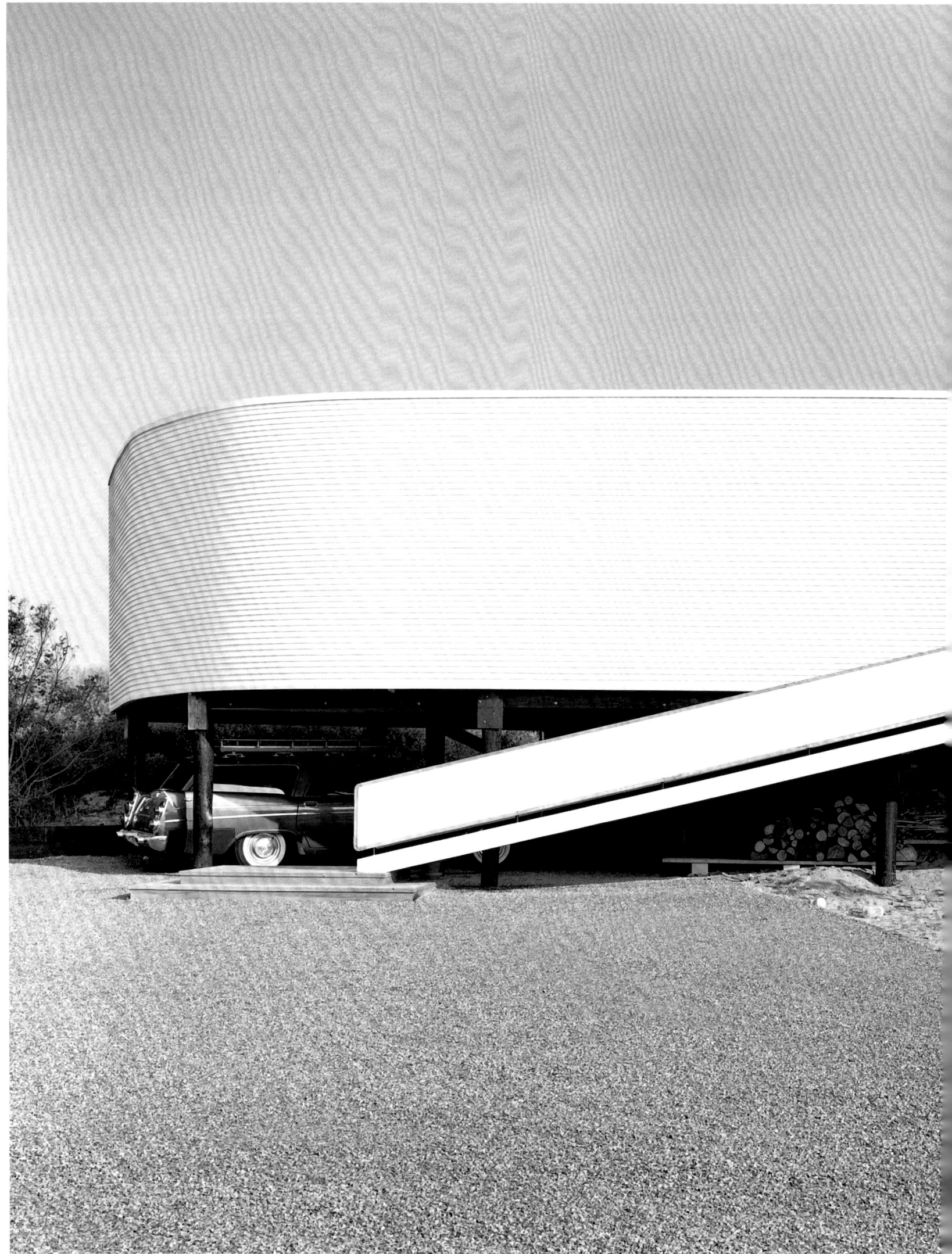

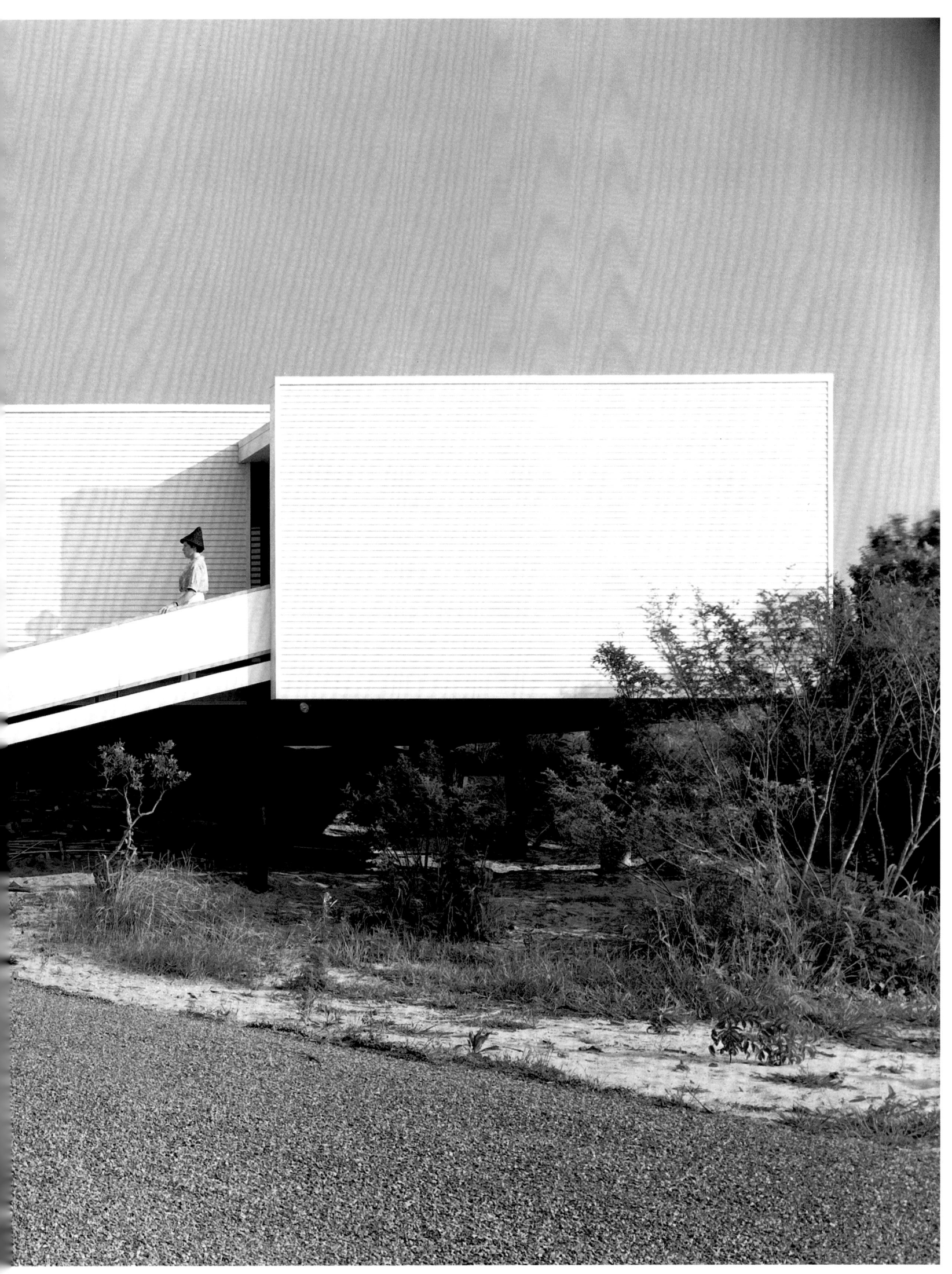

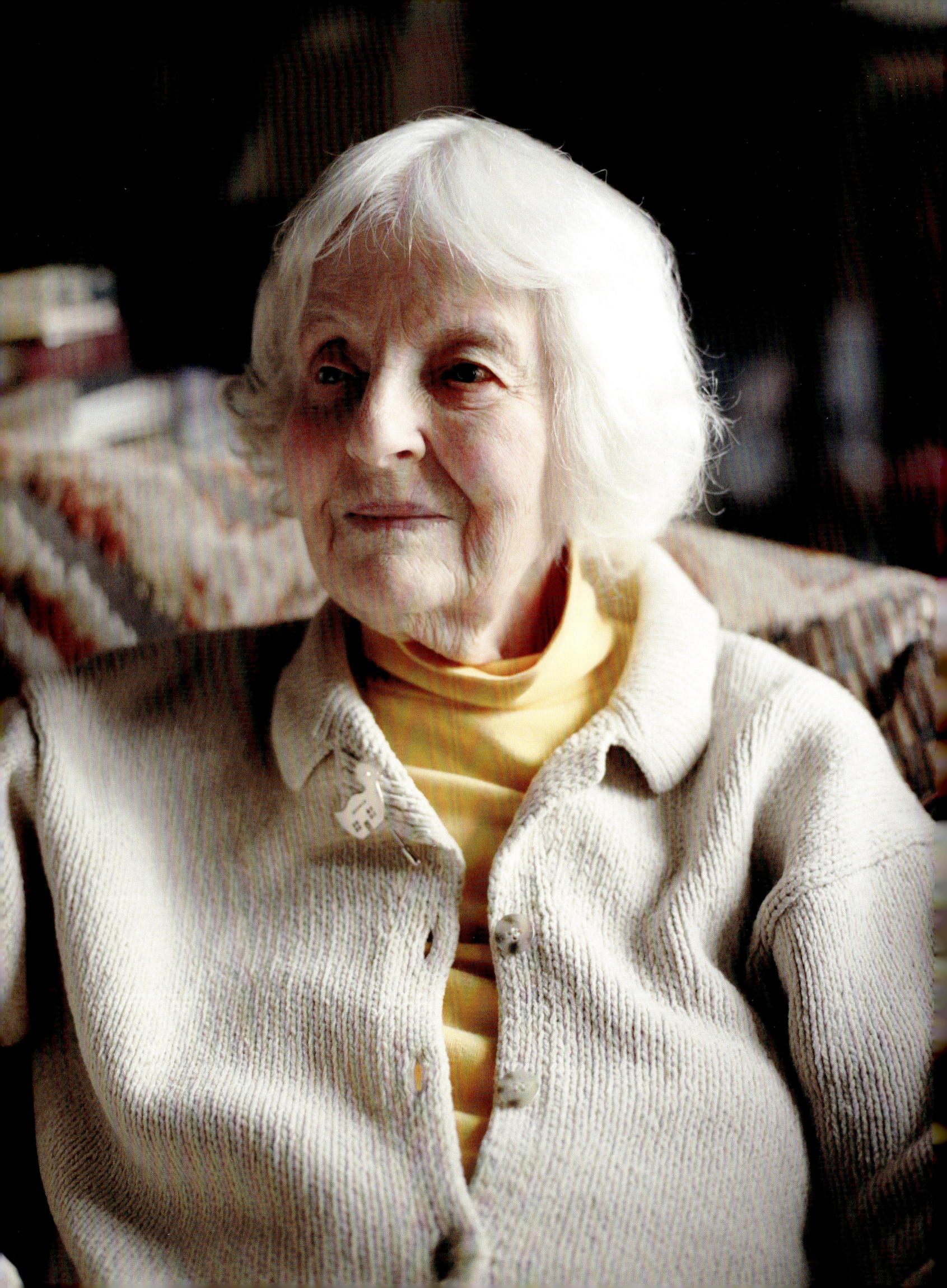

Denise Scott Brown

"Get out and see these things, and then take good photographs."

A Conversation with Peter Barberie

In her 1907 Art Nouveau home on the outskirts of Philadelphia, the architect Denise Scott Brown lives among an eclectic collection of art, furniture, and knickknacks. As in her iconic designs and writings, elements of vernacular culture mix freely with classical references. Batman pillows converse with a Piranesi etching.

Born and raised in South Africa, Scott Brown arrived in the United States in 1958 following extensive travel in Europe. She and her first husband, Robert Scott Brown, came to study with the architect Louis Kahn, bringing with them a strong commitment to urban planning that has informed her designs, teaching, and writing ever since. As a professor at UC Berkeley and UCLA in the mid-1960s, she became interested in the rapidly growing cities of Los Angeles and Las Vegas. In 1967, she married fellow architect Robert Venturi and returned to Philadelphia to join his architectural practice. Five years later, with Venturi and Steven Izenour, she coauthored the groundbreaking 1972 book *Learning from Las Vegas*.

Scott Brown's built projects range from the Sainsbury Wing at the National Gallery in London to the Mielparque Nikko Kirifuri Resort in Japan to Franklin Court, a dramatic reconstruction of Benjamin Franklin's Philadelphia house frame that blends her love of building, archaeology, and neighborhood planning. Photography has been a key element of Scott Brown's approach to architecture and urban design: she will soon publish a book of her photographs, *Wayward Eye, Photographs 1950–1970*.

Page 120:
Denise Scott Brown,
Philadelphia,
November 2019
Photograph by Jody Rogac
for *Aperture*

This page and opposite:
Denise Scott Brown's
house, Philadelphia, 2019
Photographs by Jason
Fulford for *Aperture*

Denise Scott Brown: It was said that, of all crowded rooms, there was never one so crowded as when Thomas Jefferson dined alone.

Peter Barberie: [*Laughs*] **I've heard that.**

DSB: Yes. So this house is us dining alone. These crowded things mean I can sit here and have happy memories, or be reminded of what to talk about.

PB: **I can see that you have eclectic taste.**

DSB: Well, Bob Venturi and I could spot things that other people would like in a few years and buy them when they still cost four dollars. Look at this Art Nouveau detail on this chair. One day, I'll see it in a book. Do you see it?

PB: **Yes, I do. It's delicate.**

DSB: It's so exquisite. The chairs aren't Majorelle, because they are too small. But one day we'll find someone illustrating something like them, and we'll say, "Oh, that's like our chairs."

PB: **They are made with great, great attention.**

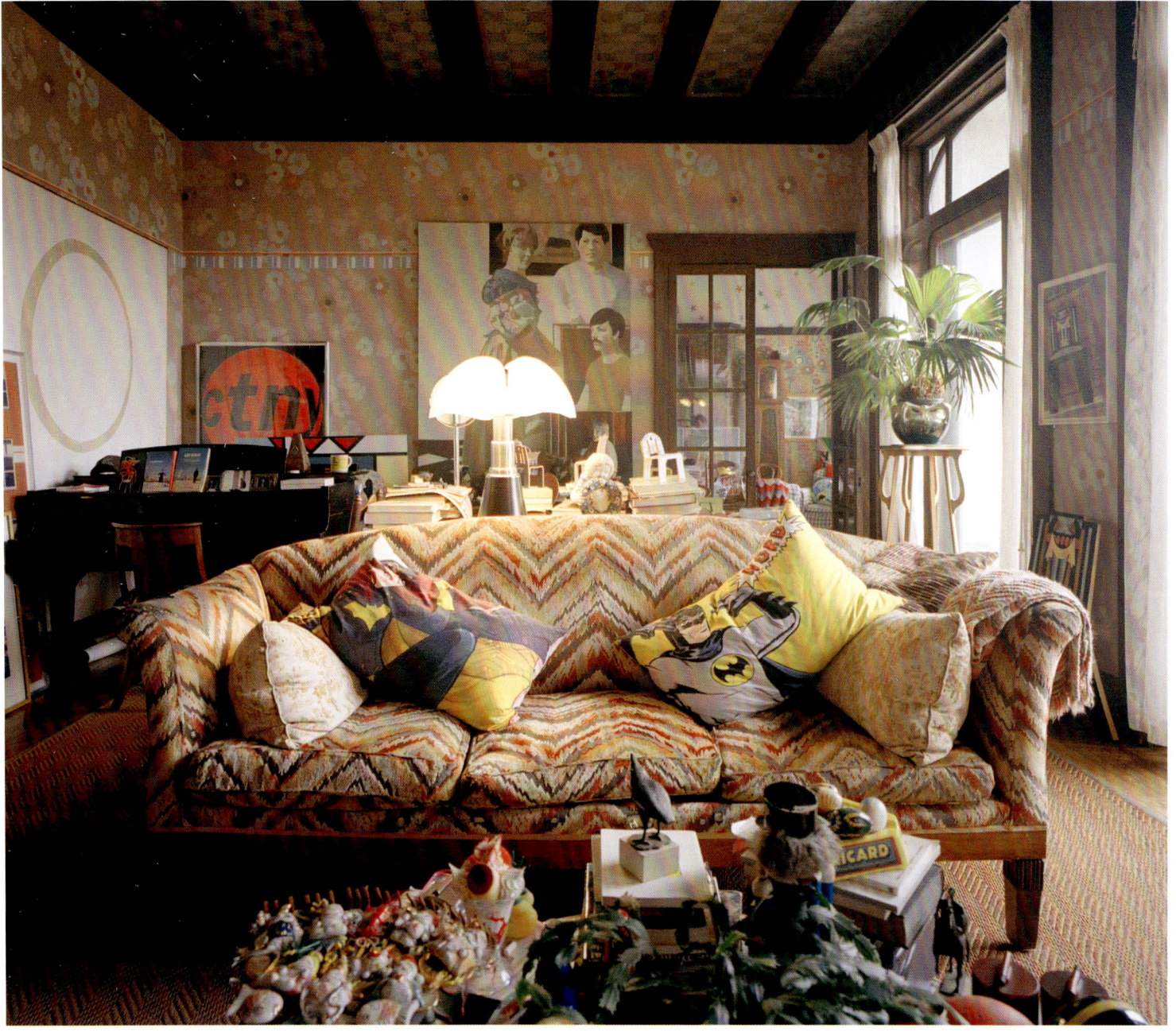

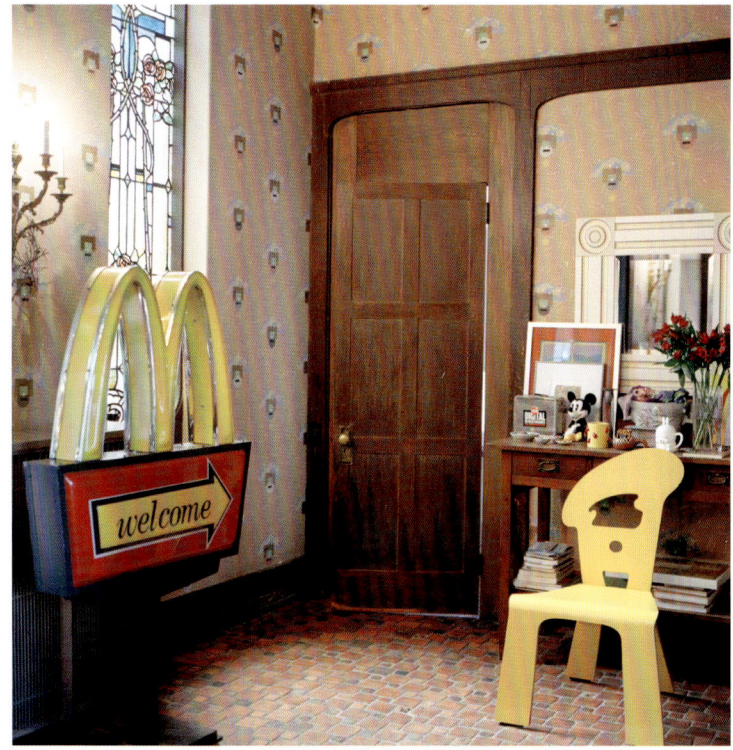

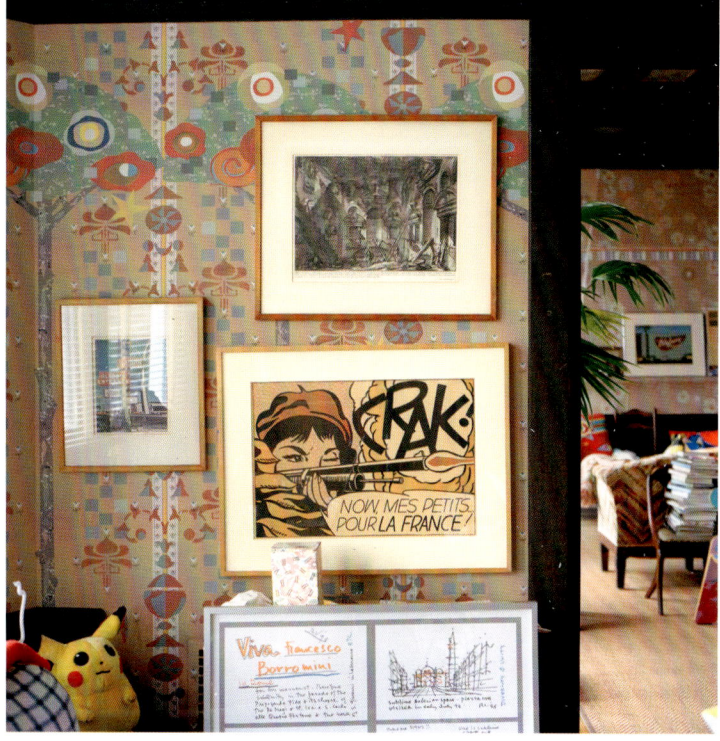

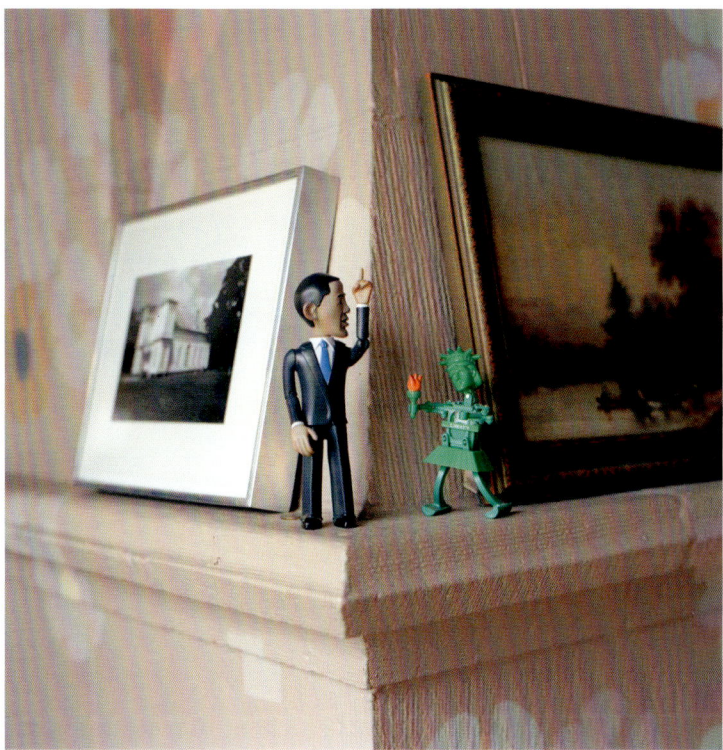

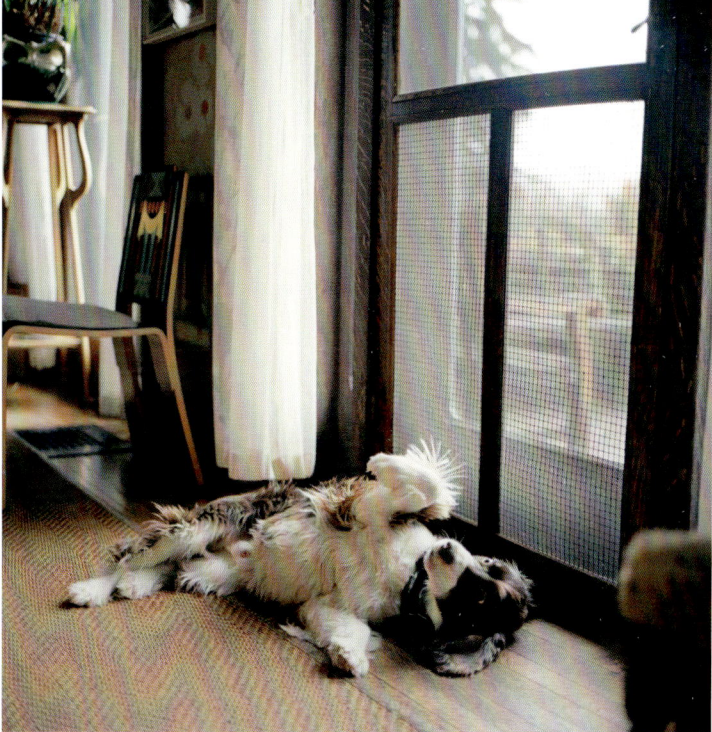

Bob Venturi and I could spot things that other people would like in a few years and buy them when they still cost four dollars.

DSB: Yes. And we had fun reupholstering them. I'd go to New York and return with a pile of samples, and we'd choose those we liked. We spent a year or so decorating, once we had a new roof. We were afraid of leaks.

That couch is from the Traymore Hotel [a grand Atlantic City hotel that was demolished in 1972]. It was exhibited in Paris in 1925. And it cost us twenty dollars. That table was in the elevator lobbies. We picked up two van loads at the Traymore.

PB: **This room is amazing, with its painted patterns on the ceiling and walls. The wall mural looks familiar to me. It's quite like the decorated skin on the Venturi, Scott Brown and Associates buildings that I've seen.**

DSB: The ceiling was painted in the 1920s. The wall is stenciled; its pattern was designed by Bob. It was a long story that began with a trip to Decorators Walk to find floral wallpaper for the bedrooms. And perhaps you could call this suite of rooms our Strip. The house is from 1907.

PB: **It's a wonderfully open house. The light that comes through this entire floor is beautiful.**

DSB: Oh, that's the first thing we saw. We drove by it regularly and were fascinated to see all the way through the house to the yard beyond. So one day we drove down the driveway, and sure enough, there was a vista through the wide glass doors, and there were stained-glass windows on either side. Art Nouveau has been my style, like this pin, you see, and my clothes. It's what I have worn since I bought my first Art Nouveau pin in about 1953. So I said to Bob, "I can't believe this; it's an Art Nouveau house in America." Because I hadn't seen even one here.

PB: **Yes, there are not too many. Do you know who designed it?**

DSB: Milton B. Medary at the age of twenty-five. He had a very distinguished later career, and his work is all over Philadelphia, but, just as he was to become dean at the School of Architecture at Penn, he died. His clients here were German. They wanted and got a German Art Nouveau house, and its woodwork was probably made in Germany. But because it's close in design to Arts and Crafts, neighbors called it the California house. The first owners were art collectors and patrons, and important works by Samuel Yellin and Wharton Esherick were housed here. They lived here from 1909 to 1970. Then a painting contractor bought it and redecorated it in "Art Nouveau" as he knew it, rubbing lye into woodwork and smearing white paint on that, to make it look like driftwood.

Not all Art Nouveau goes with this house, because its scale lies between English Romantic and automobile freeway. So I tuck this little Art Nouveau pitcher into a corner, because it's too prim for the house. This library now supports two work nooks; the one facing the bay window is a small conference space and my favorite

In Los Angeles, I was seeking an outlook on urbanism in the essence of sun and seduction.

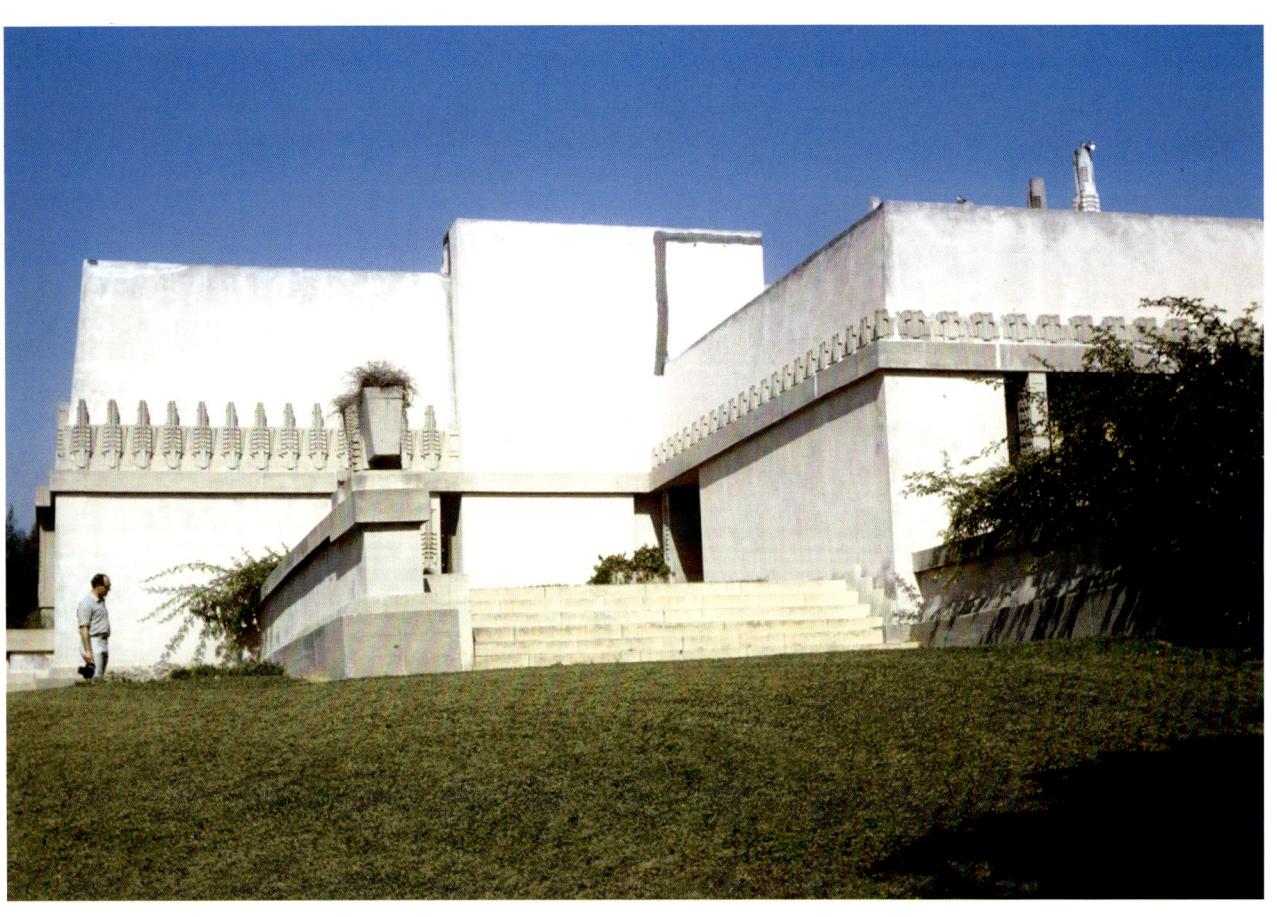

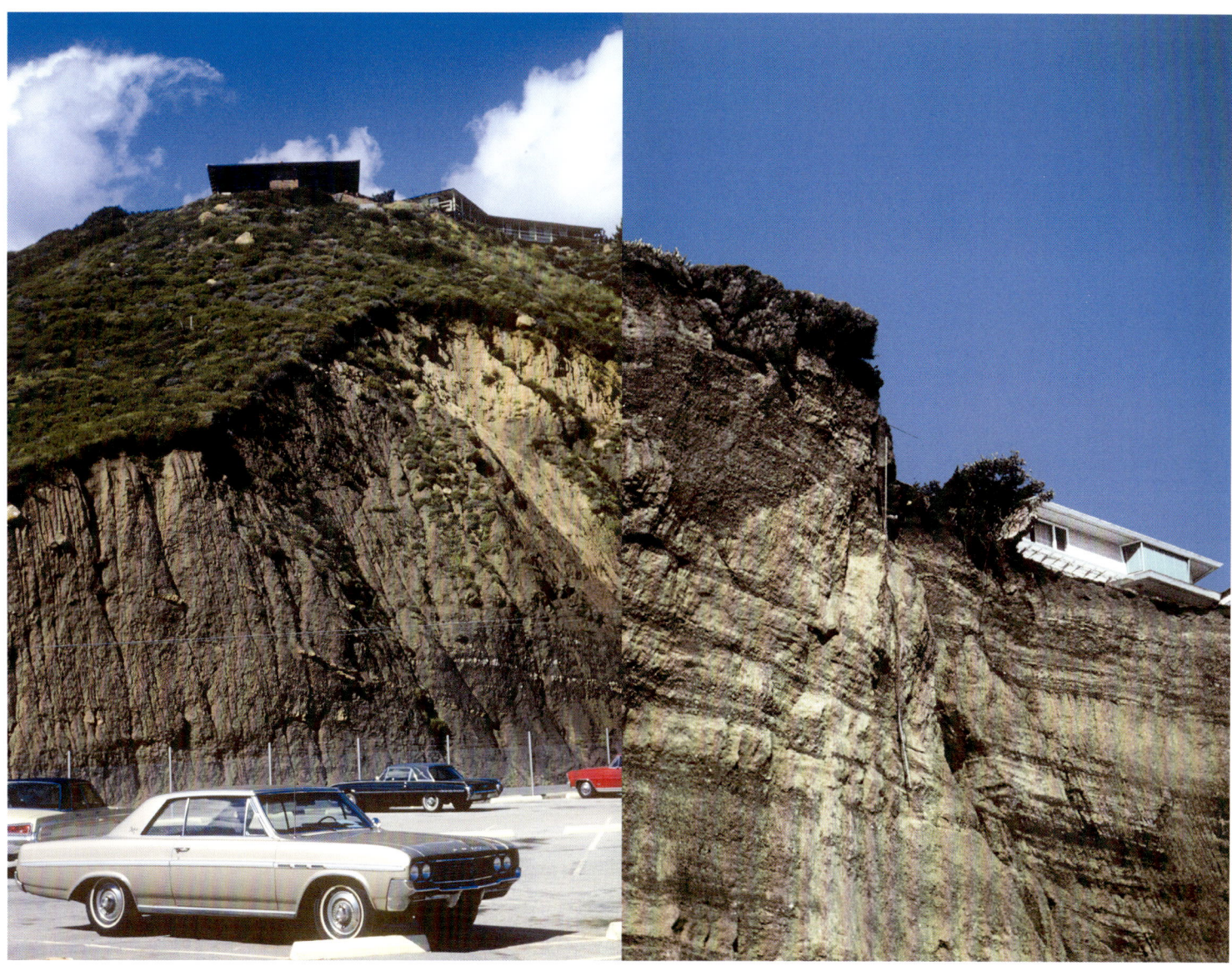

place to work. I have four such places to sit so my back doesn't die. It's like, "We need small, mass-repeated comfort enhancers distributed system-wide, to reveal places changed for new use. And they should be soft to give their users comfort." Small, mass-repeated events that make you feel comfortable are pillows. But I said, "I don't want them to be Art Nouveau; I want them to be Art Deco—related but not altogether." And then Charlotte Caldwell, who worked here, said, "Have you thought of Batman?" So people think—it was even said in one article—that I designed the pillows. I didn't. I went to the catalogs, and I looked up "little boys' rooms." I found cotton Batman pillowcases at eight dollars apiece.

PB: **I see you've got Catwoman alongside Batman.**

DSB: Yes. You see, they talk to each other, but boy, do they talk to that Piranesi etching of a Roman street. Look at the technique there, such beautiful drawing. Roy Lichtenstein learned from this. And adjacent to the Piranesi, Bob hung a Lichtenstein comic-book print.

PB: **From the way you're explaining the house, it sounds as though you think of it almost the way you think about cities.**

DSB: Very much so. Look out here at the yard. I saw one like it in front of the Mies van der Rohe houses in Krefeld. An English Romantic landscape. Our house was built for Germans who knew [Hermann] Muthesius's *Das Englische Haus*. Germans and Austrians fell in love with that style, and also with Charles Rennie Mackintosh,

but Americans and the English wouldn't touch it. This is an English Romantic landscape to go with a German house.

PB: **Is the Wissahickon Creek down there, that way?**

DSB: It's down there. That's our German linden tree, at the edge of the lawn. Its life span is one hundred years, and this one is 110 years now. Our landscape contractor gives our trees very loving attention. And I think about the garden in urban terms. Its carriage driveway, for example, is augmented to suit the geometry of cars and trucks.

PB: **[*A dog enters.*] Who is this?**

DSB: You won't believe it—his name is Alvar Aalto.

PB: **Well, he's very handsome.**

DSB: Hello, lovey. Hello, doggie. You see, he comes and leans against my knee. Bob used to say, "Where's man's best friend?"— and he'd come running. And, "Where's the dog?" And, "Poochie." And, "Aalto-ie." [*Walking from the sitting room to the dining room, she pauses to show Peter Barberie things on the mantel.*] I like this combination. This was here to amuse Bob, because, in his nineties, he liked to sit here.

PB: **So we have plastic wind-up toys of the Statue of Liberty and Barack Obama.**

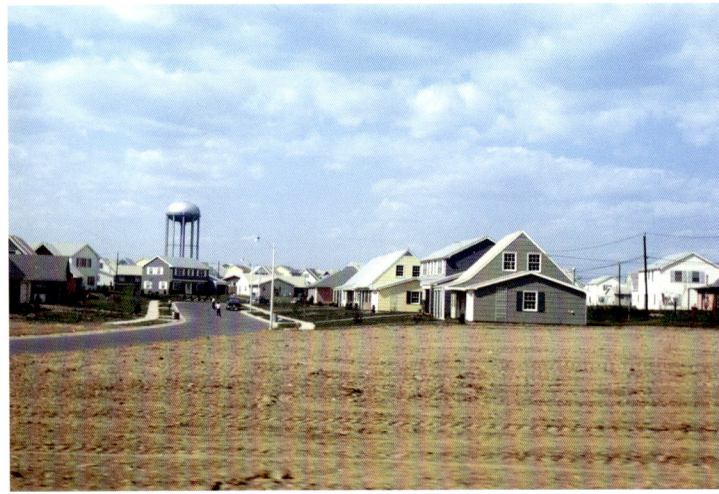

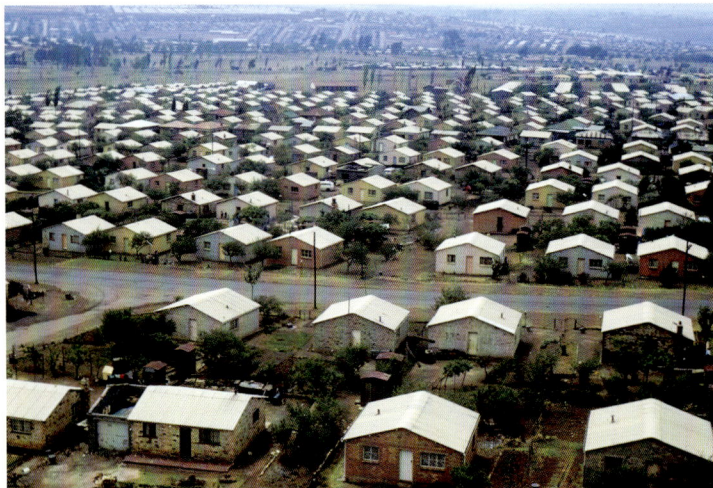

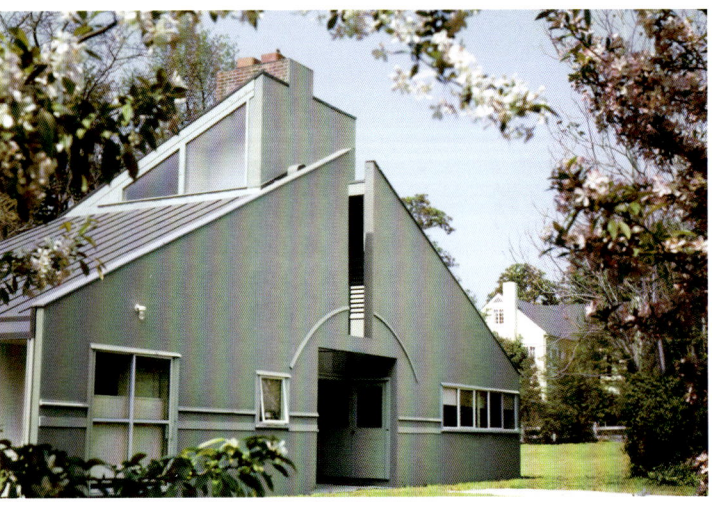

DSB: And look what the Statue of Liberty can do. [*She winds it, and noise is emitted.*] Isn't that enchanting? As I went by Bob, I'd give it a wind up. Mmmmmmm.

Bob grew up with this chair and surrounded by books filled with photographs of Italian architecture. Princeton added modern architecture, particularly Le Corbusier, and openness to the study of historical architecture. Two years at the American Academy in Rome deepened his outlook, but it was only just before he left that he discovered Italian Mannerist architecture and vocabulary.

For the Vanna Venturi House (1964), which used our postmodernism, not Philip Johnson's "PoMo" of the 1980s, his process was fascinating. He was learning about David Crane's "four faces of movement." He knew Crane, who was teaching us urban design courses about the street, the buildings, the communications systems that you can study between them, how the crossroads beget marketplaces and towns, and all of that. Bob was very eager to learn about these things—he was the only architect at Penn who was. That's why I invited him to come and look at Las Vegas.

PB: So you had been to Las Vegas prior to that?

DSB: No. My parents went to Las Vegas in 1950, and they sent back photographs. They were very strange, because of my mother's inexpertise. She'd just been on a game reserve in South Africa, and then they went to see family in America, and in one of her rolls of film of the Strip at night there's a giraffe walking down it—so two pictures are superimposed. Anyway, so I saw that then. But I was already in love with theme parks because my dad was, and because my grandparents had sent us souvenirs from Coney Island in 1936. That was my first piece of magic. Later, I was interested in Pop art and popular culture. I wanted to look at places like Disneyland or Las Vegas, where people actually liked to go. We wanted to do some work around there, and that's how the Las Vegas Studio started.

We also did a studio called "mass communication on the people's freeway." In Santa Monica, Los Angeles, we did a studio on the beach, thinking about it as a Strip too. In Los Angeles, on Sunset Boulevard, for example, I was seeking an outlook on urbanism in the essence of sun and seduction—what were these very private buildings, possibly of film stars, communicating?

PB: Did Las Vegas in the 1960s remind you of the Johannesburg that you had known a decade earlier? You have written about Johannesburg being less than fifty years old when you went there as a young woman.

DSB: Well, Johannesburg when it started was really small. It was mining camps, you see. And then it grew to a big scale.

PB: I read a wonderful quote from you about your experience traversing countries and cultures, which you said gave you a healthy perspective on things. You were in your twenties, a young woman, when you landed here.

DSB: Yes, and I was with Robert Scott Brown then, you see—it was the two of us. We'd been photographing all over Venice for a full month. When we arrived in Philadelphia, looking at our maps, I found Thirtieth Street Station and then a bridge to cross with all these little houses, and I was sure I'd find something in there. So I point to one, and I say, "We must go and look for an apartment in this house. It was Boathouse Row! It turned out I was right. They did have apartments in Boathouse Row. But we ended up in Grays Ferry, an Irish neighborhood. Pretty quickly people started telling us to avoid black neighborhoods. I said, "I think I'm in apartheid

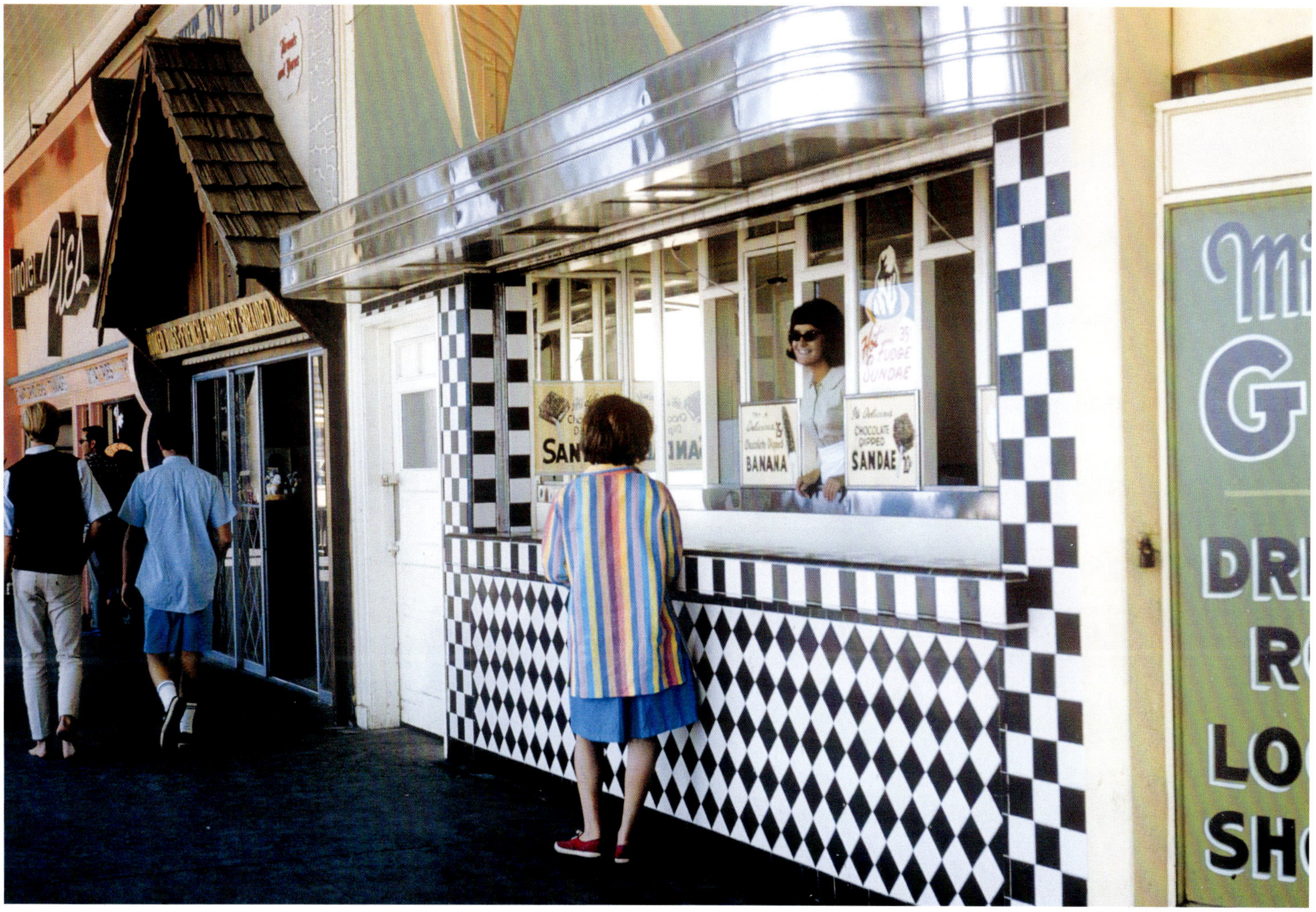
FUDGE SUNDAE
CHOCOLATE DIPPED SANDAE
BANANA

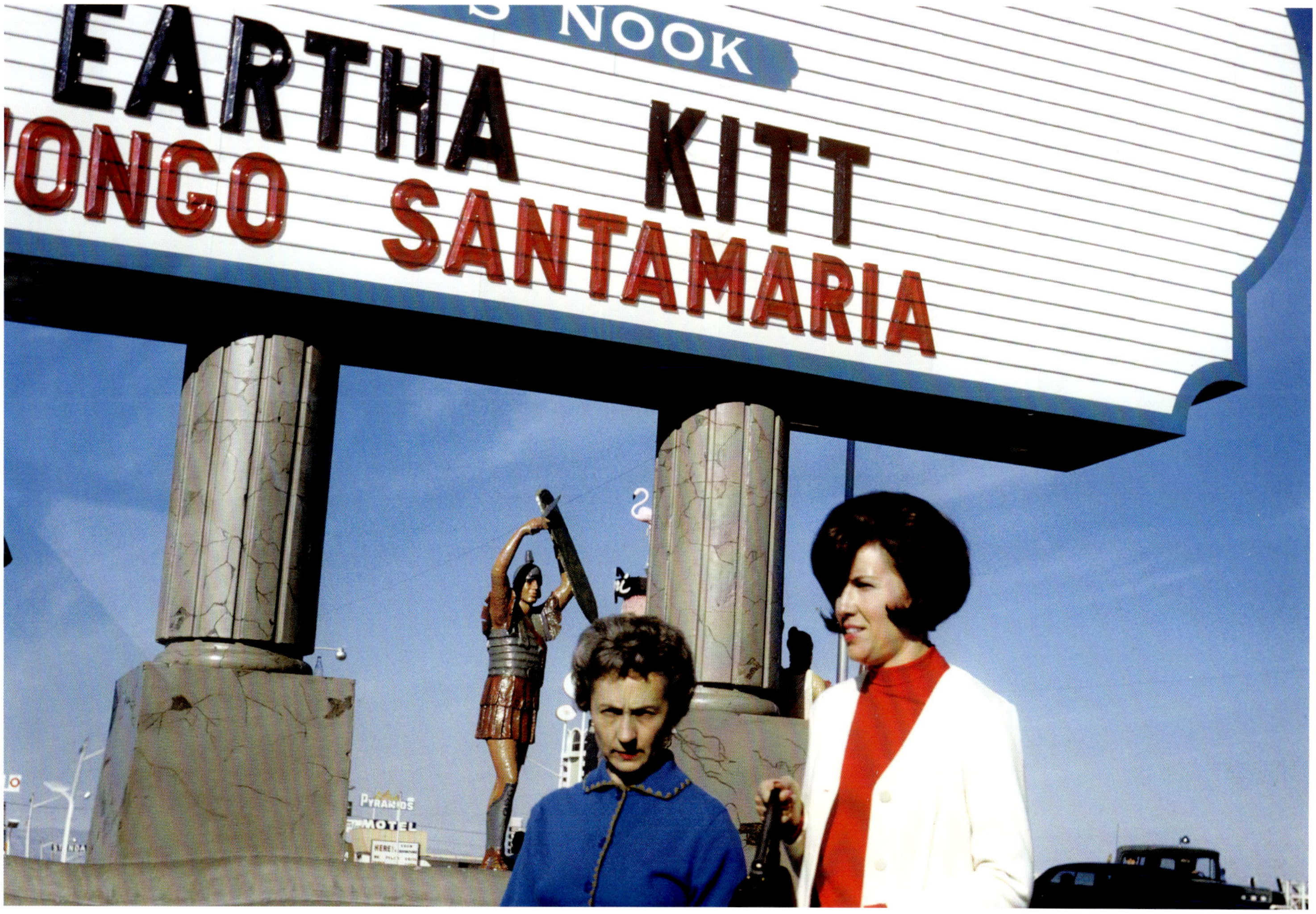
NOOK
EARTHA KITT
ONGO SANTAMARIA
PYRAMIDS
MOTEL

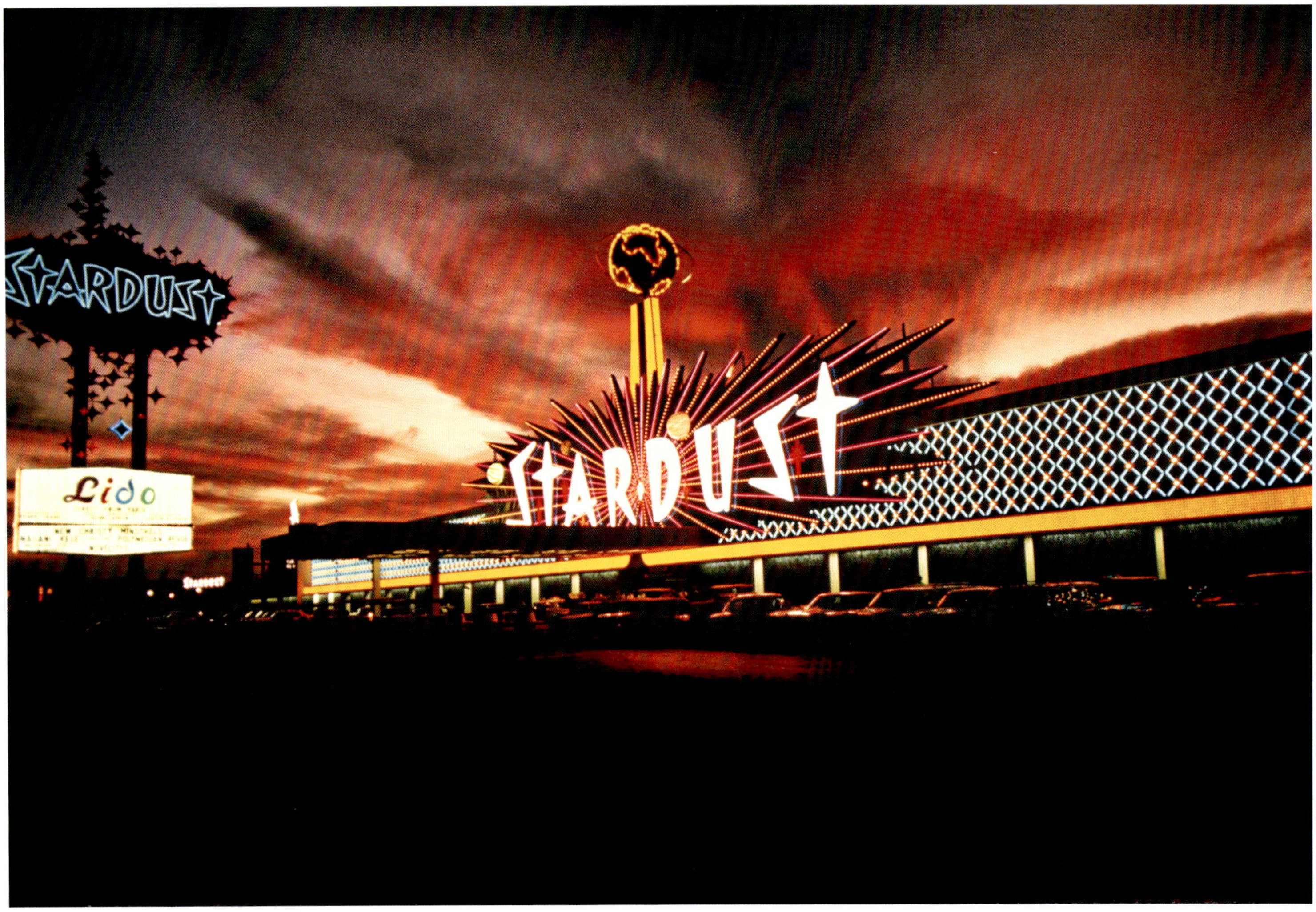
STARDUST
Lido
STARDUST

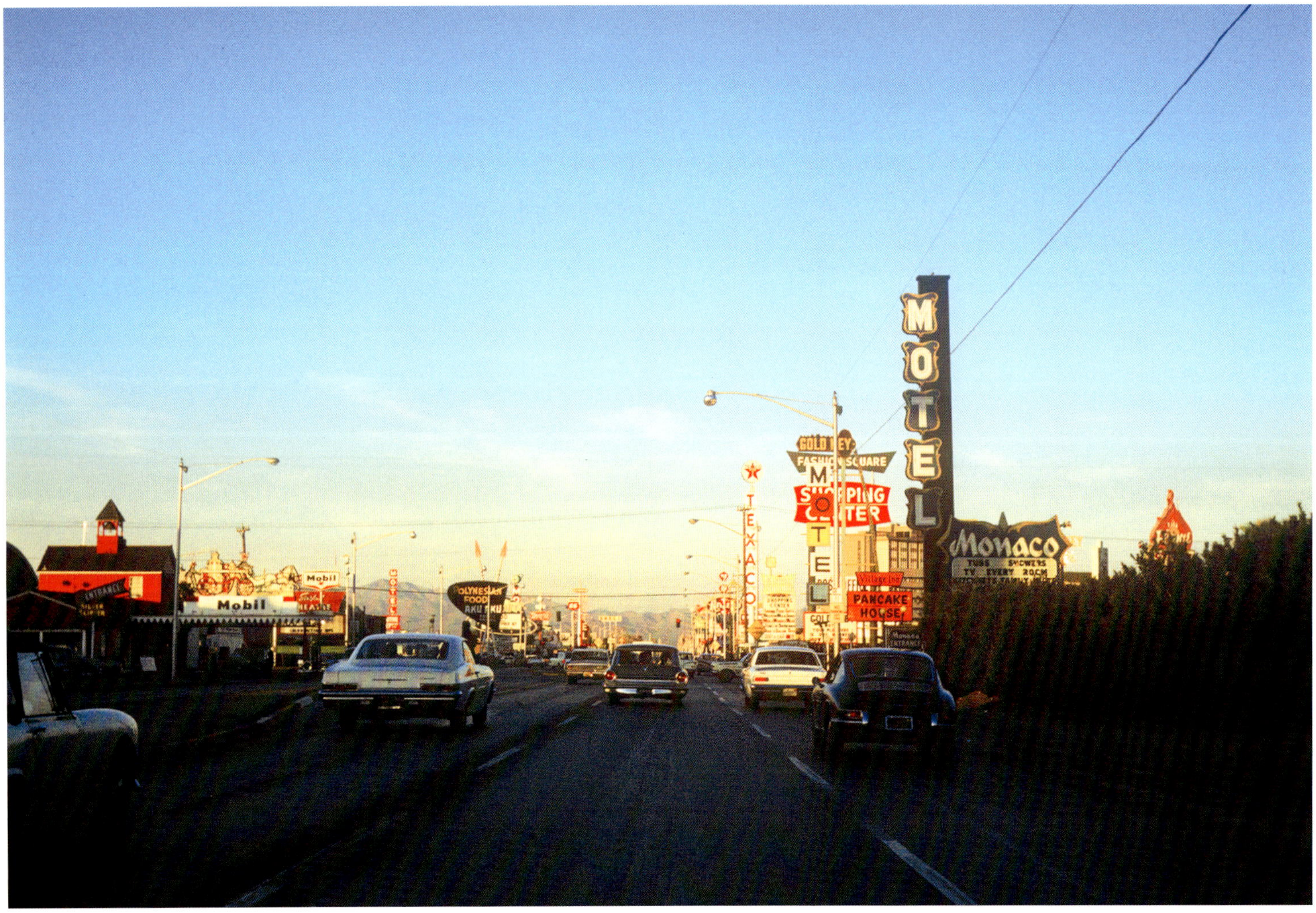
MOTEL
GOLD KEY
FASHION SQUARE
TEXACO
Monaco
PANCAKE HOUSE
Mobil

South Africa, with people saying, 'Don't go to this area because it's bad.'"

PB: **Looking at the galleys of your book—just the pictures— I could see that you're drawing a line from Johannesburg and Soweto to New York, Philadelphia, and Levittown, and even to the Vanna Venturi House.**

DSB: The book needs a little novella about Soweto. The initial, liberal aim for building the settlements before apartheid was to give shelter to the employees in the gold mines and white-owned businesses. You needed to do that if you wanted to have a workforce. Then the Nationalists said, "Yes, we must do that, and we're going to use it as our means of enforcing apartheid. We'll build townships in places far enough away from Johannesburg to never meld, but close enough so that these people can be employed in Johannesburg and in the mines." That's how Soweto developed.

Douglas Calderwood wrote about African mass housing in the 1940s. No one knows about him, but his book really shows it was a liberal activity taken up by the Nationalists. He says that housing will do better if it comes with strong strategic planning. But look at the people who do planning. In Levittown it was William Levitt, a sly developer. Follow the forces where they take you, and find a way to get the extra little business. In Soweto it was Joe Slovo, an amazing character of the African National Congress Underground, who did that sly planning.

PB: **And photography is a powerful tool to show these systems and patterns.**

DSB: Photography is crucial for ideas about architecture and urbanism, to intrigue students and win them over. And you can do that by having slides that show your ideas.

PB: **So you really were photographing, in essence, for slide-shows? To show the context for buildings and urban design?**

DSB: Robert Scott Brown and I began taking photographs on our trip through Europe, because we were planning to return home to South Africa, and we thought we would not have much opportunity to travel for a while, given the Nationalist government. When we set off to travel, I didn't take photographs until Robert arrived, and he had the camera—I didn't have one then. Though I had done photographs at home and my mother was always doing photographs. She did beautiful photographs.

We wanted a record. Everyone tells young architects, no matter which school, "You can't just look at pictures and books; you have to go and look at the real thing." We were strongly told that. "Get out and see these things; get out and see them before you can't, and then take good photographs so that you can have a memory of them when you come back." So we went out to do record shots.

We were going through all these museums. We were learning about the Japanese organization of paintings, and about [Piet] Mondrian and how he painted, and seeing all these interesting ways of putting together things, which I've lived with ever since. That whole philosophy is in how I've organized my book of photographs. Even if it looks very dour, it's made in such a way as to draw people in. A lot of it is based on the plan for Chicago in 1909.

Bob and I were at first looking for record shots, and then we got all involved with communication, streets, and the way store signs behave. So we began taking those photographs too. By then Bob had already fallen in love with Coca-Cola signs.

Then, you see, there's a tradition in America where you show pairs of slides. So I began designing lectures with pairs of slides, sometimes for contrast.

Opposite, top: Denise Scott Brown and the Learning from Las Vegas Studio, The Stardust Resort and Casino, Las Vegas, 1968; bottom: Denise Scott Brown, Las Vegas, 1966

This page: Henri Cartier-Bresson, Coronation of King George VI, London, 1937 Magnum Photos

We wanted a record. Everyone tells young architects, no matter which school, "You can't just look at pictures and books."

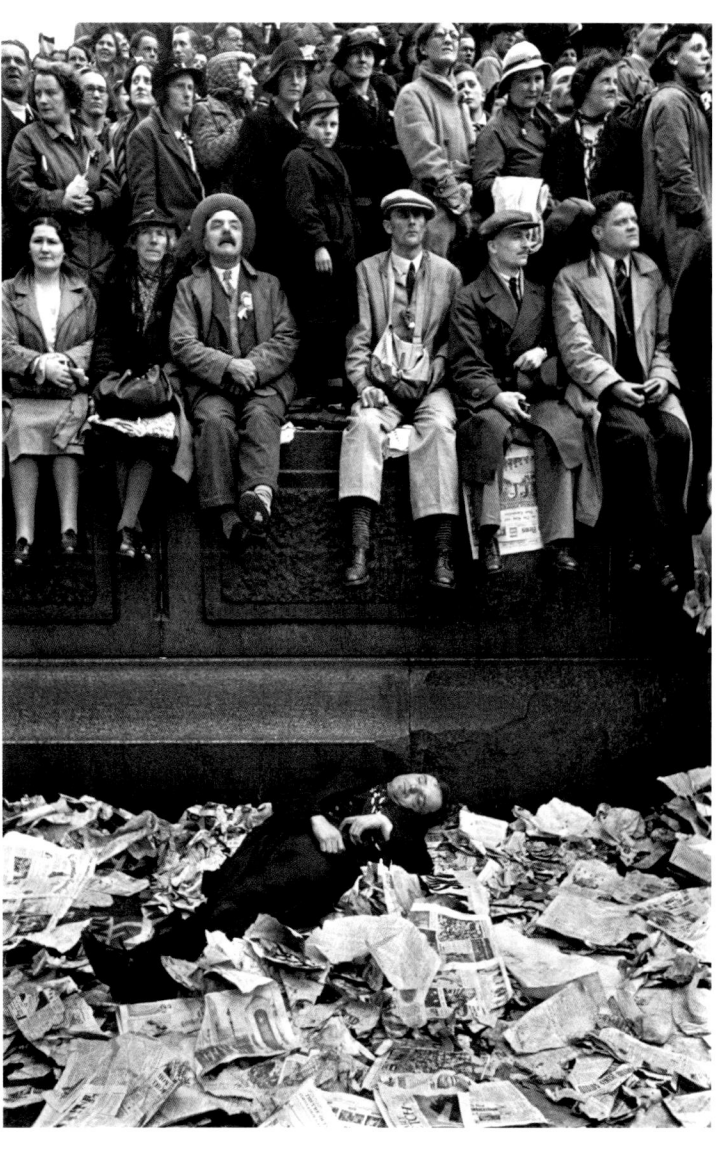

PB: **I know you and Robert Venturi commissioned Stephen Shore to make photographs for your 1975 exhibition *Signs of Life: Symbols in the American City*. Were you looking at other street photographers too?**

DSB: Yes, we moved from Las Vegas to Levitttown to the Smithsonian for that exhibition. We asked photographers to work with us. We figured, why not get some great photographers and send them on a journey? The studios were not only visual; they were sociological. Before then, I became very keen on [Henri] Cartier-Bresson. That's another interesting story, how that happened. But I found a picture in a Cartier-Bresson book that took me a little while to work out. It's got to be London. But it didn't say. At least, I couldn't find it.

PB: **Sure.**

DSB: When I saw the picture, it prompted me to utter a quote: "The mild, lumpy faces of the British."

PB: **[*Laughs*]**

DSB: So there they are, this crowd, sitting on the balustrade, looking out, and they're looking at something. You don't know what it is, but you can see it. Then, at the bottom, there's a drunken guy lying, sleeping, and there are all the remnants of a big parade.

PB: **I know this picture.**

DSB: And so he's lying on this system, like the pillow system we have here in our house. He's there, and then all these people are looking out—and what's going by is the whole might of the British Empire in golden carriages for the coronation. And Cartier-Bresson couldn't care less about the coronation. He's looking at people, or looking at one thing, and making geometric formulas. Well, I was very taken with things like that, as I was with the geometry of trees when I was lying under them while camping and just looking up.

PB: **So tell me how you became keen on Cartier-Bresson.**

DSB: Before Robert Scott Brown came to England, I traveled on my own in Europe. In Bonn, I met a young law student who offered to show me around. I was hesitant, but I wanted to see the city, so I said yes.

Later on, he invited me to join him and a friend on a road trip through Spain. I accepted the invitation, and then they wrote me and said, "We have been joined. He's an American. He's called Len. You would like him." It was an amazing adventure. Len had set out to do a grand tour, and then he discovered that if he didn't eat very much, and didn't buy anything, and just kept his camera and traveled the way we traveled, he could spend two or three times as much time there as he had budgeted for.

So there he was, falling apart, his clothes falling apart, long and lanky, about a foot taller than all the Spanish and my two German friends, with lots of dark hair, taking photographs of Spanish markets and talking about Cartier-Bresson, the monopoly of Kodachrome, and all kinds of things. He went to Columbia. It turned out Len was Len Freed—Leonard Freed. So that was a terribly worthwhile trip.

PB: **He also went on to make incredibly important photographs of the civil rights marches. Did you reconnect with him later on?**

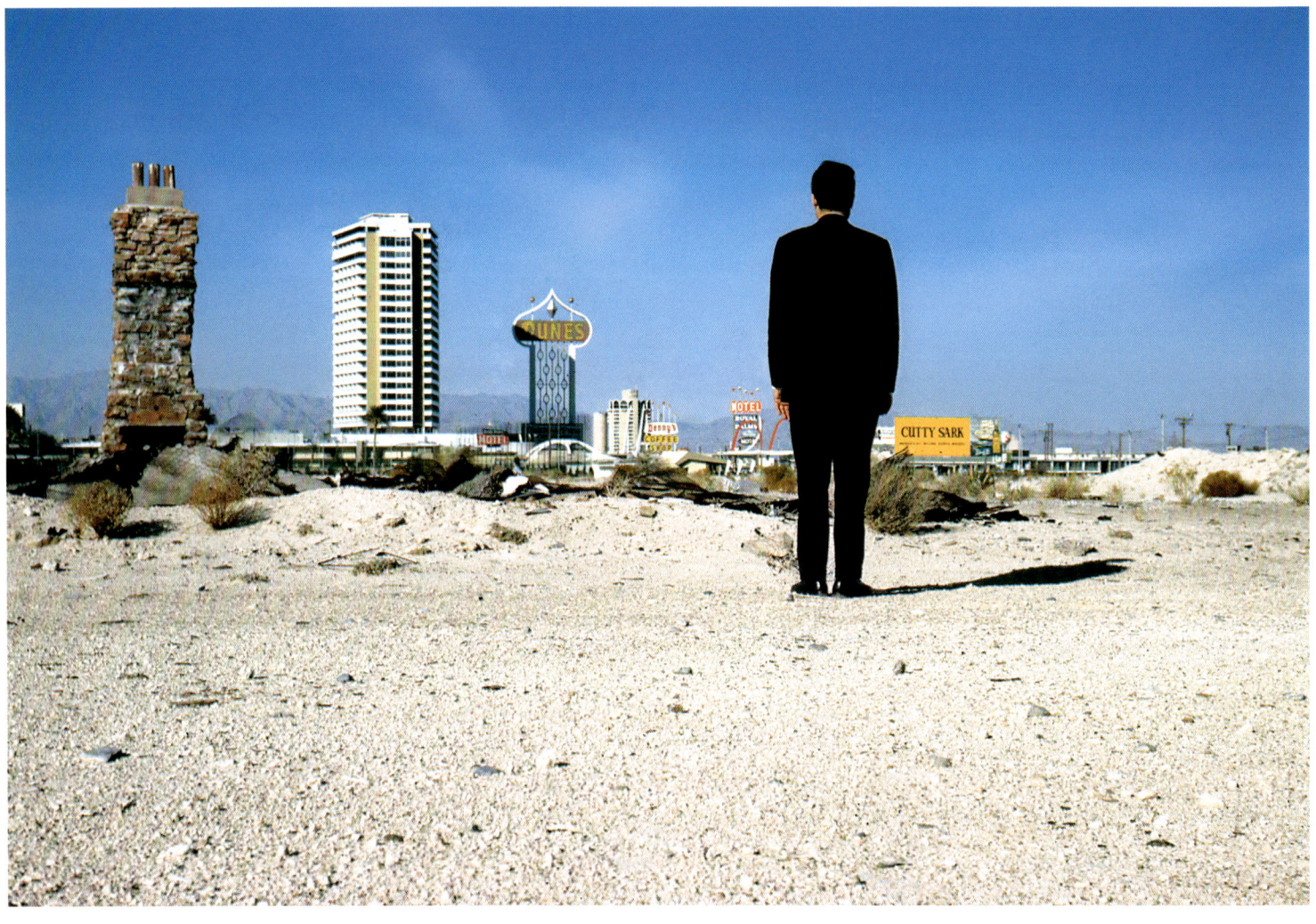

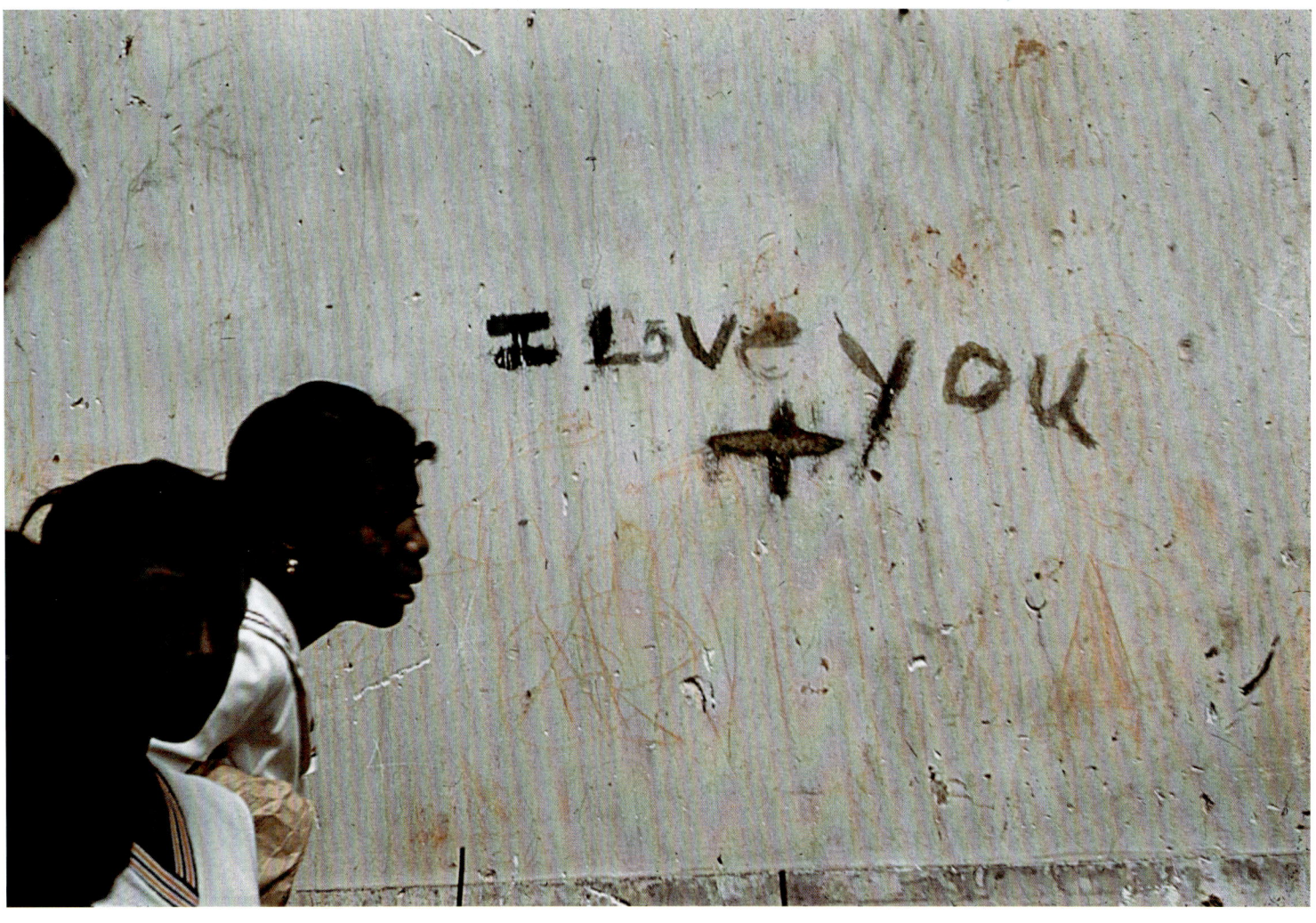

This page:
Denise Scott Brown,
Philadelphia, 1961

Opposite:
Denise Scott Brown,
Robert Venturi à la
Magritte, Las Vegas, 1966
Unless otherwise noted,
all photographs courtesy
Venturi, Scott Brown and
Associates, Inc.

Photography is crucial for ideas about architecture and urbanism, to intrigue students and win them over.

DSB: We met once, and he looked at Robert's black-and-white photographs. You see, I took the color ones (those are the fun ones), and Robert took the serious ones. Len looked at them and said, "If you're going to do this kind of photography, you'd better get to be a lot more serious about focus." Then suddenly he changed, and he wasn't so keen on focus either, and that's when he started to do the antiwar-activity pictures, which were blurred and had movement in them.

PB: Did you always love color photography?

DSB: I did. I loved the black-and-white, but I couldn't be that kind of serious photographer.

PB: Well, you're so drawn to the flavor of the street that I'm guessing color was crucial.

DSB: Very much so. But then there's my picture of a wall that says, "I love you." We'd been making pictures like that in Italy for political posters—some of the urban surfaces were peeling—and saying, "Gee, that looks like [Georges] Braque" or "That looks like Mondrian when he's learning how to abstract a tree." I remember Cartier-Bresson talking about a little girl crossing a sunny patch on the square. He said, "I sat and waited and waited, and then she suddenly was there—that was my picture." You see, it was a decisive moment. So, with the "I love you" photograph, I was sitting and waiting in Philadelphia. I'm thinking, "Something miraculous will happen, just listen and wait."

Peter Barberie is Brodsky Curator of
Photographs, Alfred Stieglitz Center,
at the Philadelphia Museum of Art.

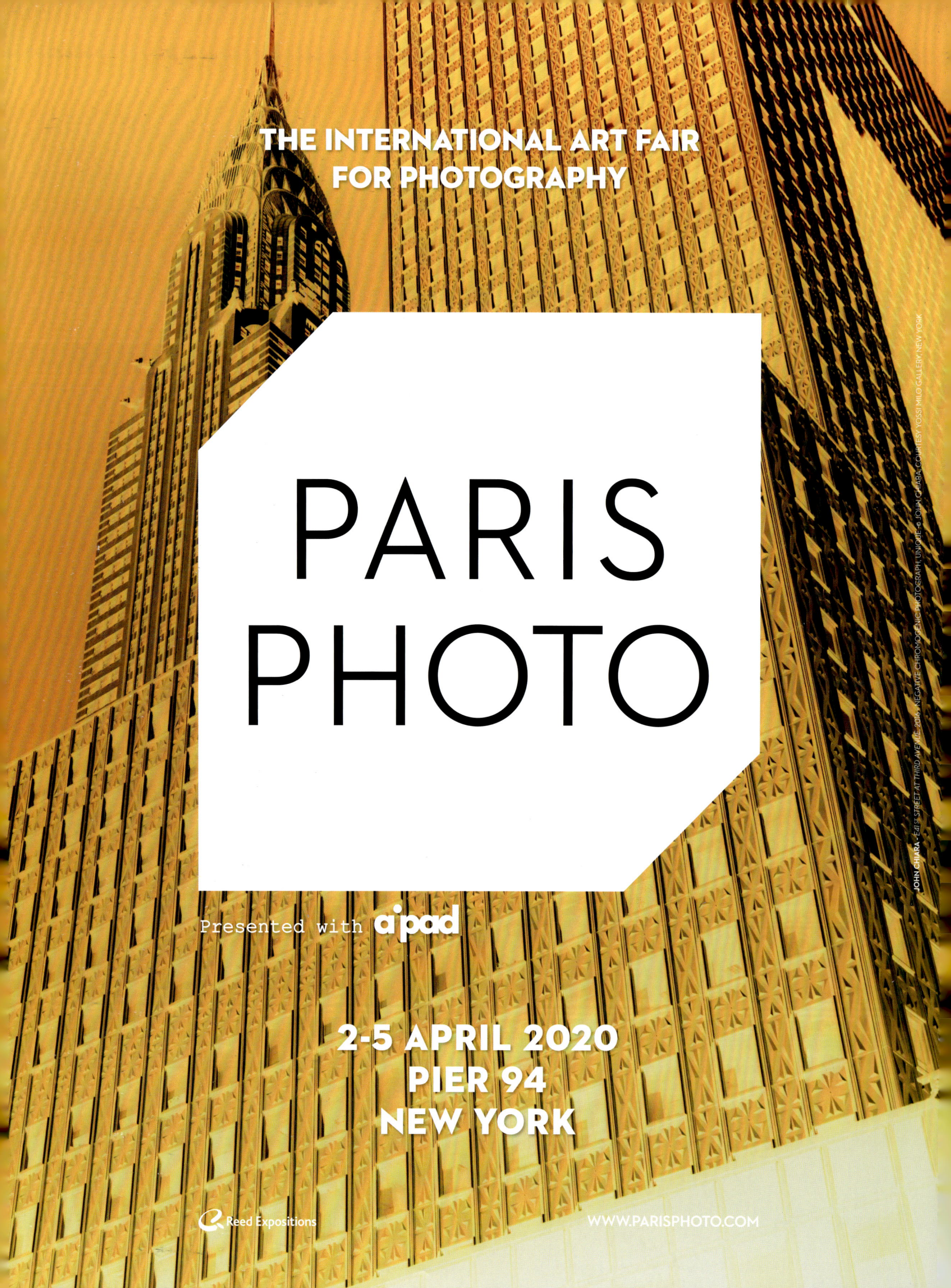

THE INTERNATIONAL ART FAIR
FOR PHOTOGRAPHY

PARIS PHOTO

Presented with a·pad

2-5 APRIL 2020
PIER 94
NEW YORK

JOHN CHIARA – E 41's STREET AT THIRD AVENUE, 2016, NEGATIVE CHROMOGENIC PHOTOGRAPH UNIQUE – © JOHN CHIARA, COURTESY YOSSI MILO GALLERY, NEW YORK

Reed Expositions   WWW.PARISPHOTO.COM

STEPHEN SHORE

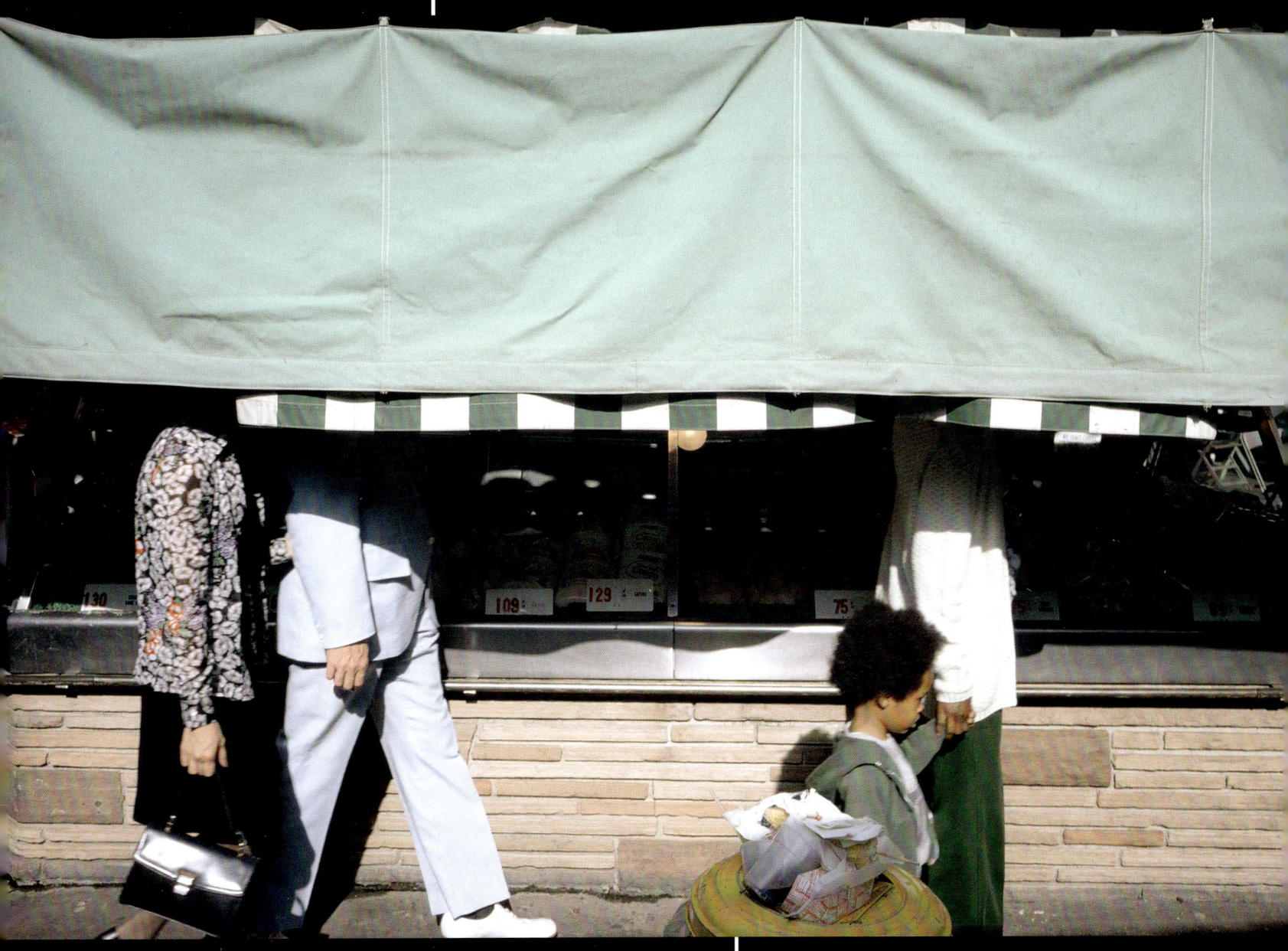

TRANSPARENCIES
SMALL CAMERA WORKS 1971–1979

MARCH 2020   MACK

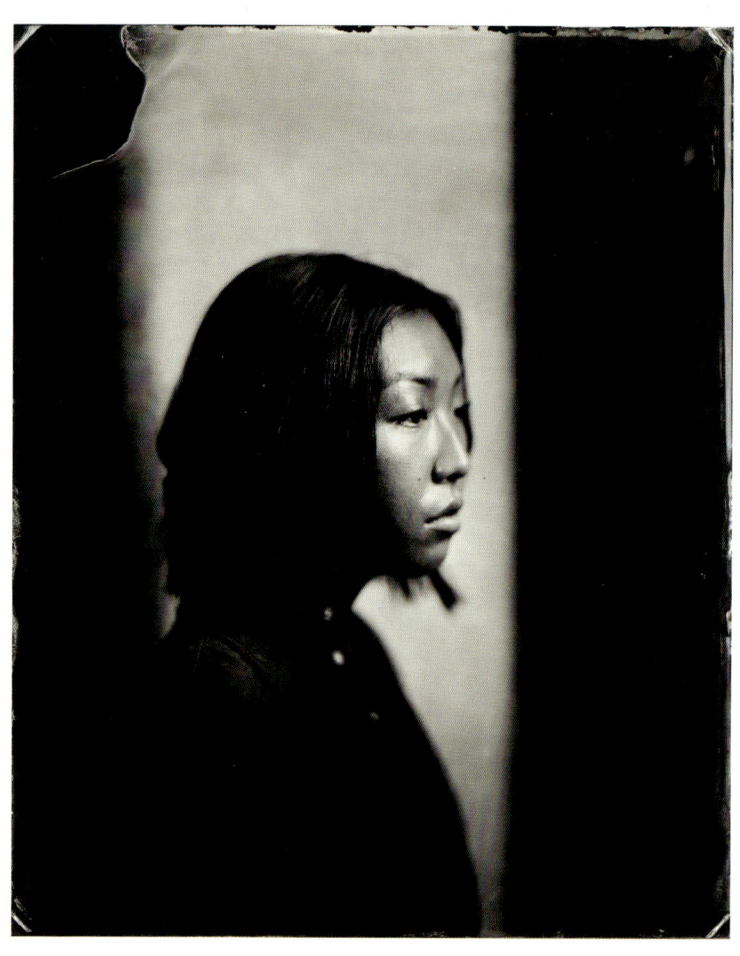
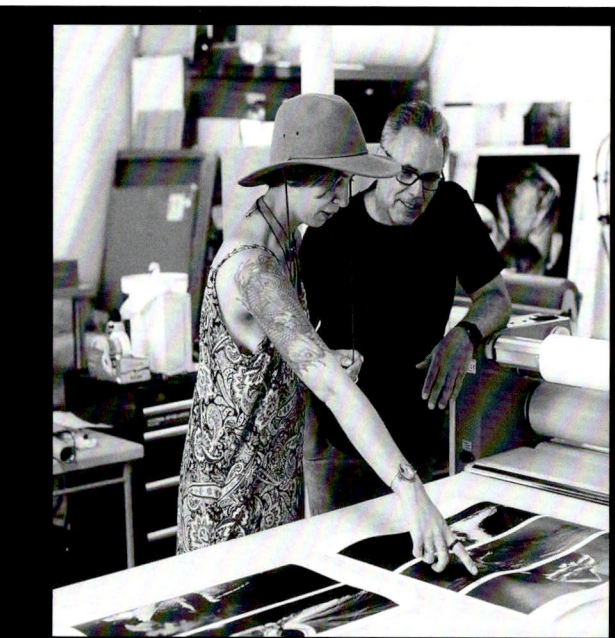
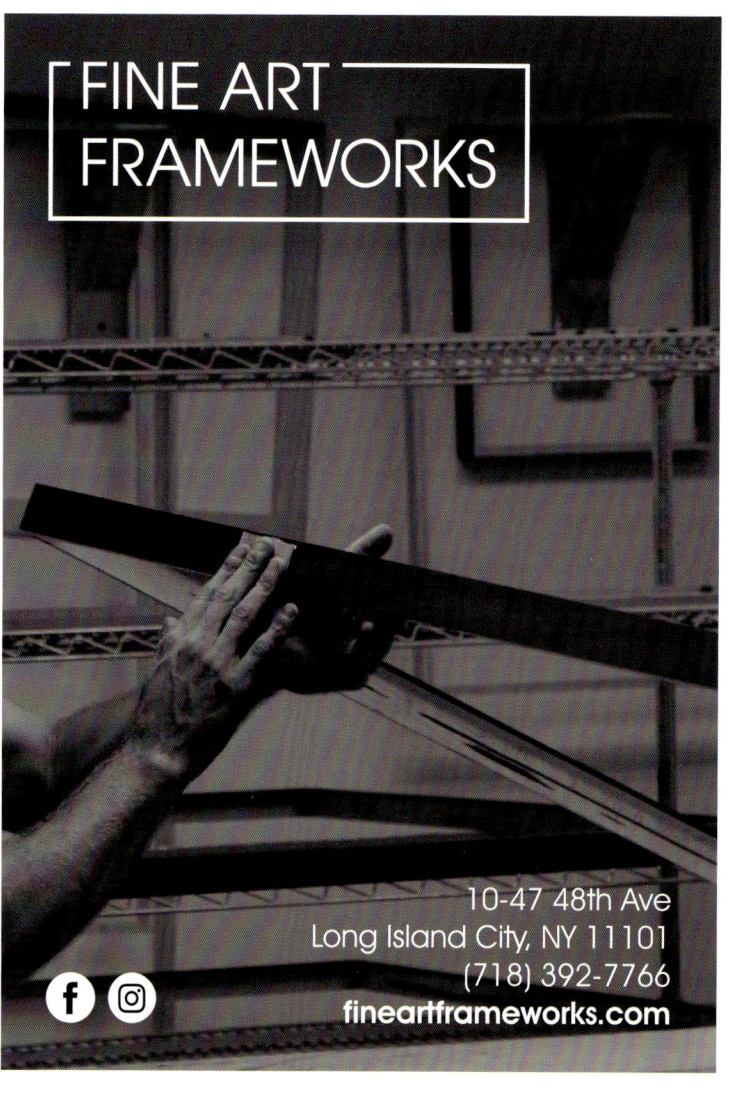